The Last Presbyterian?

The Parish Kirk at Fenwick, Ayrshire, Scotland, built 1643
(*1988 photo by author*)

Osage Presbyterian Church, rural Girard, Kansas,
Organized 1879, built 1883, closed by presbytery 2002
(*1943 family photo in author's collection*)

The Last Presbyterian?

Remembering the Faith of My Forebears

TENTH ANNIVERSARY EDITION

KENNETH L. CUTHBERTSON

Foreword by Jack Rogers

To John Philip & Ali,

With deep appreciation and gratitude
for your ministries, and our friendship
across the years.

Blessings always!
Ken Cuthbertson
7-5-2023

RESOURCE *Publications* · Eugene, Oregon

THE LAST PRESBYTERIAN?
Remembering the Faith of My Forebears
Tenth Anniversary Edition

Resource Publications
An Imprint of Wipf and Stock Publishers
199 W. 8th Ave., Suite 3
Eugene, OR 97401
www.wipfandstock.com

PAPERBACK ISBN: 978-1-6667-7973-8
HARDCOVER ISBN: 978-1-6667-7974-5
EBOOK ISBN: 978-1-6667-7975-2

VERSION NUMBER 060823

Cover image: *Nec Tamen Consumebatur* ("Yet It Was Not Consumed"), Old Scottish woodcut, Presbyterian Archives Research Centre, Dunedin, New Zealand. Used with permission.

Scripture citations are from the New Revised Standard Version Bible unless otherwise noted.

New Revised Standard Version Bible, copyright © 1989, Division of Christian Education of the National Council of the Churches of Christ in the United States of America. Used by permission. All rights reserved.

Excerpts from *The Constitution of the Presbyterian Church (U.S.A.), Part I: Book of Confessions*, copyright © 2002, published by the Office of the General Assembly are reprinted with permission of the Office of the General Assembly of the Presbyterian Church (U.S.A.).

Excerpts from *The Constitution of the Presbyterian Church (U.S.A.), Part II: Book of Order*, copyright © 2004 and 2011, published by the Office of the General Assembly are reprinted with permission of the Office of the General Assembly of the Presbyterian Church (U.S.A.).

Excerpts from *The Confessional Statement and The Book of Government and Worship*, copyright © 1948, The Board of Christian Education of the United Presbyterian Church of North America are reprinted with permission of the Office of the General Assembly of the Presbyterian Church (U.S.A.).

In loving memory of Ellen (1956–2011), my beloved lifelong friend.

In honor of Doug, my lifepartner and lawful spouse,
Hannah, our daughter, and Jean, her mother.

Contents

Contents

Foreword

KEN CUTHBERTSON HAS WRITTEN an insightful and heartwarming book. *The Last Presbyterian?*, rather than being a lament for a lost identity, shows how the values of the Scottish Presbyterian heritage can joyfully be appropriated in the twenty-first century. The history is accurate and insightful (Cuthbertson did a PhD dissertation on John Knox). He enriches the narrative with stories from his own family lore, traced back to the Covenanter village of Fenwick in Ayrshire, Scotland. Cuthbertson describes himself as being from the "Psalm-singing, Sabbath-keeping, Shorter-Catechism-memorizing branch of Presbyterianism," but he does not insist on clutching the old forms. Rather, for example, he sees reflection on the 1991 *Brief Statement of Faith* of the Presbyterian Church (USA) as an appropriate way to catechize now.

Cuthbertson channels the conservative, but not fundamentalist, version of covenant theology, represented by the United Presbyterian Church of North America (which combined several versions of the Scottish low-church tradition in 1858 and merged into The United Presbyterian Church in the U.S.A. in 1958). I was shaped by that same UPNA tradition. Surprising as it may seem, we also share having come to embrace full equality for LGBT persons in church and society. This book is a testimony to how historic values can be conserved while remaining open to new insights from "the buke," God's word in the Scriptures.

Jack Rogers,
Professor of Theology Emeritus,
San Francisco Theological Seminary
Moderator of the 213th General Assembly (2001),
Presbyterian Church U.S.A.

Acknowledgments

I WISH TO OFFER my profound thanks to Resource Publications and Wipf & Stock for their help and guidance in the publication process, particularly to Christian Amondson (2013) and Matt Wimer (2023). Deep thanks are especially due to my copy editor Shirin McArthur for her good work and gentle supportive encouragement.

I also want to thank colleagues and friends who have provided input and support to me in various ways. These include Don Tubesing, Wallace Ford,* Jim Collie, Elizabeth Nordquist, Jack Rogers,* Tricia Dykers Koenig, Cynthia Holder Rich, and Kerry Clements.

The formative role of family and friends across the years has been particularly important to this project. Thanks are due to Robert Miller,* Don Calderwood,* Frances Calderwood, Sara MacDonald, Dale Snyder,* Elizabeth Tippett, Louise Westfall, Oleta Saunders, Shoshona Blankman,* Hunter Flournoy, John Philip Newell, Nahum Ward-Lev, and Diana Butler Bass.

Among those no longer living whose influence shaped me, and this book, I must acknowledge my parents, Floyd Edward and M. Phanetta (Gibson) Cuthbertson. I would also note William C. Cuthbertson, Marvin Green, Fern Ulbrich, Merrill Proudfoot, James Spalding, and Howard Rice.

Several institutions have also played a key formative role in my life, and thus in this project: The Presbyterian Church (USA) and its predecessor bodies, Osage Presbyterian Church, Sterling College, The School of Religion at the University of Iowa, Ghost Ranch and Casa del Sol, The Program in Christian Spirituality at San Francisco Theological Seminary, The Presbytery of Santa Fe, New Life Presbyterian Church, Las Placitas Presbyterian Church, More Light Presbyterians (formerly Presbyterians for Lesbian and Gay Concerns), Covenant Network of Presbyterians, That

---

* Indicates persons no longer living in 2023.

Acknowledgments

All May Freely Serve, and my friends in the Sufi and LGBTQ spiritual communities.

I would also like to acknowledge the influence on this project of one particular book, Wallace N. Jamison's *The United Presbyterian Story*. It is a treasure.

Last, but most importantly, my unending thanks to my beloved husband and partner-in-life, Doug Calderwood, for his enthusiastic support, gentle critiques, and constant encouragement throughout this whole process. I literally could never have done this without him.

Abbreviations for Presbyterian Denominations

AP	Associate Presbyterian (US branch of Scottish "Secession" Church.)
ARP	Associate Reformed Presbyterian (A union of elements of the Associate and Reformed Presbyterians in 1782. The old southern synod remains a denomination; the northern synods merged with the remaining APs to form the UPNA in 1858.)
PCUS	The Presbyterian Church in the U.S. (1861–1983; the "southern" church, merged with UPCUSA.)
P.C.U.S.A.	The Presbyterian Church in the U.S.A. (1789–1958; this largest early Presbyterian denomination in the U.S.A. evolved from the first presbytery, formed in 1706, and the first synod, formed in 1717.)
PCUSA	The Presbyterian Church (USA) (Formed in 1983; merger of UPCUSA and PCUS.)
RPNA	Reformed Presbyterian Church of North America (Also known as "Covenanters." Formed in 1774.)
UPCUSA	The United Presbyterian Church in the U.S.A. (1958–1983; merger of P.C.U.S.A. and UPNA.)
UPNA	The United Presbyterian Church of North America (1858–1958; merged with P.C.U.S.A. to form UPCUSA.)

Introduction

I AM NOT, OF course, by any means the last Presbyterian—but I could be. Some years ago a friend suggested that he would like me to do something on the topic, "When the time comes to write the history of the last twenty-five years of the Presbyterian Church, what will it say?" From what I read and hear, the project might need to be extended out to include the Church of Scotland as well as the Presbyterian Church (USA),[2] and also to who-knows-how-many other branches of the Presbyterian and Reformed family of Christians. However, that is not what I am about here. I am really not so terribly concerned about the *history* of the declining institutions as I am about the *heritage* of a way of living, believing, and being Presbyterian that is already a fast-fading memory at best, and for many—even in the current Presbyterian Church—something largely unknown.

This is a book I have been getting ready to write all of my life, and it is an unapologetically subjective presentation. My purpose is not simply nostalgic. For all its faults, I believe in the value of much that was. My hope is that these reflections will help interested readers to reconnect with some of the formative elements of our particular faith tradition, and assist them in exploring new ways to appropriate and celebrate some of the old "distinctives" of our historical practice as "covenant communities of disciples" now living in the twenty-first century.[3] My hope, inspired by Phyllis Tickle's book *The Great Emergence*, is that, in the midst of an era of cleaning out various outworn denominational cast offs, we may also find, tucked away, some old treasures we can bring out and clean up so that they might usefully and meaningfully serve again in our common life and worship. This is an exercise, hopefully, in what my friend Diana Butler Bass calls "re-traditioning," something—I think—that Jesus himself once commended: "Therefore every scribe who has been trained for the realm

2. Hereinafter "PCUSA."

3. PCUSA, *Book of Order*, F-1.0303.

of heaven is like the householder who brings out of the treasure what is new and what is old."[4]

Without doubt, I come at this task with my own unique perspective, grounded in a long and deep heritage in various manifestations of the Presbyterian Church. I sometimes self-identify as being of the "Psalm-singing, Sabbath-keeping, Shorter-Catechism-memorizing, anti-Masonic, abolitionist, teetotaling, non-dancing, anti-gambling" branch of the Presbyterian Church.[5] As formidable as all that sounds, what I think it really indicates is a faith tradition that, at its essence, was profoundly committed to the scriptures, to an informed faith, and to lifestyles of deep integrity and commitment to justice. There is good reason, I believe, for those who, across the years, have cited the Presbyterians as being the branch of Christianity that is in various ways the most Jewish in spirit, for much of our heritage seems most deeply rooted in the Hebrew scriptures. The unfortunate part, however, is that too often we have more closely resembled the grim caricatures of the Scribes and Pharisees portrayed in the Christian gospels. Somehow we could never quite bring ourselves to embrace anything akin to the truly joyous aspects of Jewish life and culture.

I have to admit to being about as much of a genetic or ethnic Presbyterian as can still be found in captivity, being mostly of Scots and Scots-Irish descent. I was born and raised—baptized and ordained as well—at the Osage Presbyterian Church, a small country church near the town of Girard in southeast Kansas, where the majority of the old farming families shared ancestral roots back into the Scottish village of Fenwick, in Ayrshire. My family tree—counting back from my late father and my maternal grandfather—includes numerous elders and even a few ministers dating back to at least the early eighteenth century.[6] The genealogy includes members of the Church of Scotland, the United Secession Church (Scotland), the Presbyterian Church U.S.A. (pre-1958, "P.C.U.S.A."), the Associate Reformed Presbyterian Church (pre-1858, "ARP"), the United Presbyterian Church of North America ("UPNA"), and so on. Even the one branch of my family who were *not* Presbyterian belonged to an offshoot denomination, The Christian Church / Disciples of Christ.

Like various relatives on both sides of the family, I attended Sterling College in Kansas, a school originally founded by the UPNA and still,

---

4. Matt 13:52, modified by author.

5. Most of these points will be mentioned, at least in passing, as we proceed.

6. Many of the older records have fallen victim to the depredations of dampness, occasional fires, and hungry church mice.

in the 1970s, deeply shaped by that tradition. The years at Sterling also provided me with a connection to the Reformed Presbyterian Church of North America ("RPNA"), known as the Covenanters, which to this day retains many of the more particular—or peculiar—Presbyterian distinctives long since abandoned by the rest of us. It was at Sterling that I first met my beloved husband and companion-in-life, whose family roots stretch as deep and far as mine . . . even to that same ancestral village in Scotland where we discovered that our great-great-grandfathers lived less than two miles from one another, and that several of our kin worshipped together in the United Secession congregation.[7]

So far as I can tell, both of our families have been Presbyterian at least since the Reformation, and possibly even before that. The part of Ayrshire where Fenwick lies was long a hotbed of radical Protestantism. The parish was famous—or infamous—for its ardent adherence to the cause and the number of its martyrs during the Covenanter era of the seventeenth century. Back into the sixteenth century, various of the local lairds and nobles were adherents of the "Lords of the Congregation" . . . the group of nobles and gentry through whom the Reform movement finally prevailed in Scotland. Even before that, according to local lore, some of the tenant families living out in the moorlands were descendants of medieval heretics . . . perhaps spiritual heirs of the Ayrshire Lollards (followers of John Wycliffe) mentioned by John Knox in his *History of the Reformation in Scotland*.[8] The type of Christianity described in the pages that follow certainly meshes with what little is known about the Lollard underground of the fifteenth and early sixteenth centuries.[9]

All of that being said, I want to reiterate that my love for the old ways of Presbyterianism is not just historical or genealogical. My hope is to be more of a conservator than an archivist. It seems that nearly every political, economic, social and religious system and institution in the world is currently undergoing the sort of change that only happens about every five hundred years.[10] In times like these, many things that are good and worthy can be lost or forgotten, possibly forever. Before these treasures disappear, I want at least to record what I know of them because these

---

7. We even share one local surname in our ancestral lines, and suspect that we may be some sort of fifth or sixth cousins.

8. See Dickinson, vol. I, 7–11.

9. Knox himself, I strongly suspect, may have had his own faith shaped by contact with the Lollards.

10. Tickle, *The Great Emergence*, 29–31.

were the *folkways* of the people, the ways in which they lived out their faith in Christian community. Many of these ways served as a grounding for my own spiritual formation, profoundly shaping my life and faith journey even as it has unfolded in a variety of totally unexpected ways, and for that I remain deeply and truly grateful. What is best in them can be adapted and continue to serve in the new ways that are now emerging.

In what follows, my intention is to blend stories and reflections that convey some of the spirit of what has gone before, and from which some jewels might be retrieved to be placed in new settings. I'll start with the Bible and a bit of theology, then move on to the formative disciplines of family and corporate worship, and eventually finish with some thoughts on how all of this invites us to do and be in the world . . . treasures old, and new.

2023

Looking back now, ten years after its initial publication, I remain very happy with the contents of this book. Much has changed in my life and in the PCUSA, things which I address in Postscript 2. At the outset, however, it seems important to note the deepened awareness in myself, and in the PCUSA, of the often-unconscious *privilege* and dominance long enjoyed by white Euro-Americans in the cultures of both church and state. This is, rather unavoidably, the case in this account of my family and community of origin.

Even those of us whose ancestors were not directly engaged in either the enslavement of African Americans and subsequent segregationism, or the policies of cultural and actual genocide inflicted on Native Americans, must now acknowledge that our forebears—and we ourselves—have benefitted from both and share complicity with those who imposed them. Black, indigenous, and other racial-ethnic groups continue to struggle with the economic and socio-cultural impact of our historic white privilege. For that previously unacknowledged aspect of this ancestral account, I do apologize, and I look to the day when the fullness of "liberty and justice for *all*" is really realized among us.

1

The Bible and the Covenant Tradition

ONE OF THE LEGENDARY figures in our little rural Kansas community was "Scotch John" Gemmell, a tall and sinewy old bachelor who lived with his small and birdlike sister Annie on their little farm a couple of miles west of the church. John and Annie were the last of the community to have immigrated, coming over with their elderly father and another single sister in the 1880s to join cousins in the US. Among the many stories about John are those of how he could quote almost any passage of the Bible from memory. Whenever a question arose in discussion, those present would turn to John Gemmell, and he would respond, "Weel, the buke says . . . ."

John's use of scripture was not without the wry humor typical of the old Scots. As a young man (sometime circa 1914) my Uncle Jesse remembered plowing in the field adjoining John's. Uncle Jesse's family had a modern—for those times—gang plow on which he rode behind the team, but John Gemmell in his field had the old single-bottom walking plow, pulled by his one horse. John's furrows, nonetheless, were the straightest Uncle Jesse had ever seen. Coming to the adjoining ends of their fields at the same time, Uncle Jesse shouted over to Scotch John, "Excuse me, Mr. Gemmell, but how do you manage to keep your furrows so straight?" John shouted back, "Nae man, having put his hand tae the plough, and looking back, is fit for the Kingdom of Heaven!"[1] Then, chuckling, he and his horse walked on.

The old Presbyterians were a "People of the Book" par excellence. Many knew it almost literally "kiver tae kiver." One of my most treasured possessions is a small Bible printed in Edinburgh in 1727 that belonged to my Anderson ancestors from Fenwick. Although it has long since lost its front cover, and even the first few pages of Genesis, it remains a tangible link to those who once used it regularly. Like many old Scottish Bibles, it has the metrical psalms printed in the back, so it could serve as

1. Luke 9:62.

Bible and "hymnal" all in one. Wherever Presbyterians were found, from the moorland cottages of Scotland to the log cabins and soddies of the American frontier,[2] if none else there were likely to be three books in the house—sometimes with two bound into one. There was a Bible for reading, a Psalter for singing, and a copy of the *Westminster Shorter Catechism* for memorizing. All were in regular use, with the Bible being read daily in family worship.

Not only was the Bible regularly read by the Presbyterians, as it was in all Protestant traditions; it was read in a particularly Presbyterian way. It was read through the lens of "covenant theology" as a sacred pact between God and God's people.[3] Although we Presbyterians are notorious for our long association with the doctrine of predestination, in my opinion the truly distinctive element in our theological tradition is the emphasis on the idea of the divine covenants[4] between God and humanity that was brought to the fore by the Reformers of the sixteenth century (Calvin, Knox, etc.) and by the so-called "Divines" of the seventeenth century. For some (Calvin, et al.) the focus was on God's gracious promises in calling and redeeming a people, while for others (Knox, et al.) the stress was put on the obligations of the covenanted community to live in strict obedience to God. In either case, the casting of the history of redemption—from Noah, through Abraham, Moses, and David, to Jesus and the apostles—was set in terms of covenant theology, of being in "right relationship" with God and neighbor. That focus continues among us right down to the present day, as witnessed by the PCUSA's *Brief Statement of Faith*:

> In everlasting love,
> the God of Abraham and Sarah chose a covenant people
> to bless all families of the earth.
> Hearing their cry,
> God delivered the children of Israel

2. My mother used to tell stories of her mother, as a young girl, briefly living (ca. 1890) in a soddy in the Sand Hills of western Nebraska, a barren place of isolation, wind, and blinding blizzards. The stories resembled those of Laura Ingalls Wilder in some of her Little House books, except that Grandma Gibson's father, Horace Greeley Davis, was a strict and staunch member of the UPNA, and was of a sterner disposition than the kindly Pa Ingalls.

3. Although deeply grounded in the scriptures themselves, the particulars of covenant theology began to be emphasized by proponents of the *via moderna* school of thought during the late middle ages by scholars such as William of Ockham and Pierre d'Ailly. Later on it particularly influenced the Reformed/Calvinist branch of Protestantism. See McGrath, *Historical Theology*, 150–155.

4. I.e. the progressively unfolding series of covenants from Abraham to Jesus.

from the house of bondage.
Loving us still,
God makes us heirs with Christ of the [new] covenant.[5]

The Presbyterians' covenantal understanding of Christianity came naturally, because it is so deeply grounded in the Bible itself. The narratives of the Hebrew Bible, and the writings of the prophets, are expressed in terms of the covenants said to have been made directly between God and Abraham, God and Moses, and so on. Both the writings of the apostles and the traditions of the gospels also draw deeply on the covenantal understanding of God's relationship with humanity. The church was, and is, understood in terms of the covenanted community. The sacraments of Baptism and the Lord's Supper are understood as covenantal ceremonies. Marriage, too, is understood in covenantal terms. God relates to us via covenants; we are bound to God and each other in covenantal relationships.[6]

The old Presbyterian bugaboo doctrine of predestination is really just a twist on the covenant notion. What was debated long and hard over the centuries was the question of "to whom?" God chose to offer the covenant of grace, and whether those to whom God offered grace could refuse it. The tortured permutations over "double predestination" and "irresistible grace" that haunted at least three centuries worth of Presbyterians finally received a happy resolution in the first half of the twentieth century when the Swiss theologian Karl Barth went back and read the writings of St. Paul with fresh eyes, noticing that all of the predestination passages really talk about Jesus as the "chosen" or "elect" one, and that the rest of us were and are chosen "in him" before the foundation of the world. Jesus is chosen and, by relating to him in faith, we share his election.

In very practical and secular matters, our covenantal understanding of God's dealings with humanity provided one of the essential bases for the emergence of constitutional government in Britain and the US. In the sixteenth century, John Knox and his English friend and fellow exile Christopher Goodman spent some of their time in Geneva writing study notes for an English translation of the Bible, later known as the Geneva Bible. The study notes made the covenantal understanding accessible to the laity. They shaped the perspectives of both Scottish Presbyterians and English Puritans for over fifty years before the appearance of the King James Version ("KJV") of the Bible, and they continued to be used for another fifty

5. PCUSA, *Book of Confessions*, C-10.3, lines 41–48.

6. Even when the seventeenth century Scottish Presbyterians wrote about witchcraft, it, too, was primarily understood in terms of a covenant: the "pact" made with the devil. See Christina Larner, *Enemies of God: The Witch-hunt in Scotland*.

years after the publication of the KJV. In those notes, Knox and Goodman pioneered the radical, and thoroughly biblical, political notion, derived from the book of Deuteronomy in particular, that kings and rulers are subject to the laws—i.e., the covenant—of God just like anyone else, *and* that the people are empowered by God to hold them accountable. Rulers who turn away from the covenant may be resisted, and even deposed, by the people, because they (the rulers) have broken the covenant.

John Knox actively pursued this belief in his opposition to his Roman Catholic nemesis, Mary, Queen of Scots. The coup that forced Mary from her throne and into exile (prison, and eventual execution) in England was a singular instance of a political revolution occurring as an integral part of the Reformation. Later Scots like Samuel Rutherford[7] promoted exactly the same notion in opposition to the tyranny of King Charles I in the 1640s. During the era known as the "Killing Times" in Scotland, following the Restoration of Charles II in 1660, the "Covenanters"[8] resisted the new Stuart absolutism in the name of "Christ's Crown and Covenant." Simultaneously, among the heirs of this way of thought in England was John Locke, a philosopher raised in a Puritan household, whose notions on limited government were passed on to architects of American independence such as Thomas Jefferson. Consequently, as we read the most famous lines of *The Declaration of Independence*, those "with ears to hear" note the echoes of John Knox, and of words attributed to Moses in Deuteronomy:

> We hold these truths to be self-evident, that all men are created equal, that they are endowed by their Creator with certain inalienable rights, that among these rights are life, liberty, and the pursuit of happiness.—That in order to secure these rights governments are instituted among men, deriving their just powers from the consent of the governed.—That whenever any form of government becomes destructive of these ends, it is the right of the People to alter or abolish it, and to institute new government.[9]

7. Rutherford, who lived ca. 1600–1661, was one of the Scottish Westminster Divines (i.e. a participant in the Westminster Assembly that wrote the Westminster Confession of Faith and catechisms) and professor of Divinity at the University of St. Andrews. His book *Lex Rex* makes the covenant theology case for holding rulers accountable.

8. The Covenanters were the radical adherents to the Scottish National Covenant of 1638 and the Solemn League and Covenant of 1643.

9. National Archives, "Declaration of Independence," lines 5–9.

Needless to say, I take great pride in my Covenanter ancestors, the common folks of Scotland whose faith inspired them in the seventeenth century to resist the tyranny of kings who wanted to dictate the form and order of the church, and also of the state. In the Killing Times the little parish of Fenwick had more martyrs than any other parish in Scotland. Some of the surnames of the Fenwick martyrs appear in the family trees of our kith and kin: Wyllie, Bicket, Tod, Gemmell, and so on. For nearly thirty years (1660–1688) the men, and women, of the *moss-hags*[10] put life and limb on the line for what they understood to be the "Crown Rights of the Redeemer" over and against the so-called "Divine Right" of any earthly king, and in due course their cause, mostly, prevailed in the wake of the Glorious Revolution that brought William and Mary to the British throne. Without doubt, those old Covenanters could be a rather daunting and even scary lot . . . in a way they were, at their most extreme, something like the Presbyterian Taliban of their time. (I do *not* in any way say that glibly!)

One of the dangers inherent in the Knoxian approach to covenant theology—one that John Calvin himself took pains to warn about—was a tendency toward forms of legalism and biblical literalism that could, and *did*, lead zealous extremists to try to re-create the conditions and systems of biblical times and cultures in their own times and places. Knox, I believe, verged repeatedly on this type of extremism and passed along the tendency to many of his spiritual heirs. Calvin, on the other hand, took a comparatively more progressive view, that the literal biblical mandates were given in particular historical contexts, and that other peoples and cultures had evolved and developed in their own particular sets of circumstances. Therefore, as Calvin saw it, while the broad principles and teachings of scripture were applicable across the centuries in various lands and cultures, there was no need to impose what we today would call a Fundamentalist (or an even more extreme Reconstructionist or Dominionist[11]) view onto society. It was both a strength and a weakness of the later Scottish Presbyterians that they took a very long time to move to the

10. A *moss-hag* is a pit or hole from which peat has been dug for fuel. They became the shelters and hiding places of the Covenanter fugitives.

11. Christian Reconstructionism (which is *very* different from the Jewish Reconstruction movement) is an extreme right-wing Calvinist movement that began in the 1970s. It promotes the use of the law code of the Hebrew Bible as the proper God-given basis for contemporary society. Dominionism is seen as an outgrowth of Reconstructionism, and holds that the United States, in particular, should be ruled by conservative Christians, or at least governed according to conservative Christian values and understandings of the law.

same conclusion as Calvin. Without that rigorist bent they might not have survived, let alone prevailed, over the Stuart kings, but it kept them caught "aye long" in a very stern and austere place.

It has to be admitted that a "plain," face-value reading of much of the Bible, especially the historical books of the Old Testament, can come as quite a shock to those who are not familiar with it. The repeated assertions that the God of Israel commands the expropriation of lands, holy war, murder, atrocities against non-combatants, acts of genocide, religious persecution, and the execution of religious and cultural non-conformists, has struck many across the centuries as, in fact, contrary to the true nature of God . . . at least as portrayed and taught by Jesus Christ. Unfortunately, some of the old Scots-Irish (among many others) were not shy about citing such texts as justification for their own crimes against Native Americans during the westward expansion of the United States. The continued use, and misuse, of such texts, right down to our own day, to justify actions like the ongoing Israeli occupation and settlement of Palestinian lands, makes plain the dangers and pitfalls of an overly literal and uncritical reading of scripture.

By the late nineteenth and into the twentieth centuries, groups such as the UPNA had come to see that they had to adapt themselves, carefully and mindfully, to the changes in the times and circumstances in which they lived.[12] By the early 1900s, they saw that the beliefs and practices of seventeenth-century Scotland were not necessarily suited to the America of Theodore Roosevelt and Woodrow Wilson. However, as they tried to adapt to the times, they were also at pains to remain mindful of the testimonies and heritage of their past. The task, as they saw it, was to speak to their times in a manner similar to that used by earlier witnesses in speaking to theirs. In the preamble to their 1925 *Confessional Statement*, the UPNA affirmed its adherence to the heritage of the Westminster standards, but then went on to say:

> Along with this [the UPNA] affirms the right and duty of a living Church to restate its faith from time to time so as to display any attainments in truth it may have made under the guidance of the Holy Spirit.[13]

12. While all the denominations were dealing with these issues, I cite the UPNA because, as I read the history, they seem to have been pioneers of the particular "middle" way into which Presbyterian thinking eventually moved.

13. UPNA, *Confessional Statement*, 7; reproduced also as Appendix 1 in this book. This statement appears in the Preamble.

This shift in the way of approaching and understanding the faith is seen most clearly in the way Presbyterians came to understand their creeds and confessions of faith as witnesses and testimonies to particular times and circumstances. It is also central to what we have since come to acknowledge about scripture itself . . . that it is both divinely inspired *and* addressed to the very human contexts in which it was originally written:

> The Scriptures, given under the guidance of the Holy Spirit, are nevertheless the words of men, conditioned by the language, thought forms, and literary fashions of the places and times at which they were written. They reflect views of life, history, and the cosmos which were then current. The church, therefore, has an obligation to approach the Scriptures with literary and historical understanding.[14]

As part and parcel of this approach, Presbyterians have also relied on the teaching that John Calvin derived from his own mentor, Martin Bucer of Strasbourg, that the Holy Spirit of God is at work among us, helping us to listen and hear the Living Word speaking through the written word in our day and time. This is true from the pulpit—which is why preaching is virtually a Presbyterian sacrament—and in the councils of the church, but also in the quiet of our own closets,[15] where we individually—layfolk and ministers alike—study scripture and pray.

In taking this approach to the scriptures over recent generations, Presbyterians have found new vistas opened to us on many of the key issues of our changing times. New understanding of issues regarding slavery, race, gender, sexuality, divorce, and marriage have moved beyond a literal proof-texting approach to the Bible to a broader understanding rooted in the deeper implications of the gospel, particularly in the Rule of Love given by Jesus himself.[16] There are times, we have discovered, when the Spirit actually overturns and moves beyond the letter of the law, with examples being found even in the scriptures themselves.[17]

That said, I think we have to admit that some of the very methodologies and approaches that produced the Reformation in the first place (textual and critical studies, etc.) have gotten in the way of our *common* access to the scriptures. Biblical study has become dauntingly technical and specialized, with claims and counterclaims from linguists, archaeologists,

14. PCUSA, *Book of Confessions*, C-9.29.

15. "Closets" were small private sitting rooms in seventeenth-century usage.

16. For example, see Rogers, *Jesus, the Bible, and Homosexuality*, Chapter 4.

17. Isa 56 and Acts 10, for instance.

historians, form critics, and so on. The various "quests" for the historical Jesus have often left people wondering if there is anything that we can reliably know about his life or teachings. On the other hand, current post-modern approaches to scripture invite us to view it more as story and symbol, to seeking the truth within it that transcends the merely factual and rational interpretations that have characterized our approach over the last five centuries. Current scholars like Marcus Borg invite us not only to be aware of the historical-critical work, but then also to shift perspective and read the stories with what he calls "a second naiveté," which, I think, is basically a mindful return to Scotch John's, "Weel, the buke says . . . ."[18]

However, to do that, we still have to know the book! Perhaps the biggest challenge for our "brand" of Christianity in the present day is the pervasive biblical illiteracy that has become the norm. Not only are people in the general culture unacquainted with the most basic stories and teachings of scripture; even lifelong church members now have a minimal (at best) knowledge of the Bible. Often, in conversation with church members, I hear them express the feeling that they lack the knowledge and tools to really understand scripture. Nor do they feel that they are equipped to undertake the practices of devotional reading (*lectio divina*) promoted by many authors and spiritual guides. Time and energy are at a premium in the hustle and bustle of daily life, and the distractions of the constant buzz of media and technology make it hard to create the life-space required for scriptural study and devotional reading. Yet, according to our tradition, the scriptures provide us with the teachings that open to us the two-fold knowledge in which all Wisdom consists (a la John Calvin): the knowledge of God and of ourselves. So, ways *must* be found.[19]

18. See, for instance, Borg, *The Heart of Christianity*.

19. The first sentence of *The Institutes of the Christian Religion* reads: "Nearly all the wisdom we possess, that is to say true and sound wisdom, consists of two parts: the knowledge of God and of ourselves." McNeill, 35.

2

"The Cotter's Saturday Night"

LIKE MANY OF SCOTTISH ancestry, I have a special affection for the "Immortal Bard," Robert Burns. Unlike many American Scots (at least), I even *ken* a fair amount of what he's saying . . . at least after I sit and study it a bit. Burns was an Ayrshire man, and that's where our *ain* folks came from. In one of his church satires, Burns took a poke at one of the ministers ("Wee Miller") who baptized some of my ancestral uncles and aunts at Kilmaurs and, in another poem, he made mention of the troubles at Fenwick ("lately . . . sair forfairn") that led to the founding of the Secession congregation there.[1]

"Rabbie" Burns is mostly viewed as the irreverent rascal that he often was but, in my opinion, he was a genuinely good-hearted sinner, a uniquely Scottish incarnation of the Prodigal Son who had several occasions to stand in the "public place" of discipline while the minister admonished him before the congregation for his sins . . . repeatedly fornication. Our Rabbie responded with some of the best satire ever written against the Kirk, and its not-always-humble ministers and elders, in works like "Address to the Unco Guid," "The Kirk's Alarm," "The Holy Fair," "The Ordination," and (my personal favorite) "Holy Willie's Prayer." Though those at whom he took aim might not have agreed, I think those poems were really a great gift to the Kirk and still bear a good reading; a true "speaking truth to power" for those with ears to hear.

That said, it is a bit surprising to find among Burns's musings what is perhaps the most warmly affectionate description in existence of what

---

1. The references to "Wee Miller" and to Fenwick are found, respectively, in Burns's "The Holy Fair" and "The Ordination." See Burns, *Poetical Works,* 19 and 34.

was probably *the* central practice of Presbyterian spiritual life across the centuries: family worship. While he was no great fan of the ministers and elders, Burns's brother Gilbert later told of how Rabbie bore a profound reverence for the way in which their father always presided over the family at prayer, and how that informed his portrayal of the simple "cotter" gathered at the fireside with his family, after a very simple but adequate supper, on the eve of the Sabbath at the end of a hard week's labor. Reading "The Cotter's Saturday Night," I can imagine myself just a few miles away, sitting with my own kin on a late November night beside the smoking chunks of peat on the hearth:

> The cheerfu' supper done, wi' serious face,
> They, round the ingle, form a circle wide;
> The sire turns o'er, with patriarchal grace,
> The big ha'bible, ance his father's pride:
> His bonnet rev'rently is laid aside,
> His lyart haffets wearing thin and bare;
> Those strains that once did sweet in Zion glide,
> He wales a portion with judicious care;
> And "Let us worship God!" he says with solemn air.[2]

The worship proceeds in three parts, beginning with the singing of a metrical psalm:

> They chant their artless notes in simple guise,
> They tune their hearts, by far the noblest aim;
> Perhaps Dundee's wild-warbling measures rise;
> Or plaintive Martyrs, worthy of the name;
> Or noble Elgin beets the heaven-ward flame;
> The sweetest far of Scotia's holy lays:
> Compar'd with these, Italian trills are tame;
> The tickl'd ears no heart-felt raptures raise;
> Nae unison hae they with our Creator's praise.[3]

Next, the reading of the Word:

> The priest-like father reads the sacred page,
> How Abram was the friend of God on high;
> Or Moses bade eternal warfare wage
> With Amalek's ungracious progeny;
> Or how the royal bard did groaning lie
> Beneath the stroke of Heaven's avenging ire;

2. Burns, *Poetical Works*, 98.
3. Ibid.

> Or Job's pathetic plaint, and wailing cry;
> Or rapt Isaiah's wild, seraphic fire;
> Or other holy seers that tune the sacred lyre.[4]

If not from the Hebrew Scriptures, then from the pages of the New Testament:

> Perhaps the Christian volume is the theme,
> How guiltless blood for guilty man was shed;
> How He, who bore in Heaven the second name,
> Had not on earth whereon to lay His head:
> How His first followers and servants sped;
> The precepts sage they wrote to many a land:
> How he, who lone in Patmos banished,
> Saw in the sun a mighty angel stand,
> And heard great Bab'lon's doom pronounc'd by Heaven's command.[5]

And finally, the prayer:

> Then, kneeling down to Heaven's Eternal King,
> The saint, the father, and the husband prays:
> Hope "springs exulting on triumphant wing,"
> That thus they all shall meet in future days,
> There, ever bask in uncreated rays,
> No more to sigh, or shed the bitter tear,
> Together hymning their Creator's praise,
> In such society, yet still more dear;
> While circling Time moves round in an eternal sphere.[6]

And so the poet turns to offer his own assessment, with a none-too-surprising jab—though again, mayhap, not undeserved—at the clergy:

> Compar'd with this, how poor Religion's pride,
> In all the pomp of method, and of art!
> When men display to congregations wide
> Devotion's ev'ry grace, except the heart!
> The Power, incens'd, the pageant will desert,
> The pompous strain, the sacerdotal stole;
> But haply, in some cottage far apart,
> May hear, well-pleas'd, the language of the soul;
> And in His Book of Life the inmates poor enroll.[7]

4. Ibid., 98–99.
5. Ibid., 99.
6. Ibid.
7. Ibid.

Though not regarded among the greatest of Burns's poems, "The Cotter's Saturday Night" was for many years one of the most popular and beloved of his compositions, and it impresses me as one of his most heartfelt. It speaks to the historic Presbyterian psyche. With few exceptions, I have been struck over the years with the genuine warmth of the memories of family worship I have encountered among older relatives and friends, and in the written memoirs of others. With only minor variations, the pattern they recall was that described by Burns, and the thing that most vividly stood out, regardless of the years that had passed in the interim, was the recollection of their parents (traditionally led by the father) at prayer. Family worship—usually done in the morning, immediately after breakfast—was an essential thing, at the heart of family life. For at least three hundred years, it was the primary discipline of spiritual formation in the Presbyterian way of being Christian.

The inspiration for this tradition comes directly from scripture, from a passage that lies at the core of both Jewish and Christian life and practice, the *Shema,* found in Deuteronomy 6 and incorporated by Jesus into the Great Commandment:

> Hear, O Israel: The LORD is our God, the LORD is One. You shall love the LORD your God with all your heart, and with all your soul, and with all your might. Keep these words that I am commanding you today in your heart. Recite them to your children and talk about them when you are at home and when you are away, when you lie down and when you rise. Bind them as a sign on your hand, fix them as an emblem on your forehead, and write them on the doorposts of your house and on your gates.[8]

Like any good spiritual discipline, family worship required—and requires—commitment. Almost nothing was allowed to interfere. In extreme old age, one of my cousins recalled being raised in the home of her grandparents (my great-grandparents) in southeast Kansas in the 1890s. As Hattie remembered it, there were only two or three days in the year when they did not have family worship; those were the days when the "boys" (my grandfather and his brothers) left the farm by 4:00 a.m. to drive the twenty miles to Pittsburg (Kansas), either to take the hogs to market or to fetch the winter's coal. Other than that, family worship was as much a part of each day as getting dressed and having breakfast.

---

8. Deut 6:4–9, modified by author.

Directly across the road from my great-grandparents lived my great-grandfather's brother, Uncle Alex.[9] Uncle Alex was one of the elders in the Osage congregation, and was regarded as the most devout of all the family. One of Alex's sons later recalled the day they rose from the breakfast table only to notice all the neighbors coming up their lane, following the threshing machine. Unperturbed, Uncle Alex led the family into the front room where they proceeded as usual with worship, cutting nothing short. Only after that did they emerge to greet the neighbors and get down to the day's work. So far as I know, none of the neighbors—who were also mostly relatives and fellow members of the church—took anything amiss at the delay.

Although it was certainly never an "either-or" sort of thing, I have been struck over the years by the fact that, unlike some of the historically more pietistic denominations,[10] the old-time Presbyterians did not stress doing personal devotions, such as private Bible-reading and prayer, as much as they emphasized the regular practice of praying together as a family. In a very real sense, the basic unit of the old-time Presbyterian church was not the congregation, but the family. It was there, *not* in the Sunday School, that children learned the scriptures, the metrical psalms and hymns, and the practice of prayer. The school of faith was, first and foremost, in the home, and that applied beyond just the regimen of family worship. The principle components of Presbyterian family religion extended also to the practice of giving thanks—"saying grace"—at table before meals, to the "holy resting" of Sabbath observance, and to the study of the catechism.

Catechizing is a practice that goes back to the Reformation. It was one of the original tools for the widespread religious instruction of the laity, and came to be focused primarily on children and youth. When the minister came around to visit, particularly during the lead-up to the celebration of the Lord's Supper (which in earlier times occurred, at most, only four times a year), part of his job was to examine the family on the catechism. Knowledge of the catechism was an essential part of the preparation for church membership.

When I was twelve years old and about to join the church, I clearly remember my mother going to the desk in our dining room and taking a little booklet from the drawer. It was an old and slightly tattered copy of the *Westminster Shorter Catechism*. The year was 1968, and our minister

---

9. In a typical familial tangle, Alex—pronounced "Elick"—was married to my great-grandmother's niece, creating interesting degrees of double cousinage.

10. Methodist, Nazarene, etc.

had not included the catechism in his instruction, but Mother still thought I needed to take the time to read and study it a bit. In her day—she was born in 1912—she had been required to memorize it, and later on, when I was in college, I actually tried to do so, too.[11] To this day, I find myself falling back, surprisingly often, to those classic—and, alas, patriarchally framed—definitions of Presbyterian belief and practice:

Q1. What is the chief end of man?

A. Man's chief end is to glorify God, and enjoy him forever.

Q2. What rule hath God given us, whereby we may glorify and enjoy him?

A. The Word of God, which is contained in the scriptures of the Old and New Testaments, is the only rule to direct us how we may glorify and enjoy him.

Q3. What do the scriptures principally teach?

A. The scriptures principally teach what man is to believe concerning God, and what duty God requires of man.[12]

So it goes, through definitions of the godhead, the doctrines and processes of salvation (including predestination), and so on. One question in particular remains, in my mind, especially instructive when it is properly understood:

Q20. Did God leave all mankind to perish in the estate of sin and misery?

A. God, *having out of his mere good pleasure,* from all eternity, elected some to everlasting life, *did enter into a covenant of grace . . .* to bring them into an estate of salvation by a Redeemer.[13]

11. I got the doctrinal part memorized, but I never did make it through all the questions on the Ten Commandments and the Lord's Prayer.

12. PCUSA, *Book of Confessions,* C-7.001–7.003.

13. Ibid., C-7.020, italicized emphasis added. The striking bit in that answer, which too many over the generations have not known to notice, is the uniquely Presbyterian/Calvinist perspective on the atonement: the way in which God chose to redeem the world in Christ was totally voluntary; neither God's own justice nor some cosmic necessity dictated the life and death of Jesus. It was simply the triune God's "good pleasure"—Father, Son, and Holy Spirit together—to proceed in that way, working freely in and with Christ to implement the new covenant of grace. See McGrath, *Historical Theology,* 154–155.

It has to be admitted that some of the catechism questions are rather daunting, especially when one is a child:

Q14.   What is sin?

A.   Sin is any want of conformity to, or transgression of, the law of God.[14]

So far so good, but then later on it asks:

Q84.   What doth every sin deserve?

A.   Every sin deserveth God's wrath and curse, both in this life and that which is to come.[15]

Now, that gets a body's attention!

A couple of other answers particularly stick out in memory:

Q60.   How is the Sabbath to be sanctified?

A.   The Sabbath is to be sanctified by a holy resting all that day, even from such worldly employments and recreations as are lawful on other days . . . except so much as is to be taken up in the works of necessity and mercy.[16]

Q98.   What is prayer?

A.   Prayer is an offering up of our desires unto God, for things agree-able to his will, in the name of Christ, by the help of his Spirit, with confession of our sins, and thankful acknowledgement of his mercies.[17]

Those bits have been constant good reminders over all the intervening years.

Unfortunately, the major (glaring!) deficiency in the *Westminster Shorter Catechism* is the virtual absence of any adequate teaching concerning comforting things like assurance, confidence in believing, and hope.

14. Ibid., C-7.014.
15. Ibid., C-7.084.
16. Ibid., C-7.060.
17. Ibid., C-7.098.

Bits may be found, subtly tucked in when one goes searching, but nothing in the *Westminster Shorter Catechism* rises to the level of the beginning the great *Heidelberg Catechism* from Germany:

Q1. What is your only comfort in life and in death?

A. That I belong—body and soul, in life and in death—not to myself but to my faithful Savior, Jesus Christ.[18]

Not surprisingly, I cannot say that I have *ever* encountered the sort of nostalgia for memorizing the catechism that I have for the practice of family worship. Some are proud of the accomplishment, and of still re-membering the answers, but the memory of actually doing it ranks at best with those of learning the rules of grammar, or eating turnips. Others, not without reason, shudder at parts of the content of the old answers. That said, the practice had a profound impact, in the way that it formed and guided the beliefs and the practices of Presbyterian Christians across the generations, and in how it formed a common context of understanding and shaped the core identity of the community.[19]

I have not seen a study of this (if one has ever been done), but from anecdotal evidence I think that the practice of family worship, and other aspects of religious practice in the home, began to wane in the wake of World War I. For whatever reason, the younger generations began to let lapse the practices of their parents and grandparents. Not every family did, of course, but I think that is when the trend began.[20] *Not* coincidentally, I suspect, that was also when the various Presbyterian groups began our still-ongoing, long, slow decline. Various families and groups held onto the practice longer than others . . . including my husband's UPNA-raised parents who, at least until aging and health concerns intervened, still be-gan each day together with scripture and prayer.

Since the 1950s, the focus of spiritual formation for children and youth has almost totally shifted from home and family to the church's Sunday School and youth programs and, frankly, it has *not* worked very well. Our kids grow up to be great people, with amazing abilities and—by

18. Ibid., C-4.001.

19. In retrospect, for those who undertook to memorize the catechism, perhaps the greatest benefit of the process was to be found in the raising of the questions rather than in providing the answers, because it was in the posing and organizing of the questions that a thoughtful and integrated faith could be formed.

20. See, for instance, Phyllis Tickle's fascinating discussion on the impact of the automobile on family religion in *The Great Emergence*, 85–87.

and large—good social consciences. However, once they are grown and head out on their own, they, more often than not, disappear from regular participation in the community of faith.[21] There are many reasons for this, of course, but I sincerely believe that one of them is that it simply takes more than an hour or two a week to pass on faith, and a class setting is not where children and youth will truly experience faith as a lifestyle, and see it modeled.[22]

The cultural norms of the last half-century or so shifted toward the adoption of *laissez-faire* attitudes *vis a vis* sharing with our children one of the core aspects of life: our spirituality. At some point we (collectively) seem to have embraced the self-censoring notion that to be broadminded means to shy away from speaking our truth about what we hold most vital and dear. "We'll let them choose . . ." is a fine attitude to take—eventually—but it rarely occurs in a vacuum. Real choice in spiritual matters requires more than just indifferent (unbiased) information. It requires a sense that faith really matters to and for those who practice it, and that it meaningfully relates to the realities of life as we live it.

I do not think transmitting a faith tradition has to mean "imposing our values" on our children. It does not have to be dogmatic, or sectarian, but it does mean speaking about what John Philip Newell calls "our treasure."[23] It means speaking openly and honestly about what gives meaning to our lives, and what sustains us. I know families of mixed faith traditions—Christian and Jewish, Protestant and Catholic, etc.—where the vital connection of each parent to their own tradition has been richly integrated into the home, and transmitted to the next generation. Unfortunately, to refrain from encouraging and nurturing our kids in living a life of faith is also a values statement—a negative one.

I also know that we cannot simply go back to family worship after breakfast on the farm . . . at least not unless we go back to the farm. Our world has become too busy and too complex. The pace of contemporary life makes it a rarity for many families even to sit down, all together, at a meal more than once every few days . . . and that meal may have just been delivered from the local pizza place or picked up at the supermarket deli.

---

21. In recent years, it seems they have also not been returning once they have children of their own.

22. Any still-ongoing debates about prayer in the schools really are a useless distraction. As I see it, the issue is completely insignificant compared to that of the absence of spirituality at home.

23. Newell, *Christ of the Celts*, 131.

So, what is the art of the possible? One of the practices I admire is having a "family night" at home once a week, with the whole family present and interacting together. That, I think, would be achievable for almost any family that is willing to be intentional in practicing their faith at home, in something of a twenty-first century rendition of "The Cotter's Saturday Night." The devout among our Jewish faith-cousins do it all the time, each Friday night, as they come together at the family table to welcome the Sabbath. The week's work is done. Dinner is ready. The sun is setting. According to custom, the mother of the household lights the candles and the family blesses itself with the light. A cup is poured, bread is shared, prayers are recited, and holy conversation follows. It is really not so very different from what Burns described.

In our home we pray together daily, at bedtime. For much of the year I have to admit that it is just that, a brief time of prayer for those we love, for the earth, and for ourselves, followed by a version of the Prayer of Jesus (i.e., the Lord's Prayer). Over the years, it has become our practice to do a more extensive form of evening prayer during Advent and Christmas, Lent and Easter. In those seasons, we include scripture readings and the singing of the metrical psalms and appropriate hymns, along with our prayers. We light a candle as we begin, remembering the Light that shines in darkness, and at the end we close the day with a blessing and the kiss of peace. It is very simple, and very good.[24]

The other thing I would wish in regard to this subject is that Presbyterians would learn to really appreciate one of the great treasures of our current church. Not in my wildest dreams could I imagine most of us going back to traditional forms of catechizing.[25] However, ever since it was first published, I have believed that the PCUSA's *Brief Statement of Faith* provides us with a great "dynamic equivalent" of sorts to what the *Westminster Shorter Catechism* long offered our ancestors: a powerful spiritual formation tool that sums up our essential belief and identity and guides our life together as a particular community of faith. In less than two

---

24. One of the resources we use is by John Phillip Newell, who several years ago collaborated with his then-young son Cameron to put together the book *Celtic Treasure*. Intended for family worship, the book goes through a seven-week cycle of great themes, readings, and prayers covering the broad range of scripture: "Stories of Creation," "Journey and Promise," "Power and Justice," "Sayings of Wisdom," "Songs of the Soul," "The Good News of Jesus," and "Letters of Love." I know no better primer for introducing children, and adults, to many of the most important parts of the Bible.

25. Albeit the current PCUSA *Study Catechism* is a great resource for young and old alike.

pages of written text, set in poetic form, it provides a profound expression of the heart of Presbyterian Christianity—both faith and practice—set in accessible terms for our day and time:

> In life and death we belong to God.
> Through the grace of our Lord Jesus Christ,
> The love of God,
> And the communion of the Holy Spirit,
> We trust in the one triune God, the Holy One of Israel,
> Whom alone we worship and serve.[26]

Just that opening provides a sort of Presbyterian *Shema* expression and, as it continues, it reminds us of essential truths about the God "whom Jesus called Abba, Father":

> In sovereign love God created the world good
> and makes everyone equally in God's image
> male and female, of every race and people,
> to live as one community.[27]

I think it sums up who we know we are, deep in our bones, if we'll just take the time to remember, and teach our children.

---

26. PCUSA, *Book of Confessions*, C-10.1, lines 1–6.
27. Ibid., C-10.3, lines 29–32.

3

Sabbath

For many of my generation, the words "Scottish" and "Sabbath," when found together, immediately conjure up memories of the 1981 movie, *Chariots of Fire*. The movie tells the tales of two British athletes competing in the 1924 Paris Olympics, one of them being the Scottish runner Eric Liddell, who refused to compete in his principal race when it was scheduled on the Lord's Day, but then went on to win gold in a different event. One of the most beautiful scenes in the movie shows Liddell preaching in the Paris congregation of the Church of Scotland, on the day he had been due to run, and reciting from the pulpit the words of Isaiah 40:31: "But they that wait upon the Lord shall renew their strength; they shall mount up with wings as eagles; they shall run, and be not weary; and they shall walk, and not faint."

Some will find it odd that I am about to base my reflections on Presbyterian traditions of Sabbath-keeping primarily in the thought of a twentieth-century Jewish theologian, but to me it makes absolutely perfect sense. Sixty years ago, in his glorious little book *The Sabbath: Its Meaning for Modern Man*, Rabbi Abraham Joshua Heschel wrote:

> When history began, there was only one holiness in the world, holiness in *time*. [This via the sanctification of the seventh day in the creation account.] When at Sinai the word of God was about to be voiced, a call for holiness in *man* was proclaimed: "Thou shalt be unto me a holy people." It was only after the people had succumbed to the temptation of worshipping a thing, a golden calf, that the erection of a Tabernacle, of holiness in *space*, was commanded. The sanctity of time came first, the sanctity of man

came second, and the sanctity of space last. Time was hallowed by God; space, the Tabernacle, was consecrated by Moses.[1]

According to Rabbi Heschel, there was something created on each of the days of creation. The thing created on the seventh day was rest. The Hebrew word *menhua*, which we translate as "rest," means more than just stopping work. *Menhua* is a much richer concept, embracing notions of tranquility, serenity, peace, repose, happiness, stillness, and harmony. It is the stillness of the waters in Psalm 23, and the word used, in later times, for the "rest" of eternal life. It is the essence of eternity.[2]

To keep Sabbath, we have to lay aside the toils associated with the "things" of space and place that occupy us during the week. Six days are given for labor in the world of space, but the seventh is for "rest" in the realm of time:

> He who wants to enter the holiness of the day must first lay down the profanity of clattering commerce, of being yoked to toil. He must go away from the screech of dissonant days, from the nervousness and fury of acquisitiveness and the betrayal in embezzling his own life. He must say farewell to manual work and learn to understand that the world has already been created and will survive without the help of man. Six days a week we wrestle with the world, wringing profit from the earth; on the Sabbath we especially care for the soul. The world has our hands, but our soul belongs to Someone Else.[3]

Writing in the 1840s, James Taylor, a handloom weaver in Fenwick, celebrated the special quality of time he experienced at the end of a Sabbath day in a surprisingly similar vein of thought. As he wrote on an evening in early spring, the village was quiet, and from the various thatched cottages along the lane he could hear bits of song from various families at their evening devotions. He says:

> On this day no children are allowed to break from the family circle and run on the street. No Sabbath breaker, with his trotting dog at his feet, is to be seen. All keep within their dwellings, or sit in their little garden plots. Children repeat to their parents the questions of the catechism, or recite some of the songs of David. Those of more advanced years ponder over the Word of God, or investigate the writings of the practical, the pious, or

1. Heschel, *The Sabbath*, 9–10.

2. Ibid., 22–23.

3. Ibid., 12.

the more profound of our divines. It is the day of God, the day appointed for man to worship, the day of rest for man and beast, and it is meet for the children of the Father, the followers of the meek and lowly Jesus, to keep sacred his day.[4]

Taylor's rather romantic musings are not, of course, the whole story. One old story told to me years ago by a minister friend tells of the hubris that could arise among the more "o'er strict" sort of sabbatarians. As the tale goes, the young minister in a Scottish parish was "blessed" with having a rather severe old elder on the Session.[5] The day finally came when the elder disapproved of someone's misbehavior just once too often. The young minister turned to him in irritation and snapped, "Well, you know, our Lord himself broke the Sabbath!" The old man gathered himself with great dignity and replied, "Aye. And I never thought any the better of him for it, either!"

In point of fact, the New Testament is clear that keeping the Sabbath is not a requirement for Christians. The Apostle Paul, himself a highly educated rabbi before becoming a follower of Jesus, was always careful to make clear delineations between what was required of practicing Jews versus what was required of Christians of non-Jewish origin. Writing, almost certainly, about the Sabbath in his letter to the Christians at Rome, he says, "Some judge one day to be better than another, while others judge all days to be alike. Let all be fully convinced in their own minds."[6] The sayings of Jesus, too, make it clear that "The Sabbath was made for humanity, not humanity for the Sabbath."[7] That said, the words of the prophet Isaiah best sum up the historic Presbyterian attitude toward the spiritual discipline of Sabbath-keeping:

And the foreigners who join themselves to the LORD, to minister to the LORD, to love the Name of the LORD, and to be the LORD's servants, all who keep the Sabbath and do not profane it, and hold fast my covenant—these I will bring to my holy mountain, and make them joyful in my house of prayer.[8]

---

4. Taylor, *The Annals of Fenwick*, 12.

5. The "Session of the Elders Bench" was the historic terminology for a local church council. It is still called the "Session" in Presbyterian churches.

6. Rom 14:5.

7. Mark 2:27, modified by author—and it must be noted that, despite the portrayals of the gospels, the same teaching, almost verbatim, is stressed in Judaism.

8. Isa 56:6–7, modified by author.

In traditional Judaism, the Sabbath is welcomed as virtually a living being, Queen Sabbath, the very Presence that once dwelt in the Holy of Holies of the Jerusalem Temple. In some Jewish sects, the men literally went out to the fields to welcome the arrival of Queen Sabbath with joyous singing and dance.[9] Sabbath is a time of renewal for both body and spirit. There is worship, yes, but it is also a time when families gather together at the table, and in the night it is a time for couples to "sanctify the Sabbath" with their lovemaking. When the Sabbath ends, its departure is marked with wine, sweet spices, and the blessing of the light.

Unfortunately, most old-time Presbyterians were far more dourly observant of the Sabbath, giving any stereotypically-portrayed Pharisee of the New Testament more than a run for the money. In the process, I think, we never grasped the depth of the meaning of "enjoying" God or Sabbath in the way our Jewish cousins have. Though not without its consolations, old Presbyterian memories of keeping the Sabbath tend to deal mostly with what could *not* be done . . . especially, it seems, if it was fun.

There is another story about Uncle Alex, my great-grandfather's brother, which I heard repeatedly from older family and church members in my childhood. According to the legend, there was a young minister trying out for the pulpit at Osage.[10] Uncle Alex and the other elders arrived early and were waiting when the preacher arrived. As he tied his horse to the hitching rail they were shocked to hear him whistling. Uncle Alex—reportedly a cheerful whistler himself on weekdays—immediately said, "Well boys, we will *not* have a preacher that whistles on the Sabbath!" And that was that.

The focal point of the Presbyterian Sabbath was the church service, or "preaching," as it tended to be called. There were few excuses for failing to show up. Illness and infirmity counted, of course.[11] On the rarest of occasions when winter weather got too bad, services might be canceled. Even then, my mother would talk about one very icy day when it was their family's month to be janitor and she and her dad walked the three miles to

---

9. I think I can say, without fear of contradiction, that there is no known instance of Presbyterians doing that!

10. It is interesting how *young* ministers keep coming up in these stories.

11. My dad had stayed home with a bad cold on 7 December 1941, and heard the news about Pearl Harbor on the radio while the rest of the family was off at church. When the others came home—my mother and brother, and my aunt and uncle who lived just up the road—they would not believe him until they heard the news broadcast for themselves.

the church to be sure that, if anyone else showed up, there would be a fire going. No one did, and they walked back home again.[12]

Once church was over, the rest of Sabbath Day, except for works of necessity and mercy, was to be spent in "holy resting" from usual weekday activities. One time, when my great-grandmother's brother, Uncle Tom Anderson, was visiting from western Kansas, the two of them decided to venture over to visit their sister, Maggie Gemmell, on a Sunday afternoon. Maggie and Alex Gemmell were the strictest of sabbatarians—and reputedly very strict in all sorts of things—so Uncle Tom and my great-grandmother were astonished to find the family out working in the field when they arrived. They had somehow gotten the days mixed up . . . and so that week they kept Sabbath on Monday instead.[13]

For working men and women such as the Fenwick weavers and Kansas farmers—and for later factory workers in places like Glasgow (Scotland) and Pittsburgh (Pennsylvania)—Sabbath was a day of physical respite, and a blessing for that reason alone. It was a much-needed day of rest and relaxation in the midst of lives of hard physical exertion. Even as the men rested from all but the essential chores, the women—having "done ahead" much of the meal preparation on Saturday—did only the most necessary bits of cooking and washing up. Otherwise, a good nap was often at the top of the agenda.

I have to confess that, growing up on the farm, I secretly felt just a wee bit superior to some of our Methodist neighbors because, during the busy seasons of planting, haying, or harvest, *they* would go work in the fields on the Lord's Day, while the Presbyterians did not! Only once or twice do I remember my father deciding on a Sunday afternoon that, because of threatening clouds on the horizon, we ought to go out and load the wagon and the truck with some hay, baled the day before. On those

---

12. Another Osage story that I cannot resist inserting—as it is weather-related—concerns Uncle Willie Cuthbertson, another brother of my great-grandfather, and Uncle Alex. Willie had been badly burned as a child and had a wooden peg-leg. He never married and moved around among the family. Once, when he was living with Uncle Alex, he lost his wooden leg on the way to church. It was early spring and very muddy. He had stuck his leg out the side of the carriage as they rode along, and somehow neither he nor anyone else realized it had fallen off until they arrived at the church. The next carriage that came along carried Uncle Albert's family, and they had found Uncle Willie's leg standing straight up in the middle of the road, stuck in the mud. They had retrieved it, and Willie and his leg were thus happily reunited. No whistling, but I suspect there was quite a bit of laughter at church that day.

13. Uncle Tom, being a bit more liberal and flexible than his elder sister, Maggie, is said to have been extremely amused by the whole thing.

occasions we only loaded the hay, we did not unload it. The rest just had to stay out in the field and get wet, despite the extra work it would take to get it dry enough to store. Otherwise, the only work done on Sunday was the necessary chores, or taking care of sick livestock.[14]

The Sabbath was thus treasured by many, if not most, adults. For young children, however, it was a much more difficult time. They naturally wanted to play, and were not allowed to do so. One distant relative remembered asking her mother if she could go and climb the apple tree one Sabbath afternoon. "You may if you want to pick an apple and eat it," she was told, "but not if you are just going out there to play." Another time she recalled wanting so badly on a Sunday to work on the quilt pieces she was making that she went and hid behind the organ in the corner of the sitting room to do so.[15] For boisterous young boys the day could be even more of a trial, since things like ball games were particularly frowned upon. Some families, who could afford it, had a few special toys, like a Noah's Ark set, that were kept for use on Sundays.

The other social categories of people—in addition to "you, and your children"—to whom the biblical Sabbath laws explicitly applied were servants and slaves, strangers and aliens. According to the Bible, Sabbath observance was not just a privilege for the privileged, but a right (and responsibility) to be respected for and by all. The version of the Ten Commandments given in Deuteronomy does not cite the story of creation as the reason for sanctifying the seventh day. Instead, it says:

> Remember that you were a slave in the land of Egypt, and the LORD your God brought you out from there with a mighty hand and an outstretched arm; therefore the LORD your God commanded you to keep the Sabbath day.[16]

In former days it might have been easier to be mindful of the use we make of others—and not just on the Sabbath. The hired help were usually right there, in front of us: house servants and farm laborers, shopkeepers and janitors. Part of Sabbath discipline was, and is, to be aware of those whose time, energies, and skills we use . . . remembering that, before and above all else, they are our fellow humans, and they too deserve not just the physical rest but also the dignity and freedom that Sabbath betokens.

14. It did seem that some old cows deliberately waited until Sunday morning to have trouble calving, so that we not only missed church but had to call out the veterinarian as well.

15. I suspect that, on that occasion, her mother may have just decided not to notice.

16. Deut 5:15.

Nowadays it is often less clear. From the ATM to the gas pump, we are not always obviously imposing on others' time and energy as we go about our business on a Sunday. Yet we need to be mindful of the ways in which we are imposing on the cooks and servers in restaurants, the sales assistants, janitors, and security personnel at the malls, media presenters and performers, and so on. In this "service" economy, our servants (and even slaves) are usually met—if we meet them at all—in briefly transactional encounters, allowing us to be even more thoughtless of them and of what they do for us.[17]

The ongoing struggle over immigration issues in the US is also relevant to our understanding of Sabbath. Legal or not, the first and foremost fact about the "strangers and aliens" who have come among us to work is that they are people. They are not things or tools. More than *any* other spiritual discipline that I can think of, keeping Sabbath reminds us to remember our shared humanity, be mindful of the ways in which we impose on one another, and treat everyone with respect.

As in the Bible, the classic Presbyterian Sabbath was also a day of rest for working animals. My mother's forebears were Scots-Irish Presbyterians who first entered the US in 1788, via South Carolina. The Gibsons lived in Chester County, SC until the 1830s when, because of their anti-slavery views, they moved west to Illinois.[18] One of the stories that became part of the communal lore was that two groups of anti-slavery Presbyterians left South Carolina on the same day. One group decided that, due to the exceptional circumstances of the journey, they were justified in traveling on the Sabbath as on other days. The second group decided that they would not travel on the Lord's Day, and so they stopped each Saturday night and only resumed the journey on Monday morning. According to the story, both groups arrived at their common destination in Illinois on the same day, but the second group, *and* their horses, were in much better physical shape at the end of the long journey.

Other than being used to pull carriages to church and back, horses too had Sabbath Day off. The cows still had to be milked, and the eggs gathered, but that was all. Historically it was *not* a day for hunting, though the folks in our community were not always of one mind as to whether the ban also applied to fishing, especially if you went late in the day, toward sundown.

---

17. Do I dare even mention professional athletes here, particularly the football players who spend their Sundays risking limb, if not life, in the coliseums of this age?

18. More on this later.

In my dad's family, one thing deemed appropriate on Sabbath day was to go check the cows. When I was a kid we would take the pick-up and head over to the pasture late on a Sunday afternoon—dad, mother, and I—just before sunset, enjoying the beauty of the evening and the acrobatics of the barn swallows swooping low over the grazing cattle. Dad's cousin Hattie had similar memories of walking out with their grandmother on such an evening in the early 1900s, seventy years later vividly recalling "smelling the new grass" and the conversation they shared as they wandered among the calves. Sunday nights were also a good time to go see the growing crops, or to go out to the garden and, maybe, pull an onion or pick just a couple of tomatoes to go with supper.[19]

By the time I was a kid my folks had loosened up some from their upbringing, but Sunday was still very much a holy day. I had a much-loved Bible storybook, that I still have tucked away, and the papers from Sunday School included pictures that we could take home to color on Sunday afternoon. Thankfully, my parents thought *The Wonderful World of Disney* was sufficiently edifying for me to watch on television Sunday nights, along with a light supper of sandwiches or—in the winter—popcorn.

Beginning in the early 1960s, our local café opened for Sunday lunch and we often went. However, that was frowned on by some in the church. On the Sundays when we ate at home, mother had the best-ever recipe for Swiss steak, that would slow cook while we were at church. Other than the very occasional "emergency" stop to buy a loaf of bread or some milk, I never remember my parents shopping on a Sunday. Once in a while, in the summer, we would drive into town to the Tastee Freez, right about sunset, for ice cream cones. That was the sum of our Sunday commerce.

When I was in college at Sterling, many of the local United Presbyterians figured that the college cafeteria had to be open to feed the students anyway, so it was alright for them to go up there to eat after church. On Sabbath night, however, there was only a serve-yourself cold supper for the students. Some of the old UPNA and Covenanter families still refused to take a Sunday paper. I remember our pastor's wife telling us how she used to cross the street so as not to be seen with her husband when he bought the Sunday paper.[20]

---

19. Fresh tomato sandwiches with a slice of onion are a real treat! No bacon required.

20. He had been raised a Methodist, and not all of the Presbyterian ways ever fully "took" with him.

In both college and seminary I made it a practice not to study on the Sabbath. It proved to be a wonderful discipline. Sunday afternoons were a time for naps, walks, spiritual reading, reading for pleasure, and visiting with friends and family. Sometimes, rather than having the cold supper at the college, I would "just happen" to turn up at the minister's house in time to have a cup of tea and some cinnamon toast with him and his wife. Those times were always accompanied with wonderful conversations and deep laughter.[21] Back then, the United Presbyterian and Reformed Presbyterian churches in Sterling still had evening worship on Sabbath night, followed by the college fellowship hosted in the homes of various church members. Rich memories, all—things I would not have experienced had I not taken the time.

Over the last fifty years, American culture has tended more and more toward forgetting, rather than "remembering," the Sabbath (whether it be Christian—Sunday, Jewish—Saturday, or Muslim—Friday). From brunch bunches to Sunday morning kids' soccer, from charitable 10k runs to farmer's markets and art studio tours, the traditional Christian Lord's Day has lost ground to its ever-growing multitude of competitors. That shift is reasonable, given the realities of our diverse and secularized culture, but it is also challenging, not just because of the problems it creates for church programming but also because of how it reduces the space *for* time in our lives. Once again Rabbi Heschel speaks wisely:

> Technical civilization is man's conquest of space. It is a triumph frequently achieved by sacrificing an essential ingredient of existence, namely, time. In technical civilization, we expend time to gain space. To enhance our power in the world of space is our main objective. Yet to have more does not mean to *be* more. The power we attain in the world of space terminates abruptly at the borderline of time.[22]

Time is *not* money. Time is the fleeting context we have for life, and for the love of God and one another. Mindless distraction—including too many hours spent browsing the internet—can be as much a violation of the Sabbath as digging a ditch. Sabbath is the sacrament of time, and an invitation to being present in the moment.

---

21. Harriette was one of the most joyful Christians I ever knew, and when she laughed it was from her toenails up.

22. Heschel, *The Sabbath*, 3, emphasis added.

In the last few years, a new emphasis on observing Sabbath has come into vogue as a spiritual discipline.[23] This neo-sabbatarianism differs from the old ways in not necessarily focusing on the particular day, or on specific "forbidden" activities. It is not even necessarily Christian, or Jewish. Instead it looks to the common human need for *taking time* on a regular basis, time to pause in the busy-ness of life to seek physical and spiritual "holy resting" and renewal. I totally commend and recommend this move but, in all honesty, I know that I personally still need *the day* itself.

In the ever-more-manic pace of the last twenty-some years, we have still tried to remember the Sabbath day in our home. Even now, on the "clear Sabbath mornings" in our beloved mountain congregation, I get to "list to the clear-ringing bell"[24] and then sit in church lifting—at the odd moment—my eyes "to the hills," and to the apricot tree in the churchyard. After church and Sunday lunch we usually head home, maybe to take a nap, or read. Sometimes I do a bit of contemplative puttering in the garden.[25] In the evening we have a light supper and maybe watch a DVD, in place of Disney. Sometimes we call our relatives in others parts of the country to catch up. Part of my current Sabbath rest is to attempt—not always successfully—to leave the dishes and all but the most necessary kitchen clean-up for Monday morning.

What it all comes down to, in the end, is choice. Will we choose to honor Sabbath, or not? Will we *take* the time? American culture has not historically been "user friendly" to the Jewish Sabbath, but it persists because it is a practice at the heart of their faith. Modalities may change, but the Presbyterian and Christian practice can also continue if we will it to. Presence awaits.

> O teach Thou us to count our days
> And set our hearts on Wisdom's ways;
> Turn, Lord to us in our distress,
> In pity now Thy servants bless;
> Let mercy's dawn dispel our night,
> And all our day with joy be bright.[26]

—PSALM 90 (TUNE: ST. CATHERINE)

23. A great resource is Wayne Muller, *Sabbath*.

24. Words from the 1857 hymn "The Church in the Wildwood" (aka, "The Little Brown Church in the Vale"). Pitts. Online: http://nethymnal.org/htm/l/i/littlebc.htm.

25. Recalling, as I do so, C.S. Lewis's beloved teacher Professor Kirk, an atheist who, out of respect for his Scots-Irish Presbyterian roots, always put on a better suit to garden on Sunday.

26. UPNA, *The Psalter* (1912), #246.

4

Psalmody—Singing the Word of God

IT WAS SABBATH MORNING at the Sterling United Presbyterian Church, sometime about 1977. The service was just beginning and the first song was the old Scottish Psalter version of Psalm 23, sung to the tune "Evan":

> The LORD's my shepherd, I'll not want,
> He makes me down to lie,
> In pastures green He leadeth me
> The quiet waters by.[1]

As we sang I noticed Chase, the minister, suddenly staring strangely from the pulpit, and saw tears begin to well up in his eyes. Following the direction of his gaze, I saw why. There in the second row, standing next to Harriette (Chase's wife) was her father, Dr. Willie Sutherland. Dr. Sutherland was a retired UPNA missionary to Pakistan who, some years before, had suffered a stroke that left him unable to speak anything but muttered nonsense . . . even though we all could tell his mind was perfectly clear.[2] But on that Sabbath morning he was singing, singing every . . . single . . . word! Among those who saw, there wasn't a dry eye in the house, and even now I find myself tearing up as I remember.

If miracles are defined as happenings beyond the range of scientific explanation, what happened that day was not a miracle, but it was the closest I have come to actually experiencing one. From similar accounts, I have come to understand that the part of our brain dealing with singing is different

1. UPNA, *The Psalter* (1887), #72.

2. Quite the charming rascal, he was; a Highland Scot with sparkling eyes and always courtly manners. The first kilt I ever donned was his, a loan from Harriette for an event at church.

than the part that deals with speech—which is what sometimes allows such events to occur. From my limited experience, with Alzheimer's and other diseases and conditions, the things that come through at such times are some of the deepest and most ingrained memories in our minds. They are the things we *know* at the core of our beings, perhaps beyond memory itself.

One thing is sure: Willie Sutherland knew those psalms. One of the stories Harriette loved to tell on her father was how, one time during his earlier years as a missionary in India (up in the tribal region of what is now Pakistan), her dad got a fever and was out of his head. In his delirium, Dr. Sutherland sang through the entire Psalter, twice! He sang it once in English and once in Urdu, the local language. "Poor Mama!" Harriette would chortle, "She had perfect pitch, and he was off key the whole time!"[3]

The practice of "exclusive psalmody" may be the least known of the old Presbyterian distinctives among contemporary church members. At the Reformation, the practice of congregational singing was itself an innovation. After centuries in which music in worship had increasingly become a performance done by specialized choirs in monastic communities, cathedrals, and collegiate churches, singing was restored to the people as a distinctive component of Protestant piety. In Calvin's Geneva, the metrical paraphrases of the Psalms became the dominant, though not exclusive, source of hymnody. Once again, however, it was among John Knox's Scots and the English Puritans that it came to be so fiercely adhered to.

Their rationale was simple enough. The so-called "Regulative Principle" of those times—adopted in reaction to the perceived "idolatry" of the Roman sacramental and liturgical system—said that only what scripture commands is to be allowed in worship—nothing else. The Psalms were seen as the Bible's hymnbook. God had inspired the Psalms to be sung in worship in both temple and synagogue, and that was (assumed to have been) the practice of the New Testament Church as well. Jesus sang Psalms; hence, only the Psalms were meant to be sung during worship. No merely "human" compositions were allowed.[4]

Beginning in the eighteenth century, parts of the Presbyterian family began to open up to singing hymns as well as psalm paraphrases. Englishman Isaac Watts (1674–1748) was a pioneer in the movement, first giving his psalm paraphrases a Christological interpretation, and then including

---

3 Fittingly, on the day Willie Sutherland died, his two daughters, Harriette and Ruth, sat by the bed singing psalms to him until he had passed "beyond the veil."

4. Instrumental music and choirs were excluded on the same grounds, their use having been tied to the now-defunct ceremonial regime of the Jerusalem Temple.

new poetry, based in Christian experience, among his compositions.[5] In the Church of Scotland John Morison's "Scottish Paraphrases" added texts from outside the Psalter to the congregational repertoire and helped open the door for the eventual embrace of hymnody. Mainstream American Presbyterianism embraced Watts and evangelical hymnody by the time of the American Revolution. Among the stricter sorts of Presbyterians, however, exclusive psalmody continued to hold sway throughout the nineteenth and on into the twentieth centuries. The UPNA came out with its first *Psalter-Hymnal* as recently as 1927, and the RPNA continues to sing only the metrical psalms, without instrumental accompaniment.

I was raised in a hymn-singing congregation, but my mother often talked about her parents having come from the psalm-singing tradition and she would show me her mother's old UPNA Psalter . . . which is another of my treasured possessions. When I went off to Sterling, the United Presbyterians still often included metrical settings of the Psalms in worship, particularly during "requests" in the evening services. I also sometimes used to slip over to the Reformed Presbyterian service on Sabbath night, or join them for occasional psalm-sings in private homes. What voices they had! They were vigorous singers, with good four-part harmony.[6]

Although, as today, some congregations had dreadful singers, the commonality of Scotland carried a deep affection for the metrical psalms and the traditional tunes . . . as witnessed by Burns in "The Cotter's Saturday Night." Our Fenwick ancestors were notable singers, and even composers. The familiar tune, "Martyrdom," that is regularly used for Watts's "Alas and Did My Savior Bleed," was composed by Hugh Wilson, the village schoolmaster in the early nineteenth century, and was originally called "Fenwick."[7] An early twentieth-century memoir of former days in Fenwick includes the following account, probably dating to the mid-1840s:

> Fenwick was famed for its excellent singers in old time, and especially for its congregational singers. In those days, when any church in the neighboring towns was in need of a precentor,[8] the first place where they made enquiry regarding a qualified man was Fenwick, and generally Fenwick was able to supply the want . . . .

5. "Joy to the World," which we all consider a Christmas carol, is in fact Watts' rendition of Ps 98.

6. Somewhat ironically Ps 98A, "Oh Sing a New Song to the Lord," was a great favorite.

7. In the PCUSA's *The Presbyterian Hymnal* the tune is also, more appropriately, used as the setting for Ps 116.

8. The precentor was the song leader in a Scottish congregation, armed only with a tuning fork and a knowledge of tunes in the right metre to fit the chosen Psalms.

There is a tradition that on one occasion a city minister, who himself possessed some gift of song, was so impressed with the full harmony with which the opening Psalm was rendered that he proceeded to put the congregation to the proof. Those were the days before it was customary to supply the leader of praise with a note of the Psalms and hymns to be sung previous to the commencement of the service. No precentor would then have been considered fit for his office if he had not been capable of selecting an appropriate tune while the preacher was reading over the verses to be sung. So this minister had a free hand, and this is how he made use of it to test the musical abilities of the congregation, as he himself afterwards explained:

"To open with I had given out a common metre Psalm. They sang it so well that I thought next I would try them with a short metre Psalm. This they sang even better than the first. Then, thinking I might puzzle them with a peculiar metre I gave out the 124th, 'Now Israel may say, and that truly,' but they carried this through best of all with heartiness and birr, each part going, and all in perfect time and harmony. I'm sure it was not better sung even that day when the Edinburgh folk sang it till heaven and earth resounded, as they marched up from the Netherbow Port leading home again their banished minister, John Durie. Next time I preach in Fenwick I must have St. George's Edinburgh to 'Ye gates lift up your heads on high.' It would be grand."[9]

I like to think that my great-grandmother, then a young girl, might have been in the congregation on that day.

On the other side of the world, the early United Presbyterian missionaries in what is now Pakistan are said to have gone through the bazaars listening to the popular tunes of the time, which they then noted down and used as the settings for the Punjabi/Urdu versions of the metrical psalms (the *Zaboors*) used in worship. Among the largely illiterate population of the nineteenth century, the Punjabi *Zaboors* served as a great evangelistic tool, and as their de facto Bible. In more recent times these *Zaboors* have come to be regarded as cultural treasure for all of Pakistan. That, at least, is how the retired UPNA missionaries told it.[10]

Modern biblical and patristic studies have long since shown, pretty convincingly, that the Psalms were not the exclusive hymnal of either the Jews of Jesus's time or the early church. The New Testament itself contains

9. Fairlie, *Matthew Fowlds, Centenarian Weaver,* 45–46.

10. Because they are spoken of in the Koran, and because of the somewhat analogous cultural settings, these settings of the Psalms appealed more broadly to the Islamic populace than evangelical Christian hymnody.

a few brief bits of what are believed to be early hymns, and other early writings do so as well. That said, psalmody in its various forms lies at the heart of Christian spiritual tradition. For a millennium and a half, the Psalter has provided the liturgical framework for Benedictine monastic life, with the monks chanting all one hundred and fifty Psalms every week! Whether done "exclusively" or not, the regular singing of the Psalms remains one of the best ways to learn to know and love them deeply. They are a great tool of spiritual formation, as testified by the old paraphrase of Psalm 119:11 that I grew up singing: "Thy Word have I hid in my heart, that I might not sin against Thee."[11]

The tradition of metrical psalmody, of bringing the texts into versified form set to regular tunes, was the particularly Reformed and Presbyterian contribution to the wider practice of psalmody in Christian worship. Although current musical trends toward chant and praise music have value, the great benefit of versification, in my experience, is the memorization of the sung texts. On many a Sunday I find myself not having to look at the hymnal as the congregation sings a familiar old psalm paraphrase or hymn. It is simply inside me, hopefully like it was inside Willie Sutherland.

Some of the metrical texts are particularly iconic. Besides the various versions of Psalm 23—and others cited elsewhere throughout this text—they include the following . . . with some of the wording adapted to inclusive language:[12]

Psalm 1 (tune: Arlington, CM[13])

> How blest and happy is the one
> Who walketh not astray
> In counsel of ungodliness,
> Nor stands in sinners' way . . . .[14]

Psalm 8 (tune: Dunfermline, CM)

> O LORD, our Lord in all the earth
> How excellent Thy Name!

---

11. Psalm adaption by E.O. Sellers from the 1908 hymn "Thy Word Have I Hid in My Heart." Online: http://nethymnal.org/htm/t/h/y/thywhihh.htm.

12. The versions that follow are mostly found in the 1933 and 1955 Presbyterian hymnals, but are drawn from older Scottish and UPNA Psalters.

13. The names of the tunes are given along with their metre. All the tunes are Common Metre (CM), except *Ajalon*, which is 77.77.77. I previously cited the tune St. Catherine, the metre of which is 8.8.8.8.8.8.

14. Adapted by the author from UPNA, *The Psalter* (1887), #1.

Thou hast Thy glory spread afar
Upon the starry frame . . . .[15]

Psalm 42 (tune: St. Agnes, CM)

As in its thirst the panting hart
To water brooks doth flee,
So pants my longing soul, O God,
That I may come to Thee . . . .[16]

Psalm 46 (tune: Winchester Old, CM)

God is our refuge and our strength,
In straits our present aid,
Therefore although the earth remove,
We will not be afraid . . . .[17]

Psalm 51 (tune: Ajalon, 77.77.77)

God be merciful to me;
On Thy grace I rest my plea;
In Thy vast abounding grace,
My transgressions all erase.
Wash me wholly from my sin;
Cleanse from every ill within . . . .[18]

Psalm 103 (tune: Fenwick/Martyrdom, CM)

O thou, my soul, bless God the LORD;
And all that in me is
Be lifted up God's holy Name
To magnify and bless . . . .[19]

Psalm 121 (tune: Dundee, CM)

I to the hills will lift my eyes;
From whence shall come my aid?
My help is from the LORD alone,
Who heaven and earth has made . . . .[20]

---

15. UPNA, *The Psalter* (1912), #14.

16. UPNA, *The Psalter* (1887), #142.

17. Ibid., #157, adapted.

18. RPNA, *The Book of Psalms for Singing*, #51D.

19. UPNA, *The Psalter* (1887), #324, adapted.

20. UPNA, *The Psalter* (1912), #344, adapted. I shall never forget singing this on a Sabbath morning in 1988, at the rather plain and simple little church in Aviemore,

The ultimate Reformation era psalm paraphrase is the traditional Old Hundredth sung to the Long Metre tune of that name, composed by Louis Bourgeois in John Calvin's Geneva and subsequently embraced by Scots and Puritans alike. It is essentially our equivalent to Martin Luther's "A Mighty Fortress is Our God" and it has been used across the centuries by Presbyterians all over the world:

> All People that on earth do dwell,
> Sing to the LORD with cheerful voice;
> Serve God with mirth, God's praise forth tell,
> Come ye before God and rejoice.
>
> Know that the LORD is God indeed;
> Without our aid God did us make;
> We are God's folk, God doth us feed,
> And for God's sheep God doth us take.
>
> O enter then God's gates with praise,
> Approach with joy God's courts unto;
> Praise, laud, and bless God's Name always,
> For it is seemly so to do.
>
> For why? The LORD our God is good,
> God's mercy is forever sure;
> God's truth at all times firmly stood,
> And shall from age to age endure.[21]

The benefits of embracing the practice of psalmody stretch beyond mere memorization and internal integration. In the current era of interfaith interaction between the three great Abrahamic religions—Judaism, Christianity, and Islam—the Psalter stands as a shared treasure (explicitly honored in both the New Testament and Koran) of the three faiths. The Psalms can, and do, speak across boundaries that divide. The Psalm texts also contain a treasure trove of the ecological spiritual content found at the very heart of the Judeo-Christian tradition, witnessing to God's presence and revelation in, with, and through the natural world.[22]

Scotland. The small tour group I was with attended worship, and this psalm setting opened the service . . . with the highland hills clearly visible through the plain glass windows.

21. Ibid., #313, adapted. Besides being iconic, that particular paraphrase amply demonstrates some of the awkwardness of "translating" the Psalms into metre, and also the pervasiveness of the use of masculine pronouns in reference to God.

22. Take a "green" glance at Psalms 8, 19, 23, 24, 29, 42, 46, 65, 84, 90, 104, 121,

Saying this, I am fully aware that there are more than a few problematic texts in the Psalms, Psalm 137—with the lines on bashing in the heads of Babylonian babies—being the infamous case in point. Many Psalms contain apparently vengeful, and even hateful, sentiments that are, in fact, unworthy of transmission in the context of Christian worship and spiritual formation—period. In my experience, however, many of the troublesome portions can also yield themselves to sensitive re-interpretations (i.e., paraphrases) that retain the spiritual integrity of the original texts without necessarily perpetuating the prejudices of ancient authors.[23] In much the same way that Isaac Watts once interpreted the Psalms in his Christological renderings, contemporary interpreters can and should seek ways to let them speak in life-affirming and inclusive versions.

Although there are times when I also question the theology of *many* hymns—particularly all the "bloody fountain" ones of my childhood, and the sappy "cotton candy clouds" songs from college years—I have no desire to return to exclusive psalmody as the practice of the church. What I do wish, though, is that present-day Presbyterian congregations would at least take seriously the option of using metrical versions of the Psalm of the Day listed in both the weekly and daily lectionaries of the church. That alone would ground us more fully in both scripture and the heritage of our faith community, and it would quite possibly help in re-forming us, in our awareness of God's earth and in the forging of new bonds of fellowship with our kindred of other faiths.

> Behold the goodness of our Lord,
> How blest it is to be
> A company of God's beloved,
> In holy unity.

—PSALM 133 (TUNE: CRIMOND, CM)[24]

136, 139, and 148, for example.

23. Nan Merrill's *Psalms for Praying* does this beautifully, though not perfectly, and not in a form set for singing.

24. Anderson, *Singing Psalms*, 67. (Also in PCUSA, *The Presbyterian Hymnal*, #241.)

John Knox presiding at the Lord's Supper at Calder House,
Sir David Wilkie, 1839
(*Engraving in author's collection*)

5

Sacramental Occasions

I WAS ORDAINED AS a Minister of the Word and Sacrament in the Presbyterian Church on Friday evening, October 22, 1982, at the Osage Presbyterian Church outside of Girard, Kansas, the congregation in which I had grown up and where my family had belonged since 1879. On Sunday morning, October 24, 1982, I preached there, performed my first baptism, and presided at table celebrating the Lord's Supper for the first time. The child I baptized on that Sunday was my eldest grandnephew, Nathaniel. My dad (Nat's great-grandfather) stood as the elder assisting at the baptism. I know I used the 1946 version of *The Book of Common Worship* that day, for both the Baptism and the Communion liturgies. The baptismal service in that edition begins with the following scriptural sentences:

> The mercy of the Lord is from everlasting to everlasting upon those that fear Him, and His righteousness unto children's children;
> To such as keep His covenant, and to those that remember His commandments to do them . . . .
> For the promise is unto you, and to your children, and to all that are afar off, even as many as the Lord our God shall call.[1]

That last sentence is Acts 2:39; it is from the Apostle Peter's response to the first Christian converts on the day of Pentecost. I know of no better proof text for the covenantal understanding of child and infant baptism in

---

1. P.C.U.S.A., *The Book of Common Worship* (1946), 121. I still love and use this book for various services, but nowadays I modify them to make the language more inclusive.

the Presbyterian tradition. God's promise is for us, *and* our children. The children ultimately have to embrace that promise in faith, but the promise *per se* extends to them just as the promise, and sign, of the covenant made with Abraham extended to his descendants.

Strangely enough, I was not baptized as an infant, or even as a small child. The influence of my father's mother—already long deceased when I came along—was strong. Her family was from the Christian Church (Disciples of Christ) with a history stretching back to the early days of that movement in the 1820s, and the Disciples practice "believer baptism." As a result, neither my brother nor I, nor my aunt's son, were baptized as infants. Even though we were Presbyterians, our parents had us wait until we joined the church . . . in my case, at age twelve.[2]

It was Easter Sunday, 1968. My friend Ellen and I were baptized and joined the church together. At this point, over forty years later, I have no memory of the specific questions asked of us that day, but I know we affirmed our faith in Jesus as Lord and Savior, and our intention to be faithful members of the church. I know the congregation also promised to receive us as full members and to support us in living a life of faith. I remember the old silver bowl on the table—the same one I later used for baptizing Nathaniel—and kneeling on the hard floor. I remember the feeling of the water on my head, and drips running down and off my forehead. Afterwards I did not feel "saved," but I did feel like I finally *belonged*.

Anyone who has ever gone through a church membership class in the Presbyterian Church probably recalls that, in our tradition, there are only two official sacraments, Baptism and the Lord's Supper.[3] By no stretch of the imagination is there anything "magical" in the Presbyterian understanding of the two sacraments, though there is something truly *mystical* in the rites. The words, actions, and elements—water, bread, and wine—used in the celebration and administration of the sacraments are "signs and seals" of the covenant relationship established, according to the promise of Christ, between God, the believers, their children, and the entire faith community. The physical symbols serve as "outward and visible" signs of that relationship in much the same way as a wedding ring serves as the symbol of the covenant established by a couple when they

2. I had *really* wanted to join at age eight, but my folks and the minister talked me into waiting until age twelve. I think that was a mistake on their parts, but they all meant to do what was best.

3. Other things, like marriage and ordination, were and are regarded as ordinances established by God, but they were not specifically *instituted* by Jesus as integral parts of the New Covenant of grace.

are married. The tangible symbols are set aside from "common use" to "sacramental use" in the prayers, but the holiness resides in their use and not in the things themselves. In the bread and wine of Communion, the Real Presence of Jesus is not *in* the elements (as in Roman Catholicism), or *with* them (as in Lutheran tradition), but *through* them as they serve as the designated means of encountering the risen and living Christ anew.

Presbyterians regard the sacraments as the making of a covenant, not just between us and God, but also between us and one another. Although we now tend to allow friends and family to stand with the parents at a baptism, specifically designated godparents have long been forbidden in our tradition because the entire congregation—representing the entire church throughout the world—is seen as responsible for bringing up all the children among them in the faith.[4] Likewise, in the Lord's Supper we *are* the "body" of Christ, together receiving the tangible symbols of the body and blood that bind us together in faith as one mystical body in and with him.

The story of Jesus's Last Supper is the oldest story we know of him. It is the one actual story about Jesus that St. Paul tells in his letters,[5] and Paul's letters were written some twenty years before the gospels (ca. 55 CE). So, from the beginning, the church has been concerned about coming to the table to share bread and cup as Jesus did.

Back in Scotland, all the way back into the days of John Knox himself, it was the custom for congregations to actually come to the table and sit together at Communion . . . in a mode seen as equivalent to Jesus and his Disciples gathering at the Last Supper. The people would come to the table, where the minister would offer an exhortation, repeat the words of Jesus, offer a prayer of thanks, break the bread and pour the cup, and then pass the elements to the elders and the people to share with one another. When all was done there was another prayer, and the people returned to their places in the kirk. It was simplicity itself.[6]

The Knoxian way of doing Communion was peculiar to him, and his Scottish successors, among the Reformed and Presbyterian churches.[7] It is

4. In the "fear and admonition" of the Lord, as "the buke" says.

5. I Cor 11.

6. Thomas Cranmer, the first Protestant Archbishop of Canterbury and the author of much of *The Book of Common Prayer*, had little patience for folks of John Knox's ilk, and once wrote a colleague to the effect, "If brother Knox wants to receive Communion in the manner of Christ and his Apostles, then let him lay upon the floor!" For the exact wording see Lorimer, *John Knox and the Church of England*, 103–105.

7. My suspicion is that it might have come from the Lollard influence that I note elsewhere.

clearly another instance of the "regulative principle" of worship stringently applied in practice . . . doing absolutely only what scripture directs to be done. It also provides a uniquely vivid demonstration of the Presbyterian understanding of the sacrament. Not just the elements, but the entire setting, the words and the actions, are meant to be the *means* through which the living *remembrance* of Jesus is enacted. [8] The minister at the table speaks, not his or her own words, but the words of Christ. The minister gives thanks, as Christ did. The minister breaks the bread and pours the cup in the sight of the people, as Christ did. The minister gives the bread and cup to the people with the words of promise that Christ spoke. The speaking, praying, breaking, pouring, giving, and receiving are really as sacramental as the bread and wine. Each is a means through which the living Christ is re-membered within the context of the body assembled to share the feast. In a very real sense, although the minister presides, it is the body together that celebrates the Supper, and it is hosted by Christ himself.

Although many Presbyterian churches (including ours) still occasionally have a "Scottish Communion" at the table on special occasions, most long ago gave way to the practice of the elders serving Communion in the pews, or—more recently—to having the people come forward to be served by "intinction."[9] I grew up on the bread cubes and tiny cups of Welch's grape juice passed among us in the pews, but our minister had at least introduced the (allegedly) Scottish custom of the Great Entry, in which the elders withdrew during the Communion hymn, and then came processing in during the last verse with the elements, making the table ready. I remember the whole building, which was just a small clapboard structure, shaking a bit as the half dozen farmers "with heavy tred" came down the center aisle. It made a lasting impression!

Presbyterians have been notoriously "snippy" across the centuries over any hint of idolatry in regard to the Lord's Supper.[10] The attitude extends beyond how we regard the elements of bread and wine to even what

8. The late Scottish biblical commentator William Barclay discusses the Greek word *anamnesis* (the act of remembrance) as something in which an ancient memory was made sharply and vividly alive for the participants. Passover is such a divinely mandated "memorial" for the Jewish community, and the meaning of the Supper of Jesus is seen by Barclay as a "reorientation" of that memorial of deliverance. Barclay, *The Lord's Supper*, 51–52.

9. Intinction entails the communicants each tearing off a bit of the bread and dipping it in the cup.

10. More on this to come in Chapter 7.

we insist on calling the table. It is a "table." It is the Communion Table, or The Lord's Table. It is never, ever, called an "altar" in the Presbyterian Church. Why? The answer that I have long had burned into my memory is: "We have no altar, for anyone who erects an altar overturns the cross of Christ, where one sacrifice was made."[11]

For a long time it was not thought proper to put anything on the table except at Communion. Over time, some churches began to put a plate, chalice, and flagon on the table to remind the congregation of the sacrament. Only in the later nineteenth and on into the twentieth centuries did crosses, Bibles, offering plates, and candles regularly begin to appear on the table. Opinion remains divided on whether it is appropriate to have flowers placed there, or not. The simple, and relatively unadorned, Communion Table stands at the center of our worship—literally, always reminding us to remember.

Unfortunately, over the generations we Presbyterians—like most western Christians—developed our own particular quirks and superstitions around the Lord's Supper. While Protestants gave up any notions of the sacrament as an atoning "sacrifice" in and of itself, we remained grimly and somberly focused on the atoning death of Jesus as the *crux* of the rite. As a child, the only Communion hymn I can remember being used in our congregation was Watts's "Alas and Did My Savior Bleed." Communion was solemnly funereal.

It was also an occasion for somewhat fearful self-examination and feelings of guilt. As I recall, the Words of Institution from 1 Corinthians, said by the minster, always included St. Paul's admonition:

> Wherefore whosoever shall eat of this bread, and drink this cup of the Lord, unworthily, shall be guilty of the body and blood of the Lord . . . . For he that eateth and drinketh un-worthily eateth and drinketh damnation unto himself, not discerning the Lord's body.[12]

Words like that tended to get one's attention, particularly that of a rather sensitive and already angst-ridden teenager.

The solemnity and fear of "unworthy" participation surrounding the Lord's Supper meant that, for a long time, it was infrequently celebrated among Presbyterians. In many places in Scotland, Communion was held

---

11. I have heard this quote attributed to John Calvin, but cannot find where it occurs in this exact form in his writings. It also sounds like something John Knox could have said.

12. 1 Cor 11:27–29. KJV.

only once, or maybe twice, a year. Standards were supposedly strict, and the tables were rigorously "fenced" (i.e., unrepentant sinners were warned off). Sometimes, however, by the late eighteenth century, observances had degenerated into the type of "Holy Fairs" satirized by Burns where:

> There's some are fou o' love divine;
> There's some are fou o' brandy."[13]

When I was growing up, we had Communion only four times a year, on the first Sabbath of each quarter of the year (January, April, July, and October). There was no intentional connection to any of the holidays. Occasionally the spring Communion coincided with Palm Sunday or Easter, but that was always totally accidental. The Supper itself was seen as a major occasion, sufficient unto itself. Notice was always given the preceding Sabbath, with the expectation that the church members would take time to prepare themselves beforehand.

Stricter sects of Presbyterians used to practice "close" ("closed") Communion, admitting only members of their own congregation to the table. The reason, according to the old church manuals, was not to imply that others were not Christian, but rather out of a pastoral concern to make sure that all who partook were sufficiently prepared in heart and mind to participate. Even among the broader mainstream, it is only within the last thirty years or so that baptized children have been permitted to participate in the Lord's Supper before becoming fully professed (confirmed) church members. I remember having a great longing to partake as a child . . . and a wee bit of curious fear as the plates and trays passed me by.[14]

In former days these "sacramental occasions" were preceded by a day of fasting, preparatory church services, and a round of visits by the minister and elders to all who wished to come to the table. After being examined, both in their knowledge of the faith and catechism, and in regard to their conduct and state of life, approved communicants would be issued a communion token[15] that had to be presented to the elders as the person came to the table on the appointed day. Those found wanting in their preparedness were suspended from participation. Following the Communion service itself, the Communion "Season" (i.e. the entire series of services) concluded with a separate service of Thanksgiving, usually later the same

---

13. Burns, *The Poetical Works*, 21. "Fou" means "full," but it also means "drunk."

14. I loved it when it was our family's turn to provide the elements, as that meant I could have some of the bread and juice later, at home.

15. Usually a small lead coin—I actually have one from Fenwick.

afternoon or evening. Some of our older relatives remembered such services at Osage and, the last I knew, the RPNA still has them . . . though, as I understand it, they no longer use tokens or even strictly require the practice of close Communion.

The Disciples of Christ movement was originally sparked, in large part, by the severity and control of Presbyterian traditionalists over things like Communion. Thomas Campbell (1763–1854), who started the movement in 1809, was a Presbyterian minister from Northern Ireland who settled in the US and eventually rebelled against the rigid theology and severe discipline of the church. Joined, and ultimately succeeded, by his son Alexander (1788–1866), the Campbells sought to return to the simplicity of the apostolic church of the New Testament. In addition to adopting believer baptism by immersion, their movement soon came to include the weekly celebration of the Lord's Supper, shorn of the obsession over "worthy" participation.[16] Communion was, after all, an ordinance of grace, and faith.

Communion is about grace and faith, and it is about the gathered body. I think it also needs to be clearly recognized as a sacrament of the *living* Christ, not just the dying Jesus. When the UPCUSA and two other Presbyterian denominations produced *The Worshipbook* in 1970, they included several small and very simple, yet revolutionary, additions to the Communion liturgy. First and foremost, the invitation to the table in that service shifted the emphasis away from the traditional mournful solemnity towards a joyful celebration of the risen Jesus in the midst of the people:

> Friends: This is the joyful feast of the people of God!
>
> People will come from east and west, and from north and south, and sit at table in the kingdom of God.
>
> This is the Lord's table. Our Savior invites those who trust him to share the feast which he has prepared.
>
> According to Luke, when our risen Lord was at table with his disciples, he took the bread, and blessed and broke it, and gave it to them. And their eyes were opened and they recognized him.[17]

The revised service proceeds on with the essential traditional components—words of institution, prayer of thanks, breaking and pouring, etc.—and a few more small tweaks, but just the initial "spin" of the invitation made, and makes, a huge difference.

---

16. Either Thomas or Alexander is said to have been particularly incensed over the issue of using Communion tokens.

17. UPCUSA, et al, *The Worshipbook*, 1970, 34.

The thing I treasure the most, as a Minister of Word and Sacrament in the PCUSA, is the privilege and responsibility of presiding at the table. There is a sense of awe that comes in enacting the holy mystery, and in watching what happens among the people as they participate. In my experience, most ministers share this sense, at least when we allow ourselves the space to do so in the busy-ness of leading worship.

One of my great regrets is that I have never happened to be present for a Communion service at which my husband's father has presided.[18] I understand that he had a reputation among the missionaries in Pakistan for the meaningful way in which he led the service, moving some to tears. One time I did at least get to receive the bread from him, as he assisted in serving at a Thanksgiving Eve service. He had to sit in a chair beside the minister as the congregation came forward to partake, but his face glowed with joy and peace as he offered the plate to each one, calling us by name as he offered "the body of Christ . . . for you." It was truly a holy moment.

In recent years I have tried more and more to find the appropriate balance at Communion of stressing God's gracious and inclusive welcome, and the Living Presence of Christ, along with the older emphases on the solemn remembrance of Jesus's death, and the self-giving love that consecrates the New Covenant. As the authors of one of my current favorite books point out, it was the living Christ who shared himself at table with those he loved *before* he submitted to those who would violently take his life.[19] It was to those same beloveds that the risen Christ came again, to reveal himself at table in the breaking of bread.

I personally want more Communion. I don't say that as a minister, but as a follower of Jesus. Like the old Campbellites, I wish we had it weekly, at least, but I would also like to integrate it even more fully into home and family life. At the time of the Protestant Reformation, private Communion services were strictly prohibited. The prohibition was a reaction to the perceived idolatrous abuses of private masses during the era leading up to the Reformation. It was (and is) based on the absolutely true understanding that Communion is inherently communal. At the same time, there is a deep richness and appropriateness to sharing the tradition and story together at the family table, as the first Christians apparently did. If we think about it, simply pausing to give thanks for the food as we

18. Doug's dad is living, but due to issues of his age and health it seems unlikely that I will ever have this experience.

19. See Brock and Parker, *Saving Paradise*, 160. Rita Nakashima Brock is a Disciples of Christ minister.

sit down together connects us to the Table of Jesus. It only requires a small step or two beyond that for a meal to become the intentional sharing in the Bread of Life and Cup of Blessing.[20] The precedent and potential is self-evident as we look yet again to the practice of our Jewish cousins, whether gathered year by year at the Passover Seder or week by week at the Sabbath table with wine and challah.

For all the differences, John Knox and the Campbells' common desire was for Jesus's followers to share the Supper as he intended it to be shared. Like Knox, I prefer a simple celebration . . . but one more cheerful and even less verbose than his. Like my Disciples kin, I long to see Communion shared regularly. Whether at church, or gathered with a small group—duly authorized—around someone's dining table, all that is necessary are a few appropriate words of invitation, a prayer of thanks, the repeated words and actions of Jesus, and the sharing of bread and cup. Like Jesus, I like to conclude with a song (I like to begin that way, too). For the prayer of thanks, I prefer to go with the bare basics, beginning with two brief blessings I have adapted from Jewish tradition:

> Blessed are you, O Lord, who holds and guides the universe. You give us bread from the earth. It will be for us the Bread of Life.
> Blessed are you, O Lord, who holds and guides the universe. You give us the fruit of the vine to make our hearts glad. It will be for us the Cup of Blessing.

This is followed by a brief "free" prayer of thanks, remembering the creative and redemptive work of God and Christ, asking the blessing of the Spirit on the elements and those present, and offering petitions for the world and people in need. The prayer concludes with a version of The Prayer of Jesus (The Lord's Prayer). It is enough.

> In this the covenant is sealed,
> And heaven's eternal grace revealed.
>
> —JOHN MORISON, *SCOTTISH PARAPHRASES*[21]

---

20. The liturgy for an Agape in *The Worshipbook* comes very close to it.

21. The full text of Morrison's 1781 paraphrase is found in both the P.C.U.S.A.'s *The Hymnal*, 360, and the UPCUSA's *The Hymnbook*, 448. Over the last several years we have used the paraphrase in the congregation where I serve as Parish Associate on Maundy Thursday as a way of everyone joining together in the "words of institution" of the Lord's Supper. As all sing, the pastor and I do the sacramental actions of breaking the bread and pouring the cup.

6

"Thy Will Be Done"

O Thou, that in the heavens does dwell,
Wha, as it pleases best Thysel',
Sends ane to heaven an' ten to hell,
A' for Thy glory,
And no for ony guid or ill
They've done before Thee!

I bless and praise Thy matchless might,
When thousands Thou hast left in night,
That I am here before Thy sight,
For gifts an' grace
A burning and a shining light
To a' this place.

—ROBERT BURNS, "HOLY WILLIE'S PRAYER"

THE PRECEDING ARE THE first two stanzas of what is regarded as Burns's greatest satire, and—in my opinion—the greatest single satirical piece ever written about the Presbyterians. In it a self-righteous elder of Mauchline Kirk is supposedly overheard at his hypocritical (but totally candid) devotions. The very familiarity of the form of prayer and popular—if exaggerated—beliefs give a certain credibility to the brilliant send-up. Holy Willie's is the ultimate Presbyterian "anti-prayer" . . . a lesson to *ane* and *a'*!

As noted earlier, the *Westminster Shorter Catechism* defines prayer as the "offering up of our desires unto God, for things agreeable to God's will."[1] The core prayer of all Christian tradition—Jewish and Muslim, too—is "Thy will (O God) be done." It is not just a part of the formal Lord's Prayer but also the prayerful response of Mary to the angel Gabriel at the annunciation, and the agonized outpouring of Jesus to his "Abba," Father in the Garden of Gethsemane. Prayer is where human desire and God's desire come together, and the human task is not so much to lobby God for what we want as it is to learn to weigh (discern) our desires over against the desires (will) of God, for the well-being of all. Prayer is also, however, a formal part of religious culture, both in church and home.

On any given Lord's Day, in a typical Presbyterian church in the US, the assembling worshippers are likely to find several prayers listed (and some printed) in the worship program:

1. Prayer of Adoration after the Call to Worship

2. Prayer of Confession (said by all) and Assurance of Pardon

3. Prayer for Illumination (of the scripture readings) just before the readings or sermon

4. The Prayers of the People and Lord's Prayer (supplications and petitions) after the sermon

5. The Prayer of Dedication (of the offering)

On a Communion Sunday two more prayers appear:

6. The Great Thanksgiving (over the Communion elements)

7. The Prayer After Communion (giving thanks for the Supper)

The service concludes with a Benediction or Blessing, which technically is not a prayer, but rather the pronouncing of God's blessing by the minister, in God's Name, using words of scripture.

The preceding pattern of prayers is both historic and recent. It is historic in that it follows the liturgical order that was set forth by John Calvin in Geneva, Switzerland, in the sixteenth century, and then was carried over to Scotland by John Knox in an English translation. It is recent because, from the late sixteenth until the early twentieth centuries, written prayers and formal liturgies were mostly spurned by both Presbyterians in Scotland and their descendants in America. Only in 1906 did the

---

1. PCUSA, *Book of Confessions*, C-7.098.

P.C.U.S.A. issue its first *Book of Common Worship* with written prayers and liturgies for "optional" use. It took the smaller Presbyterian bodies another generation, or two, to follow.

Most of the intervening era (ca. 1600–1900) was dominated by a simpler order, set down in the *Westminster Directory for Worship* in the 1640s.[2] In that order there were basically three prayers offered on a typical Sabbath Day. There was an opening prayer of adoration and illumination (items 1 and 3 above) at the beginning of the service. There was a lengthy prayer of confession and intercession (items 2 and 4) between the reading of scripture and the sermon. Finally, after the sermon, there was a prayer of thanksgiving, revisiting the points of the sermon. The prayer in the middle was the "long prayer" . . . for which the congregation typically stood.[3]

My father used to tell of a Welsh preacher they had when he was a kid. In those days, the rule of thumb was for the long prayer to be half the length of the sermon, and the Welshman usually preached for an hour, meaning the congregation then stood for half an hour of prayer. (For some strange reason, Dad didn't remember that preacher very fondly.) I never had to endure that long a prayer from Rev. Stephens, but I do remember getting rather twitchy before he finished. I think the secret was in learning how to lean on the pew in front of you for support.

The only "set" prayer allowed by most Presbyterians of earlier times— and even it, not by all—was the Lord's Prayer. Set or not, it was for Presbyterians, as for all Christians, the formal "rule" of prayer, on which all teaching on the practice of prayer (in the catechisms, etc.) was based. All other prayers were supposedly extemporaneous (if very predictable) and, in congregational worship, they were offered by the minister alone. If the minister was not present on a given occasion, then the elders would pray. If not one of the elders, then any person might be called upon . . . usually men first, then widows, and so on. I really can't remember married women leading in prayer, except in Sunday School classes. The prayers offered in the closing exercises at Sunday School were virtually the same prayer, whether offered by Uncle Jesse, my dad, Marvin, Lyle, or Mae . . . except that Lyle tended to mutter his prayer so softly that you could barely hear:

> Lord, we thank Thee for this Sabbath Day, and for the blessing
> of coming to this Thy house to study Thy Word. Forgive us our

2. See "The Directory for the Publick Worship of God" in Free Presbyterian Church (Scotland), *The Confession of Faith*, 373-394.

3. In Scotland the intercessions were in the prayer after the sermon, making it the longer one.

sins. Bless those who are absent. If they are ill, grant them healing. If they are away, grant them traveling mercies. Be with us in
the week ahead and, if it be Thy will, bring us safely back to this
Thy house again next week. In Jesus's name, Amen.

If some family had a particular need, like a serious illness or death, they
would be mentioned by name. If it was a really dry year, there might be a
request for rain. Otherwise the pattern was pretty well fixed.

In the home, the round of prayers mostly centered on the family
table, with "the blessing" at meals and family worship in many households.
There were also bedside prayers at bedtime, with those of the smaller children usually overseen by their parents. In later years, one of Uncle Alex
Cuthbertson's sons still remembered the prayer his father prayed each day
at family worship, almost verbatim:

> Our Father, which art in Heaven, hallowed be Thy Name. Thy
> kingdom come, Thy will be done on Earth as it is in Heaven.
> We thank Thee, Heavenly Father, for Thy tender mercies and for
> the many blessings we receive from Thy bountiful hand. It is in
> Thee that we live and move and have our being. It is from Thee
> we receive every good and perfect gift. Enable us to draw near
> unto Thee at all times, with pure hearts and right spirits. May we
> worship Thee, a spirit, in spirit and in truth. Be with those who
> are careless and unconcerned about their soul's salvation, touch
> their hearts with the cords of Thy love and draw them nearer
> unto Thee. May they forsake the evil of their ways and follow
> after Thee, the living and true God. Hasten the time when all
> shall know Thee, from the least even unto the greatest, and when
> none shall be able to say, "I never knew Him," for Thou art not
> willing that any shall perish, but that all shall inherit eternal life.
> We thank Thee that Thou hast brought us to see the light of an-
> other day in health and strength. Bless the poor and the needy.
> Bless the sick and afflicted wherever they may be. Restore them
> to health if it be Thy will, but if not prepare them for death and
> prepare the living for serving Thee. Guide and direct us through
> the journey of life, and when Thou art through with us on earth,
> take us unto Thyself in Heaven. These things we ask in the name
> of Christ and for His sake. Amen.[4]

I find that prayer a remarkable example, in several ways, of a classic
Presbyterian mode of praying. First, that it made such a mark on the family as to be remembered so clearly half a century or so after this particular

---

4. Cuthbertson, *Memories of Ayrshire*, 93.

son had left home. Second, that it was so deeply grounded in scripture, and in a thankful response to God's gifts and blessings. Third, that the petitions were not a listing of personal wants and desires so much as an appeal to know and follow God's will, and to turn the hearts of all to the needs and well-being of neighbors.

The prayer also points up a historic conundrum of Presbyterian prayer . . . the question of whether human prayers can and do influence God. The old Presbyterian understanding of concepts like God's providence and predestination was pretty clear in asserting that God "foreordains whatsoever comes to pass" from all eternity.[5] Hence, according to the old joke, after falling down three flights of stairs the Calvinist looks up at those who have run to his/her assistance and says, "Well, I'm glad to have that out of the way!" Yet, according to the catechism, we are also to "offer up our desires unto God . . . ."[6]

This is one area where new understandings that have emerged during the late twentieth century, and on into the present day, are most helpful. Old mechanistic understandings of causation left us with the dilemma that either "God did it" or "I/we did it," insofar as who made what happen. The small amount I know about quantum theory shows a much more complex (and rather mystical) scenario of causation, where—in theological terms—our wills interact and intermingle with God's will in the "coming to pass" of whatever occurs. Prayer is not magic (thank goodness), but it can and does influence outcome.

Not that the outcome will be what we think. One of the hardest pieces of pastoral ministry is addressing prayer around healing and death. When my brother was dying of cancer twenty years ago,[7] he anxiously inquired of me, in the last real conversation we ever had, "What do I need to do to be healed? I've had the elders come to lay on hands and anoint me with oil,[8] but I haven't been healed." I did not have a good answer for him on that day. Later, remembering his feeling of responsibility for a tragic family accident a couple of years earlier, I realized that I should have told him, "Forgive yourself!" I do not think it would have healed his body—at least at that point—but I do think it might have helped him find peace and healing for his soul. There comes a point where the body's "healing" is death,

---

5. PCUSA, *Book of Confessions*, C-7.007.

6. Ibid., C-7.098.

7. We were nearly twenty years apart in age, but he was, at the time, only in his mid-50s.

8. Jas 5:14–15.

but our trust and hope is that physical death is not the last word. Thus we are back, I think, to Uncle Alex's prayer.

The other great conundrum of Presbyterian prayer is discerning God's will. "God's will" has often been cast as something rather fatal—as in the cross—or at least unpleasant. I remember quite a few of us in college being rather amazed when Chase said, from the pulpit, that it was entirely possible that what we *want* might actually *be* God's will! Our gifts, our joys, our interests, might actually be pointing us toward what God wants us to be and to do with our lives.[9]

My own thought is that God's will is more about outcome than the minutiae. It is not a set menu with (perhaps) certain optional sides. It is, instead, a dynamic, interactive process aimed . . . in the end . . . at our glorifying the Holy One and enjoying a lively relationship with the Living Presence that is God. What is God's will? God's will is:

1. Know and love God

2. Love yourself and your neighbor

3. Do justice (good) and love mercy (compassion)

4. Shalom (peace and well-being) for all beings

If that is our desire, then the Kingdom really does come into our midst as we try to live into it. Everything else is ultimately optional and changeable according to the circumstances. That, I think, is the summation of the Prayer of Jesus, and of Uncle Alex's prayer, too.

> Holy One, Father and Mother of all,
> You are the One who holds and guides the cosmos,
> May your Name be sanctified in our words and lives,
> May your realm of peace and wellbeing come among us,
> May your intentions and desires come to pass on earth
> as in the highest heavens.
> May there be bread sufficient for all this day.
> Free us from our misdeeds and failings
> even as we respond in compassion to one another.
> Do not lead us into temptation or trial, but deliver us from the
> power of evil.
> For you reign in the power and glory of life, light,
> and love forever. Amen.

—PARAPHRASE OF THE PRAYER OF JESUS BY THE AUTHOR

9. Albeit, I also recall a particular college friend who was *sure* that it was God's will for him to marry such-and-so. Unfortunately God never told her, and she and God made other plans, with someone else.

7

Worship—"The Beauty of Holiness"

MANY YEARS AGO THERE was a country mouse, a country *church*-mouse, who was in Kansas City for a meeting and stayed over to go to church with his cousins on Sunday. Those city mice were members of the (then) largest Presbyterian congregation in the country, Village Presbyterian Church in Prairie Village, Kansas. The country church mouse was probably a junior in college at the time, so it was about 1976. The exquisitely choreographed service started off in a generally familiar pattern with the call to worship and opening hymn . . . and then it happened. After the prayer of confession and words of assurance, the choir and congregation started to sing the *Gloria Patri*[1] and the clergy all turned toward the elaborate—and beautiful—cross on the Communion Table. The country church mouse, quite simply, freaked out.[2] From everything ever learned at home, or at college and the Sterling church, this felt like . . . *idolatry*!

> Thou shalt not make unto thee any graven image, or any likeness of any thing that is in heaven above, or that is in the earth beneath or that is in the water under the earth: Thou shalt not bow down thyself to them, nor serve them: for I the LORD thy God am a jealous God, visiting the iniquity of the fathers upon the children unto the third and fourth generation of them that hate me.[3]

1. I.e., "Glory be to the Father . . . ."
2. The country church had a cross on the table, but nobody turned around and sang to it!
3. Exod 20: 4–5, KJV.

When I was in graduate school in the late 1980s, I ran across Carlos Eire's book, *The War Against the Idols*, which looks at how the theme of anti-idolatry came to permeate the Reformed (Calvinist, Presbyterian, Puritan) branch of the Reformation in particular. Much more so than the Lutheran or Anglican communities, the Reformed churches regarded virtually everything Roman Catholic as idolatry—the mass and the entire sacramental system, transubstantiation, altars, the papacy and priesthood, the "cult" of the saints, the crucifix, statues and sacred art, stained glass windows, vestments and paraments, the church year, organs, choirs, formal written liturgies, and so on. Such things were "of Satan," and a temptation to God's elect, and thus they were to be destroyed and suppressed . . . hence all the old church ruins in Scotland.[4]

Out of that mindset came the austere forms of Presbyterian worship which, up until about the 1870s in both Scotland and America, dictated not just exclusive psalmody, but also no musical instruments or choirs at all in worship.[5] American ministers mostly did not wear vestments.[6] Godparents were forbidden, and baptism was to be performed by the minister only in the presence of the congregation. As noted elsewhere, they also practiced "close" Communion. While they kept the Sabbath strictly, the church year—including Christmas and Easter—was *not* observed.[7] Even burials were to be done without ceremony . . . though the custom of the funeral sermon, followed by a brief prayer at the graveside, soon prevailed. Weddings were also very simple, and most often occurred in the home.[8] In eighteenth century Scotland you could actually be fined by the parish for having too many guests or excessive festivities at weddings.

---

4. Many of the structural ruins are due to neglect and abandonment to the elements rather than active demolition, but the destruction of windows, statuary and paintings, vestments, altar vessels, organs and such is well attested.

5. The prohibition of choirs was "because it is the duty of the whole congregation to praise God with united voice." ARP *Directory of Worship*, ca. 1782, cited in Jamison, *The United Presbyterian Story*, 28.

6. Some colonial era ministers in the stream that became the P.C.U.S.A. in 1789 wore Scottish-style pulpit robes and preaching tabs. In the nineteenth century ministers generally wore soberly formal black suits, until about the 1920s when simple black pulpit robes began to be more common.

7. "Festival days, vulgarly called holy-days, having no warrant in the word of God, are not to be observed." ARP *Directory of Worship*, cited in Jamison, *The United Presbyterian Story*, 38.

8. Formal church weddings seem only to have become "the norm" after World War II.

It was only in the 1870s and 1880s that the UPNA slowly and cautiously began to permit instrumental music, first in the Sabbath School (i.e. the Sunday School). The debate leading up to officially tolerating (not approving) the use of instruments in worship proved to be the most divisive in the history of that denomination. Even in the early 1900s my mother's older sisters were absolutely mortified when my grandfather Gibson vociferously opposed switching from the pump organ to the piano at church, because pianos were used at dances!

The prohibition of "holy-days" was a strong one among the old Scots, even if the general populace eventually found it culturally needful to substitute occasions like the secular festival of New Year's for the "papist" and "pagan" traditions of Christmas.[9] Robert Burns gives us glimpses into some of the various other days and seasons observed as folk customs in Ayrshire during his time: wooing the lasses in the fields on a Lammas night in August, using divination on a Halloween night to try to discover who the inquirer might marry, etc.[10]

Even among other Reformed (Calvinist) Christians, the Scottish and Puritan rejection of holidays was viewed as somewhat extreme.[11] If there needs to be a biblical justification for the church year—as we have seen, Presbyterians traditionally want such things—it surely lies in the fact that the gospels, especially John, show Jesus observing the annual cycle of Jewish feasts. That Jesus kept Passover is clear in all four gospels, but John also has him observing the Feast of Booths / Sukkoth[12] and the Feast of Dedication / Hanukah.[13] Except for the High Holy Days (Rosh Hashanah and Yom Kippur), the Christian Calendar roughly corresponds to the Jewish cycle, with Hanukah and Christmas both being figured in relation to

9. Even so, super-strict characters like John Howie of Lochgoin in Fenwick—a simple tenant farmer who wrote the book *The Scots Worthies* about the Covenanters—regarded New Year's itself as "pagan" and kept a solemn family fast-day instead.

10. See also his lively accounts of the popular lore of witches and devils in poems like "Address to the Deil" and "Tam O'Shanter."

11. Think, for instance, of "Sinter Klaus" and the popular customs of the Dutch Christmas. The Second Helvetic (Swiss) Confession of 1566 approves of the religious celebration of the birth, death, and resurrection of Jesus, and the sending of the Holy Spirit, as exercises of "Christian Liberty," but does reject saints' days and so on. See PCUSA, *Book of Confessions*, C-5.226.

12. According to the text, he went up to Jerusalem for Sukkoth after quite intentionally skipping Yom Kippur (the Day of Atonement) because his "hour has not yet fully come" (see John 7).

13. See John 10:22 –23.

the Winter Solstice,[14] and Easter and Pentecost corresponding to Passover and the Feast of Weeks. While not commanded *per se,* such holy-days at least seem to fall among what the continental (Euro-) Calvinists referred to as "matters indifferent" in the ordering of church life.

Like musical instruments, Christmas crept into Presbyterian churches in America via the Sabbath School in the late nineteenth century, mostly beginning with community programs of songs and poems, to which were added a bit of scripture and a prayer.[15] In our little country church the program was called the "Christmas Tree." It was held each year in conjunction with the Methodist congregation two miles away, and had been for as long as anyone I ever knew could remember. It was held on Christmas Eve, and the ministers' attendance was optional.[16] By the time I came along, the scripture, carols, and poems had long since grown to include a pageant, but it was still *not* considered a church service. At the end of the program Santa arrived—once on a bicycle!—to hand out a few gifts along with sacks of candy, apples and oranges.

Until 1906 even the P.C.U.S.A.—the largest, wealthiest, and most mainstream Presbyterian denomination of the time—had no officially sanctioned prayers or services for any of the holidays of the church year.[17] The UPNA officially had nothing until at least the mid-1920s, when they finally allowed the singing of hymns . . . including Christmas carols.[18] At least in families like mine, if Christmas Day fell on Sunday we always went to church as usual and quietly kept Sabbath that day. We then had the big family Christmas dinner on Monday.

Holy Week and Easter snuck into Presbyterian usage in a similar fashion. Easter was generally recognized first. Good Friday, in particular, was suspect, as being *much* too Roman Catholic for many. On the other hand, Maundy Thursday—the day of the New Covenant—came to be a favorite observance among Presbyterians, and remains so. In our current

14. Hanukah falls at the dark of the moon closest to the Winter Solstice in the northern hemisphere.

15. Christmas observance in general underwent a major revival and transformation from the 1840s onward, in both Britain and the US, influenced by Dickens's *A Christmas Carol* and other socio-cultural influences.

16. Ours usually attended to the service at the town church and let us take care of ourselves; the Methodist preachers did likewise over the years.

17. Hymnbooks by then did include songs for Christmas and Easter, and plenty of songs about the death of Jesus.

18. As late as 1941, neither the UPNA *Confessional Statement* nor its *Directory for Worship* even mentioned observing the holidays of the church year.

congregation, we do a simple Scottish Communion at tables in the Fellowship Hall, and then move into the sanctuary to hear the reading of the passion story. The service ends with a hymn such as Isaac Watts's "When I Survey the Wondrous Cross," and we depart in silence. For most that suffices, and only the barest handful of folks show up for the brief prayer service held on Good Friday at noon.

Church seasons like Advent and Lent were considered even stranger, and ofttimes rather worrisome, innovations. Advent has proved easier for Presbyterians to embrace, but Lent still unsettles some of us who get uncomfortable with the "high church" and penitential flavor of the season . . . especially on days like Ash Wednesday.[19] Historically, Presbyterians are just not into (overtly) beating our breasts and muttering "*mea culpa!*" As I see it, the problem is that we have never quite found an appropriate Presbyterian/Reformed way to observe Lent, but we still want to do something along with our sisters and brothers in other branches of the Church Catholic.[20] It is a conundrum.[21]

The old Presbyterian caution in matters liturgical also extended to the physical spaces we occupy together. Presbyterians took a long time to embrace the arts and architecture in church life. The church buildings erected by the post-Reformation Scots and their kin in Ulster and America were very simple, very plain meetinghouses with no particular sanctity ascribed to them. In Scotland the old medieval parish churches, stripped bare of their statues and stained glass, were adapted to Reformed

19. Reacting against the abuses and abusiveness of the medieval penitential system, some early Protestant Reformers actually made a show of publically violating the Lenten fast with roast goose dinners and other acts of intentional transgression against the former disciplines. It was a *de facto* season of rebellion against the old system, and the clerical powers associated with it.

20. Albeit, in their own way, the old Covenanter Communion Seasons were a sort of mini-Lent, tied to each observance rather than a particular seasonal timing.

21. In a way, the themes of freedom and salvation from oppression associated with the Jewish seasonal observances of both Purim and Passover fit a Reformed understanding better than the seemingly individualistic and self-absorbed penitential focus traditional during Catholic Lent. The Jewish model is also more communal in nature. Other themes and models also merit exploration. For instance, as I understand the Eastern Orthodox emphasis for the season of Lent, it is specifically a time for "returning to the garden" (of Eden) through acts of forgiveness and reconciliation, creation-centered (vegetarian) fasting, etc. The rigor of Orthodoxy is daunting, but the themes are certainly worth considering. I know of at least one neighboring Presbyterian Church that has, on a couple of occasions, used Lent as a season of reflection on earth-care. Various ecumenical groups are now promoting the idea of observing a "carbon fast" during Lent.

worship centered on pulpit and table. Scottish kirks tended more toward tiny bellcotes rather than to tall spires and towers. The operational rule was, "Nothing too grand."[22]

In America the early Covenanters met in private homes, with occasional larger gatherings held in barns or the fields, as they had in the illegal "conventicles" of the Killing Times. The early meetinghouses tended to have the pulpit along a long wall, with no suggestion of a formal chancel arrangement. Pulpits were high, often with a "sounding board" overhead, for purely functional reasons: so that the preacher could be seen and—most importantly—heard. The table stood in front of the pulpit. The benches or pews were arranged to gather the people around the preacher and table, not to view them from afar. The plain architecture was an expression of the theology of being "church" in the Presbyterian way.

In the mid- to late nineteenth century, as many urban Presbyterians grew in affluence and sophistication, church edifices changed as well. Mainline Presbyterians embraced amenities like fine pipe organs and stained glass windows, befitting the social class and status of their membership, but—even so—many congregations held true to core principles in the design of their worship spaces by embracing innovations like the more in-the-round Akron Plan[23] of seating arrangement. The earliest use of stained glass in Presbyterian churches tended toward pattern, perhaps with the use of religious symbols—a chalice, a harp, the tablets of the Ten Commandments, etc.—over any pictorial representations of people.

Perhaps most surprisingly of all, it was really only in the twentieth century that Presbyterians began to widely use the cross—the empty cross, never a crucifix—in our churches.[24] When we did so, many quickly opted for the Celtic Cross—a resurrection cross, with the sun-circle symbolic of the risen Jesus—rather than the so-called Latin Cross. The few images of Jesus that came to be fairly common in Presbyterian churches from the 1890s on were portrayals such as the Last Supper, Jesus the Good Shepherd, Jesus blessing the children, and Jesus praying in Gethsemane. Like so much else, such things did not appear among the stricter UPNA folks

---

22. Or, as the PCUSA *Book of Order* affirms, "a faithful stewardship that shuns ostentation" (F-2.05).

23. Akron Plan sanctuaries were designed with more auditorium-like arrangements of the worship space. Pews were arranged in a semi-circle on a sloping floor, with the pulpit/chancel area along a broad wall or in a corner. Often Sunday School rooms with folding or sliding doors opened directly off of the periphery of the auditorium.

24. From the Reformation on, the most common Reformed/Presbyterian symbol was the burning bush of Moses.

until later . . . and still are not found among the Covenanters. We did not have a Christmas crèche at Osage until about 1970, when my Sunday School class (Ellen and I) bought a small one as a project, with our own money. I suspect that was the first time that any *image* of the Virgin Mary had ever entered those walls, except for the pictures printed on children's Sunday School papers.[25]

Presbyterian worship, at its core, is meant to focus on the Word. It is meant to direct us, through the written word and the enacted word (the sacraments), into an encounter with the Living Word (Christ) and the Living Presence of God. In that sense, we continue to reject the idolatry of focusing on the liturgical cult . . . even as we have mellowed quite a bit from our previous obsession. Worship is to be done "in spirit and in truth."[26] It is something we offer to God, but it is also a setting in which—God willing—we enter into relationship with God. Because of this, it is something that we need to be mindful about. Worship needs to be planned and executed in ways that are neither manipulative nor misleading. The old forms and orders have served us well over the centuries, but the shifts in contemporary culture indicate that we also need to explore how those forms and orders might adapt and evolve to fit the times in which we are living.

Back in the 1970s, Rev. Richard Avery and his partner, musician Donald Marsh, were pioneers in the move toward contemporary worship in the Presbyterian Church. In later years, after they retired to Santa Fe, I got to know and observe them as they led worship at Ghost Ranch and at various events in our presbytery. What I then realized was the genius that Richard, in particular, brought to designing worship. The services I experienced with him and Don were never gimmicky, but did blend in creative and artistic means for communicating the Word. Every element of the services they planned was designed to open the Word to and for the

---

25. Anyone who has seen our home now—with its fairly extensive collection of icons and sacred art—knows that I have come a long way from the fierce anti-idolatry of my ancestors . . . except that I haven't. I love the objects and find them meaningful "texts," along with scripture and nature, for meditation and reflection. However, I also deeply love the simplicity of the mostly-image-less, white-walled church sanctuary where we regularly worship, through whose clear windows we can gaze out toward the mountaintop. I love the simplicity of our liturgical traditions, and get uneasy when any ceremony—including too many words—gets in the way of the clear and heartfelt communication of the Word. Images and ceremonies are tools for communication, facilitating encounter; nothing more, or less.

26. John 4:23.

participants.[27] In other hands, contemporary worship is too often gimmicky or quirky but, done well, it is a powerful form of proclamation. My sense is that the continuing work of worship planners and leaders is to find the best ways to facilitate proclamation here and now.

Several years ago I had a dream. It was a Lord's Day morning and we were gathering for worship with the very informal congregation with which we were involved at that time. In the dream, the minister suddenly noticed that the church building was on fire. We had to evacuate. The question was, "What to take?" As I recall, several people grabbed the pottery Communion vessels, and others of us picked up and carried the table. Several people wheeled out the piano, and the rest gathered up the various hymnals (we had two different ones). Somebody, I think, brought the pulpit Bible . . . but I do not recall the pulpit itself being taken. That dream provided a pretty good read of that congregation and its liturgical priorities.

It seems that the whole Church, transcending all denominations, is having that dream right now. We are living in a time when we have to discern what to grab and carry out of the burning (or collapsing) institution. As that applies to worship, I was taught that, if scripture is read, and prayer is offered, then "worship" has occurred, in the formal sense. Add in some singing and the sacraments, and the basics are all there. Everything else—buildings, choirs, "high" or "low" liturgies, church year, candles, pottery or metal Communion ware, vestments (or not), styles of music, worship times, etc.—is ultimately negotiable. Word, prayer, song, Baptism, and Communion, all shared in gathered community: it is enough.

[P.S. But I *am* keeping Christmas! Maundy Thursday, Easter, and Pentecost too.]

---

27. I will never forget a service at Ghost Ranch with Don miming the story of Moses at the burning bush as Richard told it. He made me *see it* as I had never done before.

The Ordination of Elders in a Scottish Kirk, **John Henry Lorimer,** 1891
(Scottish National Gallery)

8

Elders and Matriarchs

THE BLACK-GOWNED AND WHITE-MANED minister stands at the table, the Bible open in front of him. His head is bowed, and his hands are raised in blessing. Around the table stand five craggy-faced old men, also clad in black, along with one who is much younger, perhaps in his thirties. Several of them look like they could be relatives of ours from the old family albums we have stashed away. The men also stand with heads bowed, the high pulpit and precentor's desk looming above them. In a pew to one side, a serious-faced young girl with a pink ribbon on her hat peeks cautiously but curiously up at the proceedings. The work is John Henry Lorimer's 1891 painting, *The Ordination of Elders in a Scottish Kirk*. The print, which hangs on the wall in our home, was an ordination gift to me from my husband's aunt, a beloved friend and mentor, in 1982.

We are called Presbyterians because our church is led by *presbyters* (elders). We have Ministers of Word and Sacrament (also called Teaching Elders) and Elders (also called Ruling Elders) who are responsible for the governance and guidance of local congregations, presbyteries (regional districts), and the General Assembly (national). Ministers and Elders together share in the oversight of congregational life and worship, particularly the sacraments, and in the pastoral care of the people. They serve together as equals in the higher governing bodies. Over the generations, Presbyterians have often had Deacons who assist in providing for the physical needs of the congregation and community, but that office has not always nor everywhere been included in our ecclesial systems, and remains optional. The office of Elder is not.[1]

1. In appropriate circumstances, elders may even be trained and commissioned

While the ministry of Word and Sacrament is traditionally traced back to Jesus and the Apostles, the eldership is—with great seriousness by some—traced all the way back to Moses who, at the suggestion of his father-in-law, first appointed elders to assist him in guiding and judging the Children of Israel during their years of traveling through the wilderness.[2] Later Moses and Aaron took the seventy elders of Israel up the Mountain of God, and there God appeared to them all. They remained for a time and even ate and drank in God's Presence.[3] In later days the elders of Israel sat in the gates of each community, dealing with local matters. As synagogues developed, the Rulers of the synagogue were seen as an extension of the traditional eldership and, as old-time Presbyterians saw it, the earliest Christian congregations modeled themselves on the synagogue.[4] The rise of the hierarchical and "prelatical" episcopate—i.e. bishops, especially the "lordly" kind—in the later church was viewed as a corruption of the original apostolic order.[5]

Looking back at the old records, it appears clear that the predominant task of Presbyterian Elders from the sixteenth up into the nineteenth centuries was often to serve as the local disciplinary body, dealing with the misdemeanors of church members. Elders assisted the ministers in examining those who applied to be communicants in the congregation. They also sat as a court—the Session of the Elders Bench—to deal with cases of Sabbath-breaking, swearing, drunkenness, gambling, and (especially, it seems) fornication and adultery. Some Session records, including a 1709 Kilmaurs case involving William Cuthbertson of Buntinhill,[6] read like rather bawdy novels. Offenders, like our friend Robbie Burns, were regularly required to stand "in the Public Place" before the congregation to be rebuked on several successive Sabbaths before being restored to full fellowship in the congregation and community. At Fenwick there was an iron collar on a chain, the *jougs*, attached to the outside wall of the kirk by the door, where the worst offenders had to stand for assigned periods of time.[7]

---

by the presbytery as a Commissioned Ruling Elder to take the place of a minister for a congregation.

2. See Exod 18.

3. See Exod 24:9–11.

4. The 1948 edition of the UPNA *Book of Government and Worship* clearly states that the office of elder originated in Biblical Israel and came into the early Christian Church via the Jewish synagogues (Chapter VI, paragraph 19).

5. The real history is not quite so simple or clear.

6. A possible ancestor, although I really hope not!

7. In neighboring Kilmaurs the *jougs* were on the outer wall of the Townhouse

Burns did a great job of "sending up" hypocritical elders like his Holy Willie, and others have given the *unco guid* types—those who "never thought any the better" of the Lord himself for violating the Sabbath—their due. However, there were also so many truly good, devoted, and beloved elders across the generations, whose lives and service were a blessing to their communities; persons of deep faith and commitment to the congregations in which they served. The oft-mentioned Uncle Alex Cuthbertson was one such, and also his contemporaries "Uncle Sandy" Dunlop and "Cousin Archie" Gemmell.[8]

In 1905 a ninety-nine-year-old handloom weaver from Fenwick, Matthew Fowlds of Greystone Knowe, was honored with a jubilee celebration marking his fifty years of service as an elder of the United Presbyterian (formerly the United Secession) congregation there. The account of the soiree held on the occasion includes some interesting remarks on the history and role of the eldership in the churches of Scotland. The achievements of the church across the years since the Reformation were acknowledged to be "as much the work of the elders as of the ministers." Great elders of the past such as John Erskine of Dun (a supporter of John Knox), Fenwick's own Captain John Paton (Covenanter Martyr), and Sir William Mure of Rowallan (who hosted illegal Covenanter conventicles at Rowallan Castle) were noted. Previous elders of the congregation—the farmers, weavers, cobblers, and others who had sat on "the crescent seat" near the pulpit—were remembered as the "stay" of the congregation and the "support and help" of the ministers. As he recalled the elders of his youth, including Mr. Fowlds, the speaker described them as "good and true" men of good feeling and kindly spirit. Such were the godly elders of Scotland.[9]

The genius of the office of Elder in the Presbyterian system of governance has been that it gives a continuity and stability over the years as ministers come and go. Ideally, elders emerge organically within the congregation, recognized for their wisdom and maturity, their gifts and calling. They are not religious professionals, but lay volunteers chosen to represent the people of the congregation in prayerfully discerning and

---

rather than the kirk, showing the intermingling of civil and religious authority.

8. Albeit, Archie reportedly could be rather severe . . . especially with some of the young men in the congregation—including, I think, my grandfather, who once got caught out for having gone to a dance. On that occasion, a young hothead in the group reportedly demanded his church letter (for transfer to another church) and Archie is said to have replied, "Young man, we do not issue letters to go to Hell!"

9. From comments by Thomas W. Orr in *Matthew Fowlds, Centenarian Weaver,* 134.

guiding the church (and the ministers) in finding and following God's will. It is not their business to "lord it over" others. Rather, theirs is a call to serve.[10]

From my own early years, I think of elders such as Marvin Green, an older cousin of my dad's, who nurtured and encouraged my interest in the larger church from the time I was a teen. Sterling's Fran Calderwood, who gave me the *Ordination* print, is another who comes to mind, as does "Miss Beryl" Crawford of the Girard church that partnered with our little country congregation. My dad took a term as elder on Session from time to time, and I am glad to recall that it was he who stood to inform the Osage congregation that we were henceforth required (not just permitted) to include women elders on the Session. My late brother was distinct in having served at one point as a Presbyterian elder, and at another as an elder in the Disciples of Christ.

The history of women in official leadership amongst Presbyterians is relatively recent. The Presbyterian Eldership and Ministry were predominantly male dominated until the 1970s. As in most Protestant denominations, biblical passages from 1 Corinthians 14 and 1 Timothy 2 (in particular) were long used to bar women from church office. That said, there has been an ongoing gradual shift, occurring over the last two centuries and picking up pace over the last one hundred years. The UPNA began to ordain women as deacons in 1906. The old P.C.U.S.A. approved the ordination of women as deacons in 1922, as elders in 1930, and as ministers in 1956, but ordinations of women elders and ministers were relatively rare at first. The Church of Scotland did not begin to have women elders until 1966, with women ministers following two years later. Beginning in 1975, after a ruling known as the Kenyon case, the UPCUSA (now PCUSA) required all ordained officers to affirm women's ordination, and to see that there was a representative balance of women nominated as deacons and elders in all congregations. In 1991 the *Brief Statement of Faith* of the PCUSA became the first official confessional document to affirm as church doctrine that the Spirit "calls women and men to all ministries of the church."[11]

The shift in Presbyterian understanding and practice undoubtedly reflects the providential changes (as I view them) that have occurred in women's role and status in society at large over time. However, it also reflects the shift in our understanding and views on scripture. Several years

---

10. See PCUSA, *Form of Government*, G-2.031.

11. PCUSA, *Book of Confessions*, C-10.4, line 64.

ago, when the Southern Baptist Convention was moving to embrace a far more restrictive and traditionalist policy on women in church leadership, one of the women in the congregation we were part of at the time asked me if I knew of any biblical passages she could use to counter the arguments of her Southern Baptist son-in-law. My response truly came in a moment of inspiration that was not my doing, although it was also based on a lot of study and prayer over the years. I looked at her and said something to this effect: "If you look only at the instructions given to women and families in the household codes of the New Testament and so on, it appears that he [the son-in-law] is right. But the fact is that *none* of the women who figure prominently in the Bible really followed those rules. They did not keep quiet, they did not just submit meekly to the men, and they did take leadership."

Our friend liked that answer a lot. I never heard back, however, on how it worked with her son-in-law.

When we really look for them, both the Bible and Christian history are full of godly, "uppity" women whose stories unfold in a rather collateral lineage to all the historical tales of the patriarchs and elders spanning the centuries. The stories of the biblical patriarchs and their heirs include many surprisingly assertive matriarchs and their successors. The roll call from the Hebrew Bible includes Abraham's wife Sarah and her servant Hagar; Rebecca, the wife of Isaac and mother of Jacob; Tamar, the daughter-in-law of Judah; Jochebed, the mother of Moses, Miriam, his sister, and Zipporah, his wife; Deborah the Judge; Hannah, the mother of Samuel; Ruth, the Moabite, who became the grandmother of David; Abigail and Bathsheba, who were two of David's wives; and others. In various instances, these strong women sometimes overshadowed their menfolk, both in faith and in bold action. Similarly, in the New Testament, we find Jesus's mother Mary; Mary of Bethany and her sister Martha; Mary Magdalene; and the various other women who followed Jesus, supported his ministry, stood by the cross while the men (all but one) hid, and were the first witnesses to the resurrection. Even the problematic Apostle Paul— who is largely misunderstood because we forget that he was writing his letters to particular communities that had specific problems at the time— shows happy inconsistencies as he worked enthusiastically together with women like Prisca, the Deacon Phoebe, and the legendary (apocryphal) Thecla. The women of the Bible, happily, did not strictly practice what its more patriarchal writers and editors preached.

Modern feminist scholarship has long since shown that, during the first centuries of the Christian era, women often did play a significant role, officially sanctioned, in the life and ministry of the church. Over time, however, they increasingly found themselves relegated to subordinate roles as the mindset of the "household codes" became more important than biblical exemplars. Still, as the church moved onward across the centuries, strong women emerged to play key roles in its story.

In the fourth century, as the Christian Church transitioned from an outlawed counterculture to the core religious institution of the Roman Empire, there emerged a new movement that began in the deserts of Egypt and Palestine. Holy hermits, both male and female, withdrew themselves from the perceived worldliness of the emerging order to seek God, just as Moses, the prophets, and Jesus had done before them. These desert *abbas* (fathers) and *ammas* (mothers) represented the first stirrings of what became the Christian monastic movement, as some of them moved from solitary lives into the organization of spiritual communes, where they worked and worshipped, studied and prayed, together. Within a relatively few years, their new modality of Christian community spread to the furthest reaches of Christendom in Britain and Ireland where, in the tribalized Celtic culture beyond the pale of empire, it became the dominant form of Church.

In Ireland, Wales, and the Scottish isles and highlands, Celtic monasticism took on a unique character. The official clergy (bishops and priests) were secondary to the abbots and abbesses who served as *de facto* lay chieftains of their religious communes. Either men *or* women could serve as the head of their mixed communities, and they included married lay "kindred" as well as vowed celibates.[12] The greatest Celtic saints—Columba, Brigid, Aidan, Cuthbert, Hilda, etc.—were mostly the heads of such communes.[13] Women clearly *led* men . . . and legend even has it that the Abbess Brigid of Kildare was "accidentally" ordained as bishop by a male bishop who turned to the wrong page in his book! During the darkest of the Dark Ages, in the wake of the barbarian invasions and the fall of the western half of the Roman Empire, the Celtic monasteries—Iona, for instance—served as home bases in which the faith was preserved, and

12. In one instance, some ancient bishops in Gaul were scandalized by two British (Welsh) presbyters who permitted women in their communities to co-host in serving the chalice at Communion (Ellis, *Celtic Women*, 142).

13. Patrick, a bishop, was an exception.

from which Christian mission was renewed and spread across the field of a radically changed Western Europe.

Over the ensuing centuries, the monastic communities of the western church became formalized, institutionalized, and hived off from the lives of the commonality as part of the feudal hierarchical system. Nonetheless, though strictly segregated by gender, the women's communities continued to be alternative venues of real empowerment for women. In the late medieval period, individuals like Dame Julian of Norwich gained fame, and some of the less formal lay women's communities (the Beguines, etc.) became dynamic centers of spirituality and service.

With the Protestant Reformation, monasticism was dismissed by the Reformed/Presbyterian stream, particularly in Britain. Folks like John Knox were vehement in their opposition, viewing the monasteries—sometimes with justification—as hotbeds of ignorance, superstition, idolatry, corruption, and immorality.[14]

In place of the monasteries, the Reformed Kirk in Scotland looked to faithful families and congregations, guided by the lay elders, as the foundation of their new order. In the process they, like virtually all Protestants, shut women out of the ecclesial power structures without questioning the assumptions of male privilege that had prevailed since at least the third century.[15] It took another four centuries for Presbyterians to really begin to address the issue. However, despite being denied an official role for so long, women have always been a potent force in Presbyterianism.

Although John Knox himself was undoubtedly something of a misogynist, some of his bold spirit was passed along to at least one of his daughters.[16] In 1622 Elizabeth Knox[17]—wife of the outspoken Rev. John Welsh of Ayr—showed true Presbyterian pluck during an audience with King James VI/I[18] in London while seeking permission for her banished

14. Worse still, in a way, they were seen as simply irrelevant.

15. John Calvin—alone of the major Reformers—went so far as to say that the day might come when women could be validly permitted to preach. See Douglass, *Women, Freedom, and Calvin*, 106.

16. While Calvin had some very positive experiences of support from learned and powerful noblewomen over the years, poor Knox had fled for his life more than once from the likes of England's Bloody Mary and the alluring Mary, Queen of Scots. Knox's infamous tract against (Catholic) women rulers, his *First Blast of the Trumpet Against the Monstrous Regiment of Women*, infuriated Elizabeth I who came to the throne just as Knox's work came off the press.

17. From earliest times down to the present, the custom is for Scottish women to continue to be known by their birth surname after marriage.

18. He was James VI of Scotland, and styled himself as James I of Great Britain

and ailing husband to return home. When James asked her about her family of origin she replied, "My father was John Knox." "Knox and Welsh!" the King exclaimed, "The Devil ne'er made sic a match as that." "'Tis right-like, sir," she responded, "for we never *speired* (asked) his leave."[19]

According to popular legend, the great covenanting struggle of the seventeenth century was kicked off by an Edinburgh woman on 23 July 1634, when an Episcopal clergyman started to read a prayer from *The Book of Common Prayer* in the High Kirk now known as St. Giles Cathedral. According to the traditional story, a market-woman named Jenny Geddes picked up her stool[20] and flung it at the man, crying out, "False loon! How daur ye say Mass at my *lug* (ear)!" A riot ensued, and a revolution. The lore of the subsequent Killing Times includes the names of women such as the Wigtown Martyrs, elderly Margaret McLachlan, and young Margaret Wilson.[21] Covenanter heroines of the era also include the likes of Lady Grisell Baillie and Fenwick's own Isobel Howie of Lochgoin.[22]

It was in the nineteenth century that organized "women's work" really developed in the churches. Some form of the Women's General Missionary Society[23] eventually existed in most, if not all, Presbyterian denominations, both in Scotland and America, and their accomplishments are well documented. Money was raised for foreign and "home" missions and the women slowly but surely proved to the resistant men that they were equal to the tasks of organization and administration. They also proved themselves more than equal to the task of serving as missionaries, on their own as well as partnered with husbands. The leaders of the missionary societies were often the only women permitted to speak and participate in the General Assemblies of the denominations, beginning (so far as I know)

(not just England).

19. McCrie, *Life of John Knox*, 362.

20. This was before churches had installed pews.

21. Margaret McLachlan and Margaret Wilson were executed together in 1685 at Wigtown. They were tied to stakes in a tidal riverbed at low tide so that they would drown as the tide rose. Eighteen-year-old Margaret Wilson bravely sang Psalms until the waters overcame her.

22. Lady Grissell Baillie, nee Hume, is famous for having, at age twelve, carried a secret message from her father to a fellow Covenanter imprisoned in Edinburgh, and then later for smuggling supplies by night to her father as he lay hidden in the family burial vault at Polworth Kirk. Isobel Howie once charged a government trooper as he entered the house at Lochgoin, making time for the several Covenanter men sheltering within to try their escapes. She herself later had to take occasional refuge in the moorlands.

23. A.k.a. the Ladies Aid.

with Mrs. Sarah F. Hanna at the UPNA Assembly of 1875. On various occasions, they skillfully and forcefully fended off patriarchal attempts to take over the management of their affairs, and repeatedly the women took up the slack when denominational funds were cut.

That said, my perception is that the broader and deeper foundations for the emergence of women's full participation in Presbyterianism are to be discovered in an even wider spectrum of contexts and roles assumed over the years, including teaching in the Sabbath Schools and participating in the ministry of music as church organists and choir members . . . as such things came into vogue. However, I think one particular and overarching role stands out, almost from the beginning. Long before women were ever officially recognized as Elders, they evolved amongst themselves the equally important *de facto* office of Matriarch. It was, and still is, to be found in almost every small- to medium-sized congregation, and even shows up in large and sophisticated urban congregations.[24] Women ministers, as well as elders and deacons, are heirs and successors to this old tradition . . . to the benefit of all.

The best description that I know of a matriarch comes from chapter 31 of the biblical book of Proverbs. Although feminists of the 1970s sometimes backed away from its portrayal of the capable wife and mother, subordinate to her husband and sons, the woman described there is an amazing figure in her own right. She is described as totally trustworthy (vv. 11–12), industrious and resourceful (vv. 13–15), and a discerning business person (vv. 16–19). She is generous (v. 20), strong and wise (vv. 25–26). She is also a teacher (v. 26).

> She opens her hand to the poor,
> and reaches out her hands to the needy . . . .
> Strength and dignity are her clothing,
> And she laughs at the time to come.
> She opens her mouth with wisdom,
> And the teaching of kindness is on her tongue . . . .
> A woman who fears the LORD is to be praised.
> Give her a share in the fruit of her hands,
> And let her works praise her in the city gates.[25]

24. The formidable Miss Fowler in the movie version of *A Man Called Peter* comes to mind.

25. Proverbs 31:20, 25–26, 30–31. The meaning of that last verse might just as easily be rendered, "let her works praise her amongst the elders" (who sat in the city gates).

In no way do I want to discount or explain away the true and profound wrongs of patriarchal dominance over the centuries, indeed millennia. However, I also think we too often neglect to appreciate the balance that often existed in fact. We tend to forget the degree to which the capable women of traditional societies were in true and vital partnership with the men. Village women and farm wives were never "stay at home moms" in the modern sense. They were essential co-workers in the family enterprise. In old Fenwick, the weavers' wives were often the spinners, making the yarn to be woven, and the women of the farm families worked alongside the men "amangst the hay" and in the harvest. The same was still true for my mother's generation of Kansas farm wives, as she drove the harvest trucks to town, kept the accounts, and tended 300 laying hens that were as much a part of the family income-stream as the hogs and cattle.[26] Like today's dual-role professionals, and the capable wife of Proverbs 31, these women also bore a disproportionate share of the day-by-day household tasks and chores.[27]

The account of the wives of the Fenwick Weavers Society (of which more, anon) in *Matthew Fowlds, Centenarian Weaver* tells of several of the village matriarchs of his day. First in honor, according to the author, was Granny Howat.[28] She was a caring soul who saw to the needs of her feebler and more infirm neighbors, and also a favorite of younger relatives who would come to visit from Kilmarnock and Glasgow. "Sunny disposition," "unaffected sympathy," and "hearty participation" are cited as the good woman's virtues, which shone forth from a "smiling, welcoming face."[29] Another notable name was that of Agnes Craig, who was described as Granny Howat's "worthy compeer and successor" in the community.[30]

26. We did not have dairy cattle, but the women of those families often played an even more massive role in the family work.

27. In our defense, I learned early on that we boys and men had constant chores ourselves: caring for the livestock, cleaning barns, mending fences, painting and repairing houses and outbuildings, and so on. As a kid I became my mother's primary assistant egg-gatherer and co-gardener. Because of my severe hay fever I also became the harvest-season housekeeper and cook while mother was out driving the trucks to the elevator in town. I think that the alienation of both men's and women's work from the domestic context, via factories and offices, needs to be held in mind, both as an aggravating factor in the dynamics of nineteenth and twentieth century gender polarization and imbalance, and in its eventual breakdown.

28. Elizabeth Young, wife of Jasper Howat. See Fairlie, *Matthew Fowlds,* 75–76.

29. Praise was also heaped on her "superlative" potato scones, and the raspberry and currant jellies she made from the fruits of her "well-tended" garden. Ibid., 76.

30. The wife of Matthew Fowlds himself. Ibid.

Similar praise is given to "Betty" Gemmell,[31] described as a "ministering angel" in "not a few homes" of the village. All, according to the author—Rev. J. Kirkwood Fairlie—were of the type of "quiet, sensible, queenlike" village matriarchs of old.

Matriarchs in US church congregations were, and are, of much the same ilk. The typical matriarch was a senior woman in the congregation whose strong (and hopefully kindly) personality combined with her organizational skills to make her a natural leader among the women. She was the one who would organize and oversee the planning of events such as the annual cleaning of the church, church dinners, providing food for bereaved families, and so on. She was often the one to suggest when it was time to buy a new piano, or re-do the cushions in the pews. The matriarch was always well informed about what was going on with everyone in the community. No wise person—woman, man, or minister—failed to consult her on pertinent matters. When one matriarch passed away or became unable to sustain her duties, another would emerge to take her place.

I wish there were formal lists of matriarchs, but it was not the sort of thing that was written down, except (as at Fenwick) in memoirs. The first matriarch I remember was my grandfather's cousin, Mabel "Grandma" Green (1885–1966). She was a solid and rather square-jawed old lady, reflecting her Anderson and Gemmell ancestry. A hard-working farm wife, she was also a wonderful pianist, inveterate letter writer, and always busy, both in church and the community.[32] I remember her as a kindly presence who, at age eighty, could still fascinate a little boy by playing elaborate runs on the piano, but also as someone respectfully deferred to by everybody in church and community. She died at home a few days before Christmas in 1966, on the night of a huge snowstorm. That year was the only time I can remember the Christmas Tree at church being cancelled . . . though I am not sure if it was because of her death, or the weather.

Grandma Green was succeeded by my dad's older sister, Aunt Juanita. "Auntie" was the pianist for church, Sunday School, or both, from 1916 to about 1980 (she alternated with Grandma Green for many of those years). Auntie's husband, Uncle Jesse, was the perennial Superintendant of the Sunday School, and was mostly quite biddable by his formidable wife. My memory of her leadership style is that she would announce during the

31. She was the wife of one of the *many* John Gemmells, or Gemmills, in Fenwick. Ibid.

32. She also headed up the Home Economics department at the Crawford County Fair for years, overseeing the canning and baking entries.

closing exercises of the Sunday School, "It is time to start planning X . . . ." Assignments would be made, and things would proceed from there. When someone in the community died, she organized the neighborhood flowers and collected the money. At least one cousin forever after recalled how "Jesse and Juanita" showed up at their door one day and offered to loan her and her husband the money they needed to buy the lot that would make it possible to build themselves a new house.[33]

Auntie was succeeded in turn by LaVerna Gemmell, whose style proved similar. LaVerna "saw to business" in all she did. When the local ministerial alliance set up a thrift shop in the late 1970s, LaVerna became one of the main organizers. She also became an elder—only the second woman ordained in the congregation—and, as the men of the congregation aged and died off, she very much kept the church going, up to the end of her life.[34]

I have crossed paths with other matriarchs, in other churches and communities over the years; whatever their racial-ethnic or cultural background, they all seem to be cut from the same cloth. They remain a potent presence among the Native American and Hispanic Presbyterians of northern New Mexico where I now live. Among the old Euro-American missionaries in India-Pakistan, such women were called *memsahib*—basically meaning "ma'am-sir"—by the local population.[35] Although this term was generally used to speak of European women during the colonial era, I have heard it quite specifically (and aptly) used in reference to those of the matriarchal personality type. The concept, if not the vocabulary, transcends place and time.

As was observed at the Jubilee of Matthew Fowlds, the accomplishments of the Presbyterian churches historically were as much the work of the elders—and the matriarchs—as the clergy, both in Scotland and around the world. Especially in smaller and more remote communities, where the minister might be seen once a week at most (or, in early days, once every few months), the elders and matriarchs were the *presence* of church, day by day, through all the joys, sorrows, toils, and challenges the

33. Over the years, my parents both chafed a bit at having his big sister living (literally) within shouting distance, just a quarter of a mile up the road. Yet her funeral was also the only time I remember seeing them *both* weep in public. She was a major force in my childhood, though I frustrated her efforts to teach me to play the piano. Sometimes, I confess, I now recognize bits of her coming out in me.

34. That church essentially ended with her, though, the last I heard, the old building is still lovingly maintained by her family and the neighbors.

35. It is a word that refers to the sort of woman to whom you would say, "Yes sir!"

community faced. What is evident in the accounts of the historic matriarchy is that—although their informal role was very different, and insufficiently valued for far too long—the ministry and vitality of the churches were as much their accomplishment as the men's. In that sense, and at their very best, I think they together assumed the mantle of the ancient *abbas* and *ammas* of the desert.

In the *flux* of our day, with longstanding institutional structures rapidly collapsing all around us, I suspect that, yet again, the future of formal Christianity depends more on these organic leaders of our base ecclesial communities. Whether the emerging modalities use the title or not, the men and women who serve as "elders" will be essential. They are the ones who will see us through as much, if not more, than any professionals. No spiritual or faith community can exist only in the ethereal abstract. (This is the fatal flaw, I think, in too much of the contemporary, "spiritual but not religious" chatter, which fails to take this into account.) Community has to be incarnated in some form of basic organization, and organization requires some form of leadership. There have always been elders and matriarchs, and I think there always will be. There *must* be.

9

Ministers

I HAVE DELIBERATELY DEFERRED my consideration of ministers until after examining the elders because I believe that, in many ways, the elders are really more foundational to the Presbyterian way. If the office of Elder/Matriarch emerges naturally—or organically—within a community, the role of the Minister (also now called "Teaching Elder" in the PCUSA) has traditionally been that of "integral other" within a Presbyterian congregation. Ministers were, and are, highly educated and trained professionals, brought in from outside the local community to provide leadership, instruction in the faith, administration of the sacraments, and pastoral care. They always stand just a bit apart—"maintaining professional boundaries," in modern jargon—even if they serve a congregation for ten, twenty, thirty, or even forty years.

The classic Presbyterian—and general Protestant—model for ministers and their ministry closely resembles the description of the Parson in Chaucer's *Canterbury Tales*:

> There was a good man of religion,
> Who was a poor Parson of a [country] town,
> But he was rich of holy thought and work.
> He was also a learned man, a clerk,
> Who would truly preach Christ's gospel;
> And he devoutly taught his parishioners.
> He was benign, wonderfully diligent,
> Full of patience in adversity,
> And such he was often proved to be.
> He was loath to curse for his tithes, [1]

1. I.e. threaten excommunication to procure the tithes.

But rather, when in doubt, he would give
To his poor parishioners roundabout
Some of the offerings, and even his own possessions.
He could get by on just a little.
His parish was wide, and the houses far asunder,
But he never neglected to visit his people,
In rain or thunder, sickness or misfortune,
Those near and far, great and small,
Walking abroad, carrying a staff in his hand.
He gave this noble example to his flock,
That first he wrought, and afterwards he taught…

And though he was holy and virtuous,
He was not scornful of sinners,
Nor was his speech disdainful and haughty,
But in his teaching he was discrete and benign;
His business was to draw folk to heaven
By fairness and good example.
But if anyone was obstinate,
Whoever it was, of high or low estate,
That one he scolded, sharply, as occasion required.
I do not believe there is a better priest to be found anywhere.
He did not expect to be treated with pomp or reverence,
Nor did he have an over-fastidious conscience,
But he taught the lore of Christ and his twelve apostles,
Having first followed it himself.[2]

Chaucer is reputed to have favored the Lollards[3] and this description of the Parson—the only churchman he describes in a positive light—certainly matches the Lollard ideal for their poor priests.[4]

Reading Chaucer's description brings thoughts of several ministers to mind. The first is the Rev. William Guthrie (1620–1665), who was the first minister of Fenwick Parish after it was divided off from neighboring

2. Adapted by the author from the Prologue of Chaucer, *The Canterbury Tales*, lines 479–499, 517–530. The Parson is described as being from a "town" but the setting portrayed is more of the countryside. It could be that a sort of "township" is more what Chaucer had in mind, or a community slightly (but not much) larger than a village.

3. As noted elsewhere, the Lollards were followers of the late fourteenth century English proto-Protestant "heretic" John Wycliffe. Chaucer was a contemporary, and allied to the party at the English royal court that favored Wycliffe.

4. As noted elsewhere, there is credible reason to believe that the surviving Lollard underground in the sixteenth century influenced the formation of both the Church of Scotland under John Knox and the Puritan movement in England.

Kilmarnock in 1643. An ardent Covenanter, he was also a dynamic preacher, conscientious pastor, spiritual counselor, and church-planting evangelist. During his ministry, people flocked to Fenwick to hear him, and some even moved to the parish from places as distant as Glasgow and Ulster to become part of his congregation. Given to humor and fond of sport (fishing and curling in particular), he once paid a noted poacher in the parish to skip his surreptitious rounds and show up at church on Sabbath Day. The poacher reportedly experienced a powerful conversion and is said to have eventually become an elder. Guthrie was turned out of the Fenwick congregation shortly after the Restoration of King Charles II, but he did not share his cousin's fate on the scaffold.[5] He was held in high regard, even by the episcopal clergy with whom he so strongly differed, and was visited by the Bishop of Brechin—his native parish in Angus—on his deathbed.

Two hundred years later, the Rev. William Orr of the United Secession congregation at Fenwick proved himself a worthy, beloved, and long-serving successor to William Guthrie. He served Fenwick from 1830 to 1879, and died there in 1882.[6] Rev. Orr's era saw the great diaspora of Fenwick folks, who emigrated to far corners of the United States, Canada, Australia, New Zealand, and various other parts of the British Empire in search of a better life. He was thus truly held in affectionate esteem around the world. Writing to Thomas W. Orr[7] in 1908 from Elgin, Illinois, eighty-two-year-old J.B. Shedden wrote of the minister:

> The first prayer meeting that I ever attended was in your father's church. When I was four or five years of age my grandmother took me with her. I can remember yet hearing your father pray ... it all impressed me with a good deal of reverence .... When I was a young man[8] I had several kind letters from your father .... Many times have I received your father's blessing with his hand on my head, even when he met me on the road .... Who that loves Jesus would not love such a man?[9]

5. William Guthrie was a cousin, close friend, and supporter of the Covenanter martyr James Guthrie.

6. Orr was pastor both to the family of my Anderson great-great-grandparents (he baptized my great-grandmother in 1840) and to the family of my husband's Calderwood and Bicket kin (he performed the wedding of Doug's great-great-grandparents in 1832). The Cuthbertsons of the day were members of the neighboring "Auld Kirk" (Church of Scotland) congregation in Fenwick.

7. Rev. Orr's son.

8. This was after emigrating with his family at age 14.

9. Fairlie, *Matthew Fowlds, Centenarian Weaver,* 47.

The first Covenanter preacher to arrive in the American colonies was the Rev. John Cuthbertson.[10] After coming to America in 1751, he itinerated up and down the eastern seaboard from his home base in Pennsylvania, preaching, baptizing, marrying, and presiding over the Lord's Supper for some forty years. In 1782, John Cuthbertson was also one of the leaders who helped to bring about the (possibly) first denominational merger in the United States, when major portions of the Associate Presbyterians ("AP"; the Seceders) and the Reformed Presbyterians (the Covenanters) came together to form the ARP Church. His diary, with entries concerning the places and people to whom he ministered, is a fascinating document.

The Rev. David Lindsay (1800–1880) was an AP, from the branch of the Seceders that did not enter the 1782 union. He was the great-great-grandfather of my husband's father. Born in County Down, Northern Ireland, he came to America with his parents and siblings in 1806. He began his studies for ministry after already being married and responsible for a large family. He was ordained in 1833 and, after several years of ministry in Ohio, he moved his family to Birmingham, Iowa, where he served from 1842 to 1854. In 1857 he was badly injured, when a stagecoach overturned while he was itinerating as a "home missionary," and he used crutches for the rest of his life. In 1867 he and his wife retired to Garnett, Kansas, joining two of their sons who had settled there in support of the Free State cause during the territorial struggle of the 1850s (more on them later). An account written by the UPNA minister at Garnett at the time of David Lindsay's death gives a sense of his spirit and character:

> Though during this period [he was] not actually engaged in preaching the gospel, he was not idle. Seldom was his place vacant in the congregation or the prayer meeting. Upon communion occasions he always took part in the table service. He was particularly attentive to strangers and to the sick, almost always cheery and in good spirits.
>
> [He lingered in his last illness for two weeks, and we are told...] They were weeks of abiding peace—no pain of body, no pain of mind. Once, when the writer visited him, and asked him how he was getting along, he looked up, with a smile, and said: "Almost through!"[11]

10. He lived ca. 1711–1791. No kin to me, so far as we know; his family was from Renfrewshire while mine was from Ayrshire.

11. The account comes from a clipping found among old family papers. The original source publication is not identified.

From my own experience in childhood and youth, I remember ministers like the Rev. Fred Lenk, who was the minister at the old UPNA church in Pittsburg, Kansas, and his successor the Rev. Bob Docherty.[12] Fred was a tall, thin, rather heady and earnest old United Presbyterian, robed each Sabbath in his austere black pulpit gown. I often used to listen to his sermons on radio via "The United Presbyterian Hour," broadcast locally on Sunday mornings. He was very precise, and a solid, but not at all showy, preacher. Dr. Bob, by contrast, was a hearty and cheerful Scot who always wore his kilt to church on the Sunday before Christmas. A good and lively preacher and caring pastor, he willingly added service out at our little Osage congregation to his duties in Pittsburg for several years.[13] Very different men, they were, but both lovers of Jesus and faithful pastors.

And then there was Chase . . . . I have mentioned Rev. Chase Stafford several times. He was the minister at the Sterling United Presbyterian Church during my college years, and taught Greek at the college. By welcoming me in various ways into their lives, their home, and their ministry, Chase and his wife, Harriette, became major transformative influences in my life. They were not perfect, by any means (he could be a bit of a gossip, etc.), but they both modeled a faith that was deeply joyful and laughter-filled. Chase modeled a Christian faith that mixed deep intellectual curiosity with compassion and generosity of spirit. He was a very good expository preacher, whose knowledge of psychology, theology, and history served well in adding depth and breadth to his sermons. In his day, the Sterling church was packed, including the balcony, on most Lord's Days as farmers, townsfolk, college faculty and students alike flocked to hear him. A number of us from his Greek classes went on to become ministers. In later years, the Staffords and I parted ways over the sexuality issue in the PCUSA, and sadly never quite managed to make it up again before age and illness set in and they both passed from this life. Nevertheless, I continually thank God that I got to know them so well, and I love them still.

Early on, I alluded to how preaching is almost a third sacrament in our tradition. Faithful ministers always have a variety of roles to perform but, without doubt, the most visible and public role of Presbyterian ministers has historically been that of preaching. Presbyterians have traditionally expected thoughtful, biblically- and theologically-based, timely

---

12. Both, by the way, were graduates and enthusiastic supporters of Sterling College.

13. He quite lovingly conducted my mother's funeral on December 12, 1989.

sermons. Until a hundred years ago, they also expected *long* sermons.[14] Today brevity—twenty minutes, or less—is considered a virtue.

A time-honored saying goes, "The preaching of the Word of God *is* the Word of God." That is, in proclaiming the written word in relation to present-day life, it becomes alive to and for us here and now. In practicing the art of preaching, there are at least four participatory elements, or agents:

1. The Bible

2. The Spirit

3. The Preacher

4. The Congregation

Ideally the preacher has carefully studied and prayerfully considered the text, seeking the assistance of the Holy Spirit. Hopefully, in the process, the preacher has heard the Word speaking in his/her own heart a message that will also speak to the hearts of the hearers in the congregation. The process is completed in the proclamation, a surprisingly interactive exercise in which, once again, we preachers trust that the Spirit is using our words to speak *the* Word. From the highly exegetical and theological sermons of the sixteenth and seventeenth centuries down to the more informal storytelling modes of our day, that has been the unvarying hope and intention behind Presbyterian sermonizing.[15]

One particular preacher serves, for me, as a great exemplar of the art, and his sermons were a major formative influence on the way I continue to approach preaching. As a high school student I first read the book, *A Man Called Peter*, the story of Dr. Peter Marshall, who was the minister of New York Avenue Presbyterian Church in Washington, DC, during World War II, and who later served as Chaplain of the US Senate until his early death in 1949.[16] His biography led me eagerly on to his published sermons, *Mr.*

14. If I recall correctly, in William Guthrie's day the beadle (sexton) at Fenwick normally turned the hour glass twice during the sermon.

15. A classic old Scottish story highlights the true deadliness of uninspired preaching. It tells of a rather meek older woman who was chosen to serve on the committee to seek a new minister. After hearing one young minister, all the committee members except her expressed their opinions. Asked by the chair what she thought, she quietly and regretfully delivered the verdict: "Weel, what he had, he had to read. He couldna read. And what he had was no worth readin'."

16. My cousin sang in the choir at New York Avenue Presbyterian Church during the war. In 1946, he and his wife were due to be married by Dr. Marshall, but Marshall's first heart attack intervened. Peter Marshall died following a second heart attack at the

Jones, Meet the Master being the best known volume. Some sixty to seventy years after being preached, those sermons still read well.

Peter Marshall was born into a working-class family in Coatbridge, Scotland.[17] After immigrating to the US in 1927, he, in due course, found the ways and means to pursue the calling he perceived to the ministry. Naturally gifted, he was a vividly descriptive preacher and a master storyteller, as well as a man of lively faith. He could make the biblical tales and the practical life circumstances of his hearers come together in dynamic and transformative combinations, and did so in sermons such as "Disciples in Clay" (imagining an interview board set up to screen all twelve potential disciples of Jesus) and "The Saint of the Rank and File" (presenting the Apostle Andrew, Scotland's patron, as the saint of simple common working folks). In one sermon, entitled "Letters in the Sand," Marshall set forth the story from John's gospel of the woman taken in adultery and, after telling the tale, he brought it home to his hearers:

> No, we do not know her name
>   nor where she lived
>   nor who she was.
> But of this we can be sure—she was never the same again.
> She was a changed woman from that moment.
> Of that we can be sure.
>
> She has looked into the eyes of Christ.
> She has seen God.
> She has been accused
>   convicted
>   judged but not condemned.
> *She has been forgiven!*
>
> And now her head is up.
> Her eyes are shining like stars,
> for has she not seen the greatest miracle of all?
>
> It is more wonderful than the miracles of creation . . .
>   more beautiful than the flowers . . .
>   more mysterious than the stars . . .
>   more wonderful than life itself . . .
> that God is willing, for Christ's sake,
> to forgive sinners like you and me.

---

relatively young age of forty-six.

17. Coatbridge is an old industrial town near Glasgow.

For we are *all* sinners . . . guilty of different kinds of sin, no
doubt.
For there are sins of the heart
   and sins of the mind
      and sins of the disposition
as well as sins of the body.

We, too, may be forgiven, no matter what type or kind
of transgression we have committed.
That we may be forgiven is the greatest miracle of them all.[18]

Through such sermons, and his lively and pertinent prayers, the Scottish
emigrant became a notable influence in the nation's capital, in the country
as a whole, and particularly (and most importantly) in the individual lives
of his hearers and readers.

As the times may have required, many Presbyterian ministers have
also been boldly prophetic preachers (and some still are). Stories of the
Scots Reformer John Knox strongly remind me of Hebrew prophets like
Elijah, Elisha, and Amos. He was fiery, blunt, and uncompromising before
Queen and commons alike.[19] Among Knox's successors, men like John
Welsh (his son-in-law) and Andrew Melville sometimes found themselves
silenced and/or sent off into exile by Scotland's King James VI/I. Melville
once famously referred to James as "God's silly vassal" . . . right to the king's
face! This prophetic line continued on down through the Covenanting era
of the seventeenth century, to James Guthrie of Stirling—the cousin of
Fenwick's William—who was unjustly executed for treason by Charles II.[20]
Various Covenanter preachers after him followed the path to martyrdom,
or hid themselves among the moorland *moss-hags*. The visionary Alexander Peden (1626–1686), called "the Prophet" because of his numerous
corroborated experiences of Second Sight,[21] was one of the latter, as he
spent many years either imprisoned or hiding out in the rough as he ministered in the southwest of Scotland and across the Irish Sea in Ulster.

---

18. Excerpt from "Letters in the Sand" in Marshall, *A Man Called Peter*, 343. The
current DVD version of the movie *A Man Called Peter* includes the bonus feature of
one of the few audio recordings of Dr. Marshall preaching, with his strong Scottish
burr, a sermon on crucifixion entitled "Were You There?" given in March, 1944.

19. John Calvin was more of an Isaiah type, though not so lyrical as Second Isaiah.

20. Unbending, yes, but James Guthrie was not a traitor.

21. "Second Sight" is the old Scots term for precognition, often in the form of a
vision.

The American Revolution was said, at least by some in Britain, to be a Scots-Irish Presbyterian Revolution in which "Cousin America" had run off with a parson. The particular parson in question was John Knox's descendant Dr. John Witherspoon, the only clergyman to sign the Declaration of Independence. On 17 May 1776, just weeks before voting for independence, Witherspoon preached a sermon at Princeton worthy of his ancestor:

> If your cause is just, if your principles are pure, and if your conduct is prudent, you need not fear the multitude of opposing hosts.
>
> If your cause is just, you may look with confidence to the Lord and entreat him to plead it as his own. You are all my witnesses that this is the first time of my introducing any political subject into the pulpit. At this season however, it is not only lawful but necessary, and I willingly embrace the opportunity of declaring my opinion without any hesitation that the cause in which America is now in arms is the cause of justice, of liberty, and of human nature. So far as we have hitherto proceeded, I am satisfied that the confederacy of the colonies has not been the effect of pride, resentment, or sedition, but of a deep and general conviction that our civil and religious liberties, and consequently in a great measure the temporal and eternal happiness of us and our posterity, depended on the issue . . . . There is not a single instance in history in which civil liberty was lost, and religious liberty preserved entire. If therefore we yield up our temporal property, we at the same time deliver the conscience into bondage.[22]

Both in Scotland and America, the prophetic tradition continued right on through the nineteenth and twentieth centuries with strong voices against slavery and for social justice. Rev. George MacLeod, founder of the Iona Community in Scotland, was notoriously outspoken in matters of peace and justice (so much so that he was not invited, or permitted, to preach on the BBC during WWII). Other more recent names, such as Eugene Carson Blake, John Fife, and the self-proclaimed "lesbian evangelist," Janie Spahr, come to mind. Those in our current churches who think that preachers need

---

22. Excerpt from "The Dominion of Providence over the Passions of Men," in Miller, *The Selected Writings of John Witherspoon*, 140–141. Witherspoon began his ministry at Beith in Ayrshire, less than ten miles from Fenwick. Records of the Secession congregation at neighboring Kilmaurs show that, in 1751, one of their members was disciplined for having gone to hear Witherspoon—a minister of the "established" Kirk—preach.

to shy away from speaking to the great issues of the day, either in church or state, just do not understand historic Presbyterianism . . . or (I think) most of the Bible.

It has "aye" been, and is, the great privilege and responsibility of Presbyterian ministers to exercise a ministry of Word and Sacrament. The sharing of Word and Sacrament is the focus of our ministry, and the basis of any authority or influence we can or should possess. We are not called to be administrators, social workers, activists, or even teachers in the general sense . . . though sometimes we find ourselves exercising some of those functions, and more. We are called, simply, to be stewards of the mysteries of God. They are the only thing we really have to offer . . . in word or deed. Our *raison d'être* is to mindfully, humbly, and sometimes boldly, speak God's words and do God's deeds in, for, and with the congregation as we all seek to follow the ways of Jesus in this world—nothing more, or less.

Unlike other Christian denominations (Roman Catholic, Episcopal, etc.), ordination is not a sacrament in the Reformed Tradition. The ordination of Presbyterian ministers (also elders and deacons) is not so much a bestowal of something as it is the formal recognition by the community of the gifts and calling by God of the persons being ordained, and their confirmation in the role and function of the office to which they are being ordained. It is a communal empowering of those ordained, and the offering of blessing in God's name. It is also a meaningful recognition of the continuity of the living Christian tradition across time, as we are touched by those who were touched by others who were touched by yet others in the succession of laying on of hands, reaching (literally) back across two millennia to Jesus and his disciples.

There can be no doubt that times are a-changing. One of the biggest questions now facing traditional institutional Christianity is the future of professional ministry. Current models probably are not generally sustainable as Presbyterian congregations shrink in size, and traditional roles have to adapt and change in the face of the cultural transitions occurring all around us. I truly have no problem with that, and find it rather exciting.[23] My biggest concern, however, is that there might be a loss of substance along the way. The mindful and careful study of scripture, history, theology, spirituality, and pastoral ministry is—in my opinion—necessary for the ongoing vitality of the church. It is a great privilege to be part of a faith tradition that cares deeply about delving into what the scriptures

23. My bias, as you may well guess, lies more in the direction of house-church than mega-church.

said and meant when they were first written, and about how to translate and apply that meaning, under the rule of love, into our day and time. It is precious to me to be part of a succession of faith and practice stretching across three millennia. How do we hold on to an awareness of all of that as we move into the unknown and uncertain future?

One of the other elements of Presbyterian worship that used to be reserved solely for the ministers was the pronouncing of the Blessing (the Benediction) over the congregation at the conclusion of worship.[24] Although we have become a bit more flexible (or lax) over time as to who can do this on a typical Lord's Day, it is still the first ministerial act of a newly-ordained pastor to offer the Blessing at the conclusion of the ordination service. The Blessing was always to be taken from scripture, for it was not *our* blessing but that of God, saying it through us. As I was once taught, it is something that the congregation should receive with eyes open, looking the minister in the eye as he/she says it. As a minister, it always feels like a great privilege—and blessing—to pronounce the Blessing. At the same time, it is very humbling.

The two most traditional, and commonly used, Blessings were the Priestly Benediction from the Book of Numbers, and the Apostolic Benediction of St. Paul:

> May the LORD bless and keep you;
> May the face of God shine graciously upon you;
> May the Holy One look upon you, and give you Peace.[25]
>
> May the grace of our Lord Jesus Christ, the love of God,
> and the communion of the Holy Spirit be with you all,
> now and always.[26]

So be it. Amen.

---

24. The rationale for this was that the minister "of the Word" was the one in the congregation with the authority to pronounce the Blessing in God's Name, on God's behalf.

25. Num 6:24–26, modified by author. LORD (in all caps) is used in various translations to indicate the divine name YHWH.

26. 2 Cor 13:13.

10

From Discipline to Discipleship

Ecclesia reformata semper reformanda secundum verbum Dei.

THIS REFORMATION-ERA MOTTO MEANS: "The church reformed, and always being reformed, according to the Word of God." The only doctrine of infallibility that Presbyterians ever affirmed was about scripture . . . and we have not always been of one mind as to what infallibility even means. The institutional church (as opposed to the mystical body of Christ) has always been seen by us as a provisional body. It is *not* the Kingdom of God. Although we trust that the Holy Spirit guides and directs, it is nevertheless subject to errors of belief and practice . . . sometimes put into place by good and well-intentioned, but fallible, human leaders. Mistakes are made and, from time to time, great wrongs have been done. Not only that, like the wonderful Tevye from *Fiddler on the Roof*, as times and circumstances change we have learned that "Tradition!" sometimes (often) has had to give way to new understandings and ways. The only, and all-important, caveat in such change always (supposedly) being, "according to the Word of God." Even then, the way we discern and understand the Word itself, and the God revealed therein, sometimes shifts and changes, too.

The changes currently occurring in Christianity are comprehensive and universal, affecting all types of churches and all their people, everywhere. Every aspect of church life is in transition: theology, worship, spiritual formation, mission outreach, and church organization and governance. Strangely enough, it is the last of these that may be the most challenging for some Presbyterians. Over the last century we have somewhat become accustomed to dealing with new trends in thought, new modes of worship, new emphases on spirituality, and new approaches to doing mission. However, the way the church organization is conceived, structured, and does its institutional business has remained fairly constant for over forty years.[1] Now that, too, is changing.

In 2011 the PCUSA adopted a fairly radical revision of the *Form of Government*, the central constitutional document setting forth our organizational structure. I am *not* one of those Presbyterians who idolizes our church polity—and, in fact, I get quite irritated at those who do—so I find myself deeply encouraged by the potential for a new way of conceiving and living out the business of being church that is envisioned in this new order. The notion behind the change was to step back from what had become an unwieldy and over-regulated legalism and to move toward a more flexible and adaptive system of governance fitted to the transitional nature of the times and to local circumstances. The parts that most excite me, however, are the re-visioning of the core principles underlying the system and a new focus on a "bottom up" rather than "top down" understanding of church organization.

For some Presbyterians, the most startling, and unsettling, change may be the emphasis that is placed on local congregations as the foundational unit of ecclesial organization:

> The congregation is the church engaged in the mission of God in its particular context . . . . God gives to the congregation all the gifts of the gospel necessary to being the Church. The congregation is the basic form of the church, but it is not of itself a sufficient form of the church. Thus congregations are bound together in communion with one another, united in relationships of accountability and responsibility, contributing their strengths to the benefit of the whole, and are called, collectively, the church.[2]

"Basic" but not "sufficient," possessing "all the gifts of the gospel necessary" for engaging in mission in a particular context, but also "bound together in communion" in broader relationships (presbyteries, etc.) of "accountability and responsibility"—I find it to be a beautiful summation of a theology of organization, starting from what Liberation theologians refer to as the "base ecclesial communities." It represents a huge shift away from the corporate hierarchy model of understanding that has prevailed over the last sixty-some years. I also believe it is, indeed, "according to the Word of God."

1. The 1983 merger of the UPCUSA and the PCUS notwithstanding.

2. PCUSA, *Book of Order*, G-1.0101.

The Bible itself, and the subsequent history of Christianity, shows that, every so often, it has been necessary to hit the "reset" button on the religious institutions of the time. The ancient Hebrew religion started with a family, that (as the story goes) grew into tribes, and ultimately into a nation with a powerful monarchy and priesthood centered in Jerusalem. Archaeological discoveries over the last couple of centuries have shown that the most ancient expressions of the Hebrew religion were more similar to those of their Canaanite neighbors than traditionally thought. However, at a certain point, the faith of Israel began to change and evolve. Beginning in about the eighth century BCE there was a major reformation, led by various prophets and by the group now referred to as the Deuteronomists, which changed the ways of belief and religious practice among the emerging Jewish People. The Hebrew Bible, as we know it, was largely a product of that reform movement.

Then disaster struck. Jerusalem fell to the Babylonians, the Davidic monarchy ended, the Temple of Solomon was destroyed, and many of the people were carried off to a foreign land. Despite all this, the religion of Israel survived and emerged into something new: Judaism. Although the priesthood was restored, and a less impressive temple was eventually rebuilt in Jerusalem, the Jewish people began to practice their religion in new ways. Devout people began to gather in circles of study and prayer, and the synagogue was born as a new form of the base community.

Some five hundred years later, Jesus gathered to himself a reforming community of disciples. The Christian Church was not necessarily preplanned. It was not immediately clear how the religious establishment of Judaism would deal with the Jesus movement. Even after the crucifixion, followers of Jesus continued to pray in the Temple. The missionary outreach to the gentiles raised challenges on how to integrate non-Jews into the new faith community. Outside of Jerusalem, the top leaders of the Christian movement were mostly itinerant, establishing and visiting emerging communities spread across the Middle East and the Roman Empire.

Then, again, disaster struck. The primary leaders of the international church—Peter and Paul—were killed at Rome by Nero. Shortly after that, the Jewish Revolt against Rome broke out. Jerusalem and its Temple were destroyed in 70 CE. The priestly and ceremonial order of Judaism (led by the Sadducees) was destroyed, with rabbinic Judaism (led by the Pharisees) taking its place. The Jewish-Christian community centered at Jerusalem was also dispersed, and soon disappeared as a significant element of the Christian movement. The New Testament documents emerged in the aftermath of all of this, and the scattered communities of predominantly gentile Christians became the base from which the Church grew.

At least two more times in its history, major segments of the Christian Church have had to revert to their base and restart under radically changed circumstances. The first instance followed the collapse of the Roman Empire in Western Europe in the fifth century, as the new monastic communes provided centers of religious life in the midst of social turmoil and anarchy. The distinctive, community-based Celtic Christianity of Wales, Ireland, Scotland, and northern England emerged, and flourished, in this era.

Nearly a thousand years later, the power, corruption, and dysfunction of the Roman Catholic Church began to give rise to a variety of heretical (i.e. dissenting) groups across Europe. These groups varied in their views from the extremes of the Albigensians (Cathars) to the more moderate proto-Protestant understandings of the Waldensians in Italy, the Lollards in Britain, and the Hussites in Bohemia.

The elements that united the heretical underground, across the board, were a strong anticlericalism and an equally strong rejection of the existing sacramental system of the church. From the Pope in far-off Rome right down to the local parishes, clergy were viewed by these folks as corrupt oppressors, abusing the Mass and sacrament of penance in particular to enrich themselves (via masses for the dead, etc.) and wield power over secular leaders (via excommunication, etc.) across Europe. From at least the fourteenth century, people began to talk about the Pope (the office itself, and often the man) as an Antichrist presiding over an evil ecclesial system.

During this time, teachers like John Wycliffe[3] of Oxford University began to give voice to alternative views and understandings of the Church. Wycliffe and his followers (the Lollards) emphasized the poverty and humility of Jesus and the first Christians, and the authority of Scripture over that of the clergy. They began to challenge what they saw as false understandings of the sacraments and of how God's grace is bestowed on humanity. Perhaps the bread and wine of the Mass were not the literal body and blood of Jesus, miraculously (magically?) transformed by the priest. Perhaps the Mass was not a sacrifice for sins that could help liberate a soul

3. Wycliffe died in 1384. He not only had influential ties at the Courts of England's Edward III and Richard II, but his teachings also influenced the rise of the Hussite movement in Bohemia.

from purgatory. Perhaps Jesus gave the authority to forgive in his name to all Christians and not just to the clergy. Perhaps the Church belonged to the people, and the poor parsons were all the churchmen that were really needed.

In the mid-1490s, during the reign of King James IV of Scotland, a group of about thirty Lollards from the districts of Kyle and Cunningham in northern Ayrshire were charged and prosecuted by Archbishop Blacader[4] of Glasgow. John Knox began his *History of the Reformation in Scotland* with their story. Among the few names he mentions is one from our ancestral Fenwick, Helen Chalmers, who was the wife of the Laird of Polkellie.[5]

In his account, John Knox quotes a statement made by one of these Lollards—Adam Reid of Barskimming in Mauchline Parish—to King James IV and Archbishop Blacader at their hearing. Asked by the King if God was in heaven, Reid replied (addressing the Archbishop):

> I neither think nor believe, as thou thinks, that God is in heaven; but I am most assured that He is not only in the heaven, but also in the earth. But thou and thy faction declare by your works that either ye think there is no God at all, or else that He is so shut up in the heaven that He regards not what is done into the earth; for if thou firmly believed that God were in the heaven, thou should not make thyself cheek-mate [boon companion] to the King, and altogether forget the charge that Jesus Christ the Son of God gave to his apostles, which was to preach his Evangel, and not to play the proud prelates, as all the rabble of you do this day. And now, Sir (said he to the King), judge ye whether the Bishop or I believe best that God is in heaven.[6]

Such is the sort of stock from which the Scots Reformers arose a few generations later. Like their continental counterparts in sixteenth-century Europe, they addressed the long-festering abuses and dysfunctions of the papal church, and also the new socio-cultural context of the time, by seeking to return to the apostolic simplicity of the first Christians. To varying degrees, all of the Reformers tried to strip away the accretions of the

4. Doubtless an ancestor of comedian Rowan Atkinson's fictional Edmund Blackadder.

5. Her husband would have been the head of a branch of the ancient Mures of Rowallan. According to lore passed down about various Fenwick families, I suspect some other Lollard connections as well . . . the Howies of Lochgoin, the Calderwoods of Blackbyre, and perhaps even the Andersons of Doghillock.

6 Dickinson, *John Knox's History*, 10.

preceding thousand years (in particular) and to restore the church to its origins "according to the Word of God."

The Scottish Presbyterians and English Puritans were some of the most pronounced in their efforts. In 1560, John Knox and five other men named John were chosen to write the Confession of Faith for the newly re-formed Kirk of Scotland. It is a fascinating document, setting forth not only the core theological views of the reforming Kirk, but also their vision and understanding of what constitutes the true Church of Jesus Christ in its particular manifestations in time and place:

> The notes, signs, and assured tokens whereby the spotless bride of Christ is known from . . . the false Kirk, we state, are neither antiquity, usurped title [i.e. the papacy], lineal succession [of bishops], appointed place, nor the numbers of men approving an error . . . . The notes of the true Kirk, therefore, we believe, confess, and avow to be: first, the true preaching of the Word of God, in which God has revealed himself to us, as the writings of the prophets and apostles declare; secondly, the right administration of the sacraments of Christ Jesus, with which must be associated the Word and promise of God to seal and confirm them in our hearts; and lastly, ecclesiastical discipline uprightly ministered as God's Word prescribes, whereby vice is repressed and virtue nourished. Then wherever these notes are seen and continue for any time, be the number complete or not, there, beyond doubt, is the true Kirk of Christ, who, according to his promise, is in its midst.[7]

The Knoxian "notes" of the true Church, then, are:

- The Word of God, truly preached and heard.
- The Sacraments, rightly administered.
- Ecclesiastical discipline, uprightly ministered.

Given the great distance we have come from the Knoxian forms of Presbyterianism over the last century or so, it came as a rather huge shock to discover that the authors of the 2011 PCUSA *Form of Government* had chosen to make Knox's notes a central organizing principle in the current reformation of the ordering of the church.[8] The introductory section on the "Foundations of Presbyterian Polity" includes an interestingly updated version:

7. PCUSA, *Book of Confessions*, C-3.18.

8. Especially—if I remember correctly—since John Calvin did *not* agree with Knox on including ecclesiastical discipline in the list.

> We affirm that, in the power of the Spirit, the Church is faithful
> to the mission of Christ as it:
>> Proclaims and hears the Word of God . . . .
>> Administers and receives the Sacraments . . . .
>> Nurtures a covenant community of disciples of Christ.[9]

In order to emphasize the point, these notes are not just stated once; they are repeated and referenced throughout as defining elements for each level of the ecclesial structure: congregations,[10] sessions, presbyteries, and the General Assembly.[11]

What I find most fascinating of all is the seemingly subtle, but in fact quite profound, shift of wording in the third note . . . from "discipline" to covenantal "discipleship." I suspect Thomas and Alexander Campbell, the Disciples of Christ founders, would be delighted! Their hope, in their time, was to help bring the church back to its apostolic roots in "Churches of Christ composed of "Disciples of Christ"[12] . . . and two centuries later that seems to be a key piece of what the Presbyterian Church has, at last, embraced.[13]

The great flaw in the old Presbyterian emphasis on discipline was that it so often nurtured a tendency toward legalism among the people, and led to a petty tyranny among the eldership and ministry. The compendium of sins listed under the Ten Commandments in the *Westminster Larger Catechism* gives the best notion of the daunting standards the conscientious "o'er guid" tried to live up to themselves, and/or see that their neighbors did. As I noted earlier, for a very long time the primary role of the eldership was to serve as a sort of local court, overseeing the morals and behavior of the congregation. It was not a pleasant task. Even with the best of intentions, it proved far too easy to slip into "lording" it over others, and mere mortals often fell short of the best of intentions.[14]

---

9. PCUSA, *Book of Order*, F-1.0303.

10. Ibid., G-1.0101.

11. Ibid., G-3.0101, etc.

12. The "Church of Christ," the independent "Christian Church," and the "Disciples of Christ" are the three main branches of the old Campellite movement.

13. From my cursory read of Alexander Campbell's thoughts on church organization—in Chapter 24 of *The Christian System*—there are several affinities with the concepts informing the new PCUSA *Form of Government*.

14. Session records of the several conflicts between Rev. Hugh Thomson of Kilmaurs and the erstwhile William Cuthbertson of Buntinhill in the early 1700s illustrate this beautifully. Sin there certainly was, in abundance, but it also appears that Thomson and Cuthbertson may have borne a longstanding and very personal dislike

If we will actually embrace the concept, then the shift from "godly discipline rightly administered" to "nurturing a covenant community of disciples of Christ" could profoundly change the focus of Presbyterian life. Discipleship is a matter of learning of Jesus and following his ways rather than of adhering to legalistic proscriptions. To what end? In Mark's gospel, we are told that Jesus called the twelve, *"That they should be with him,* and that he might send them forth to preach, and to have power to heal sicknesses, and to cast out devils."[15]

A disciple of Christ is one who has been called to be on the spiritual path, with Jesus as his/her spiritual master.[16] The author of the Acts of the Apostles depicts, quite simply, the essentials of living that out. Concerning those who first responded in faith on the day of Pentecost, we read:

> They devoted themselves to the apostles' teaching and fellowship, to the breaking of bread and the prayers . . . . All who believed were together and had all things in common . . . . . Day by day, as they spent much time together . . . they broke bread . . . with glad and generous hearts, praising God and having the goodwill of all the people. And day by day the Lord added to their number those who were being saved.[17]

Discipleship is portrayed as a path of shared spiritual practice[18] and service, in the company of others who are committed to the way. Christian disciples are those who seek to live out, as best as they can, the core principle so beautifully expressed in the new PCUSA ordination standards for deacons, elders, and ministers:

> to submit joyfully to the Lordship
> of Jesus Christ in all aspects of life.[19]

---

for one another. I pity the poor elders caught in the middle.

15. Mark 3:14–15, KJV, emphasis added.

16. As in other faith traditions, Eastern and Western, a disciple is trying to become like the "master" and to receive the particular blessing transmitted only through and by that person.

17. Acts 2:42–47.

18. The core practices being: word and sacrament, prayer and praise, and sharing resources. While I do not directly discuss the topic of stewardship (the sharing of time, skills, and possessions) elsewhere in this book, it really is an underlying assumption throughout, and it is an *essential* element of discipleship. The centrality of questions about our relationship to wealth and community in the teachings of Jesus has, from the beginning, been the greatest ongoing challenge posed by the gospel.

19. PCUSA, *Book of Order,* G-2.0104b.

I particularly believe that *covenantal* discipleship means the living of life in thankful response to God's promised grace, rather than in fearful attempts to win God's approval.[20] The Iona Community's John Bell expresses Jesus's invitation well in his hymn "The Summons":

> Will you come and follow me, if I but call your name?
> Will you go where you don't know and never be the same?
> Will you let my love be shown,
> Will you let my name be known,
> Will you let my life be grown in you and you in me?[21]

Have I known communities where this sort of discipleship happens? I have certainly seen glimpses, usually in the mundane details of daily life. (It does not all have to be about the saints and martyrs.) I think of the story of my great-grandmother Cuthbertson, known as Aunt Mary in the community, who was handy at midwifery and doctoring, delivering Nellie Wylie—a breach birth—before the doctor could get the ten miles from town in a horse and buggy. I think of occasions in my childhood when the community came together to bring in the harvest of a sick neighbor. I think of a household shower, many years ago, for a family whose house had just burnt down. I think of friends bringing Christmas dinner to a family that was spending its time at the bedside of a dying mother. I think of the volunteers serving, week by week, at our church's food bank. I think of prayers with the sick, the dying, and the grieving. I think of the congregation at our former church celebrating the baptisms of the adopted daughters of a lesbian couple who had come to us in search of a welcoming church home. I think of a minister friend who, just recently, laid down his book after presiding at a burial, took off his coat, and grabbed a shovel to help the men of the village fill in the grave. Then I think of being at table to share the Lord's Supper, and turning to the person next to me with the bread and cup:

> "Greater love has no one than this,
> to lay down one's life for one's friends."

—JOHN 15:13

---

20. I have become increasingly convinced over the years that the central aspect of Reformed/Presbyterian spirituality is gratitude, pure and simple.

21. John L. Bell, "The Summons," Copyright © 1987, Wild Goose Resource Group, Iona Community, Scotland; GIA Publications, Inc., exclusive North American Agent.

11

Vows and Promises—"Duty" to God and Man

The honest man, though e'er sae poor,

Is king o' men, for a' that.

—Robert Burns, "Is There for Honest Poverty"

Thus far I have focused mostly on the theological perspectives and the religious and spiritual practices that formed the church culture of old time Scots-Irish Presbyterianism as I have known and studied it over the course of my life. The specifically religious and spiritual culture of any religious group is, however, only a partial expression of the faith. The Ten Commandments and the Great Commandment of Jesus encompass not just love for God, but also love for neighbor and for self. Over against the Sabbath-time reality of the one day, there is also the reality of the six days. Both discipline and discipleship are lived out in the context of day-by-day life in the "here and now" of this world.

It has to be confessed—both corporately and individually—that the "love commandment" has often not been an easy one for phlegmatic Presbyterians, as we take a certain pride in *not* wearing our hearts on our sleeves. The Lowland Scots were stereotypically a dour lot, self-possessed, inhibited, and rather awkward in personal relations. (Though there was, and is, also a lovely strain of gentle humor and kindliness found in the Lowlanders.) The Scots-Irish, like my grandpa Gibson, could be temperamental and feisty. However, one thing they all respected and honored was—as Burns says—an "honest man."

A family story will illustrate this. James Taylor's "journal of local events" from the 1840s mentions the "public roup" (auction) held by order of the local sheriff on 5 April 1842 to sell off the effects of William Cuthbertson of Gardrumhill.[1] Taylor writes:

> William Cuthbertson left this country for America sometime in January this year. He had been in the dealing way for some years past, and had considerable creditors. The debts he left behind him amounted to about six hundred pounds, all in small sums from six shillings to forty pounds. He cut without letting anyone know, not so much as his wife (only a few months married), or his mother. A good number in Fenwick suffered more or less by his flight.[2]

The fugitive William came to Illinois, to the town of Sparta, where his brothers Alexander (my ancestor) and Robert had settled. Despite having their own affairs to look after, Alexander and "Uncle Rabbie" pooled their resources to send for William's abandoned wife and baby daughter, their mother, an unmarried sister, and a niece, all of whom had been left in the lurch. Then, some years later, Alexander did one thing more.

When William died in 1854, Alexander was named administrator of his estate. William's first wife and little daughter had both died by then, and the woman he had wed as a second wife apparently was willing to go along with his plan. So Alexander sold off the land his brother had acquired after immigrating and paid off all the still-outstanding debts back in Fenwick.[3] A few of the appreciative recipients in Scotland then went together and bought a gift for Alexander, a gold watch that is still in the family, which they had inscribed as follows:

> Presented to Mr. Alexr. Cuthbertson by a few Friends
> As a token of respect for his Uprightness of Conduct 1856

Accompanying the watch was a letter from Alexander Watt (an uncle by marriage) which includes the lines:

---

1. William was my great-great-grandfather's brother, and Gardrumhill was the old family home.

2. Taylor, *The Annals of Fenwick*, 29.

3. Because of international jurisdictional issues, any legal obligation for the administrator to pay off those debts was apparently moot, but the moral obligation was a different matter.

> The inscription on it when you read it will give you much satis-
> faction. Tell your children, and tell them to tell their children to
> a thousand generations to come, that duty to God and man has
> a present reward.[4]

Over 150 years, and some six or seven generations later, some of us in the family do remember.

From this and other instances I have come to think that, for the old time Scots, the honoring of one's obligations to God and neighbor was their way of living out Jesus's Great Commandment to *love* (even if they may not have been comfortable saying it in quite those terms). To be deemed "guid," fair, and honest was to be highly esteemed by the community.

Things proved to be much the same once they crossed the water. Early American culture was essentially Calvinist, and in popular culture from the eighteenth until the mid-twentieth centuries—a la *The New England Primer*, *McGuffey's Readers*, and suchlike—the primary moral messages conveyed were about trying to be *good*. To be good meant to be a moral person, with morality being generally defined by the Ten Commandments and the Sermon on the Mount. It concerns, in catechism-speak, the "duty" that God requires of humankind.[5] The generically Christian person endeavored to be good, and also to be kind to those in need. Correct behavior was typically defined by the "family values" standards of personal morality . . . with much attention traditionally being paid to private behavior in matters such as sex, dancing, smoking and drinking, swearing, gambling, and so on. Behavioral standards tended to be rigid, especially among "evangelical" church folk, and the judging of others—despite Jesus's several warnings—was a constant pitfall, and pastime.

The irony of this is that, at one and the same time as we (both Scots and Americans) were being taught to be good, we were also being told, strongly and repeatedly, that we were and are, essentially, *bad*. Protestant evangelicals in general, and Presbyterians in particular, have historically laid a lot of stress on sin, and especially on the "total depravity" of humankind. It was not just that we *did* wrong, but that the old doctrine of Original Sin[6] teaches that we *are* basically and inherently wrong, from birth, with sin being understood as almost a moral and spiritual genetic

---

4. Written at Glenleitch, Fenwick, 10 June 1857. In Cuthbertson, *Memories of Ayrshire*, 13.

5. PCUSA, *Book of Confessions*, C-7.003.

6. Dating back to St. Augustine in the fourth century CE.

disorder. According to those old teachings, we are "wretches,"[7] and even "worms."[8]

In the Augustinian view, any particular good things we do are never enough to overcome the corruption of our fallen being; only grace can do that. However, an experience of grace was, and is, often elusive. Meanwhile, the *law* remains, not just to convict us of sin, as in Lutheranism, but to serve as the ongoing (and impossible to attain) standard of morality and communal life. That, at least, was the way the theory was commonly understood. It posed a terrible conundrum, popularly expressed in an old saying:

> You can but you can't.
> You will but you won't.
> You're damned if you do;
> And you're damned if you don't.

If there is a dark side to the Presbyterian and Puritan tradition—and there *is*—then this lies at its heart.[9] In such a setting, shame and guilt were easily and deeply instilled.

Shame, in particular, is essentially social. It is something we are taught through our interactions with others. Shame is about the urge to engage in cover-up.[10] The Garden of Eden story about Adam and Eve sinning, hiding from God, and then putting on clothes to "cover" the "shame" of their nakedness is a very powerful myth in most of our Christian tradition.[11] Being seen to be involuntarily naked, and thus feeling ashamed, is a profoundly visceral fear for many of us . . . at least for those whose perceptions and attitudes were formed in the mold of previous generations—myself included. We are terrified of being exposed, and being "shameless" is about the most shocking thing imaginable: "What will the neighbors think?!?"[12]

---

7. As in John Newton's classic hymn "Amazing Grace."

8. As in Isaac Watts's "Alas and Did My Savior Bleed."

9. It haunts, for example, the writings of the Puritan-descended Nathaniel Hawthorne in works like *The Scarlet Letter.*

10. The English word is believed to derive from an ancient Indo-European root that means "to cover" something.

11. The whole story is understood somewhat differently in Judaism.

12. One of my all-time favorite movie scenes is from the 1983 film *Yentl,* with Barbara Streisand, who portrayed a young Jewish woman in Poland who aspired to study the Torah, which was not allowed for women. After much pleading, her aged father, a revered rabbi, agreed to teach her . . . but he told her to close the curtains before they

Familiar as he was with the quirks of human behavior, Robert Burns brilliantly lampoons the absurd *hubris* of it all in his delightful poem "To a Louse—On Seeing One on a Lady's Bonnet at Church." As he describes the "crowlin ferlie's" progress to the "tapmost height" of the elegant Miss's fine headgear, he warns:

> O Jenny, dinna toss your head,
> An' set your beauties a' abroad!
> Ye little ken what cursed speed
> The blastie's makin!
> Thae winks an' finger-ends, I dread,
> Are notice takin![13]

The shame of being seen and exposed to public scorn is terrible, but is also, it apparently seems to Burns, a path to liberation if embraced (and he certainly had plenty of experience). He continues with some of his most famous lines:

> O wad some Power the giftie gie us
> To see oursels as ithers see us!
> It wad frae monie a blunder free us,
> An' foolish notion;
> What airs in dress an' gait woud lea'e us,
> An' ev'n devotion![14]

As I read over Burns's works, it seems that the worst sins in his mind were hypocrisy (first), and then "lording it over" others in abusive and harmful ways. He clearly did not care very much about sins like fornication or drunkenness—so long as a body was straightforward and basically goodhearted about it—but he deeply resented falsity and social pretence. His strongest jabs were aimed at Holy Willie and those of his ilk, who justified and excused themselves for what they condemned in others.

Likewise, in the gospel stories told of Jesus, the harshest words he is said to have uttered were reserved for the "Hypocrites!" of the religious establishment. Jesus himself hung out on the margins with all the "wrong" sorts of people—even being accused as a "winebibber" and a glutton.[15] In Jesus's perspective, the old priestly obsession with purity—and the

---

began. When asked why, her father responds, "Because God will understand, but I am not so sure about the neighbors!"

13. Burns, *The Poetical Works*, 119.

14. Ibid.

15. See Matt 11:19.

"pharisaical" equivalent, respectability—were set aside in favor of the more "situational" mandate to love. Love is the gospel law, and its ethic is the Golden Rule of doing to others as we would have done to us. As I read it, then, shame and shaming behaviors have no place in Jesus's path. As he apparently anticipated, however, it did not take his followers long to rediscover and embrace what he called "the leaven of the Scribes and Pharisees," a tendency that has persisted across the centuries.[16]

The substance of the previous paragraph is not exactly traditional Presbyterianism, but I think the spirit may be. Without doubt, the thought-world in which I was born and raised was pretty well shame-based. My folks and our neighbors were deeply sincere and well-intentioned people, but that is just the way it was for them. They may not have been as harsh as earlier generations, but they were still caught up in the same old shame-based perspective. As a result, I spent the first twenty-two years of my life trying to be "the best little boy in the world."[17] I tried *so* hard to be good—and then I hit the wall.

In 1978, the UPCUSA was beginning its long and agonizing struggle over homosexuality. Asked in 1976 by the Presbytery of New York City if they could ordain an openly gay candidate for the ministry, the General Assembly had appointed a task force to study the question. Their positive recommendation nearly split the church. I was then a senior at Sterling College, and found myself profoundly disturbed (horrified, in fact) over the proposal to accept "unrepentant, self-affirming, practicing" gays, not only as church members, but as elders and ministers. It was through that struggle—God apparently having a rather perverse sense of humor—that the realization first began to dawn on me that I, myself, was a homosexual.[18]

The dawning self-realization was a true "spiritual emergency" for me.[19] From everything that I had ever been taught, directly or indirectly, homosexuality was *not* "good," and was even damnable . . . in the full theological sense. At that point, it was not about something I had *done*—I was

16. See Matt 16:6–12.

17. The phrase is also the title of the classic 1970s "coming out" book by "John Reid" (pen name).

18. Years later, Kathy Conner, the widow of the former Moderator of the UPCUSA, recalled visiting Sterling that year and having a discussion with a particularly intense young man who was strongly opposed to homosexual ordination. "That was me!" I replied.

19. A spiritual emergency is a spiritual crisis which carries in it the potential for growth and "emergence."

still far from being "self-affirming" or "practicing"—but I quickly realized, deep inside myself, that it was about something that I inescapably *was*, and *am*. At the time, I was totally ashamed.

The story continued, as I went on from Sterling to study in seminary under the evangelical theologian[20] who had authored the conservative response that prevailed in 1978. I even worked for a year as his student assistant . . . ironically learning, through him, of several books (which he was reading to refute) that ultimately proved very helpful on my journey. It took another seven years of wrestling with God in prayer, studying scripture, and undertaking conversations with a few wise friends, before I finally began to find peace of mind and start the process of "coming out" in earnest.

The reason for telling this story, in this particular context, is that, over the course of my journey to make my peace with God, and myself, I came to a new understanding of what I believe to be a core Presbyterian principle. Rather than being *good*, I think we are called to live lives of faithful *integrity*. In other words, I think we are called to be *honest* with ourselves, with God, and with our neighbors. That is a central piece of our "duty" to God and humanity.

The covenant theology that comprises the heart of distinctively Presbyterian thought is about relationship. It is about "right relationship" between God, ourselves, and others. It is about living together in faith and trust. It is about loving one another as Christ/God has loved us. It occurs to me that the essential moral requirement for any of that to be possible is honesty and integrity. We have to be honest with ourselves, with God, and with one another. Furthermore, we need to live out that honesty in lives that are as well-integrated and whole as possible. Integrity is the one thing we possess that we and others most need to respect and honor. Honest dealing, leavened with compassion, is (I think) the very heart of a covenantal understanding of morality.

Given that the existence of God (or the gods) was not really questioned in the times that the Jewish and Christian scriptures were being written, the most important teaching of the Bible in its day was probably that God is trustworthy; God is not a liar, or undependable. God has integrity. No other assertion about God is more basic. If God is not trustworthy, humans are fools for trusting in God; if God is trustworthy, then humans are foolish if they do not trust in God. That basic idea is the root of all the teachings of Judaism, Christianity, and Islam.

20. Dr. Richard Lovelace of Gordon-Conwell Theological Seminary.

The flip side of the teaching is that humans have the potential for integrity. We know ourselves to be mortal, fallible, and imperfect. We need to acknowledge ("confess") our failings ("sins") and seek forgiveness. According to the Bible, we are also creatures made "in God's image," able to grow into God's "likeness" through entering into relationship with God. We, too, can have integrity. We are capable of being trustworthy. We can know and love God, our neighbor, and ourselves.

Relationship requires commitment (trust and faith) between the parties involved. Commitment involves promises. In the Abrahamic traditions, God promises to be a compassionate and merciful God to those who put their trust in God, and believers promise to love God and follow God's ways. The Ten Commandments, for instance, are not really a statement of universal or natural law. They are the terms of the covenantal pact between God and the Israelite people, established on the basis of what God has done for them: "I am the LORD your God, who brought you out of the land of Egypt, out of the house of slavery."[21] On that basis, then, the commandments follow: "Do not have other gods . . . . Do not commit murder . . . . Do not steal" . . . etc. The promises are mutual, and reciprocal. All of them deal with God and neighbor. The human beneficiaries of the covenant owe due allegiance and obedience ("duty"). In this, the path of Jesus is the same as that of Moses (and of Mohammed), whatever difference may exist in the terms. From the integrity of the parties (divine and human) comes the integrity of the relationship, and from that comes the integrity of the promise. Or vice versa, if the parties are *not* trustworthy.

I believe this all underlies the importance attributed to oaths and vows in scripture:

> Then Moses said to the heads of the tribes of the Israelites: "This is what the LORD has commanded. When a man makes a vow to the LORD, or swears an oath to bind himself by a pledge, he shall not break his word; he shall do according to all that proceeds out of his mouth."[22]

> If you make a vow to the LORD your God, do not postpone fulfilling it; for the LORD your God will surely require it of you, and you would incur guilt. But if you refrain from vowing, you will not incur guilt. Whatever your lips utter you must diligently perform, just as you have freely vowed to the LORD your God with your own mouth.[23]

21. Exod 20:2.
22. Num 30:1–2.
23. Deut 23:21–23.

> When you make a vow to God, do not delay fulfilling it; for God
> has no pleasure in fools. Fulfill what you vow. It is better that
> you should not vow than that you should vow and not fulfill it.
> Do not let your mouth lead you into sin, and do not say before
> the messenger that it was a mistake; why should God be angry at
> your words, and destroy the work of your hands?[24]

> Again, you have heard that it was said to those of ancient times,
> "You shall not swear falsely, but carry out the vows you have
> made to the Lord." But I say to you, "Do not swear at all . . . .
> Let your word be 'Yes, Yes' or 'No, No'; anything more than this
> comes from evil."[25]

Leapfrogging forward from Jesus, across some sixteen or seventeen
centuries, the Scots of the Reformation era and the time of the Covenanters were heirs both to the biblical understanding of covenants, which they
enthusiastically re-appropriated, and to their own semi-tribal cultural tradition of "bands" or "bonds" used to form alliances in times of conflict and
crisis. "The Lords of the Congregation" were one such band, an alliance of
Protestant nobility who eventually brought the Scots Reformation itself to
pass. A few generations later, the Covenanters—in the National Covenant
of 1638 and the Solemn League and Covenant of 1643—followed in their
train. Bands, bonds, alliances, covenants, treaties . . . each and all were the
glue that connected diverse groups of people in a common purpose.

The provisions of the Solemn League and Covenant[26] included an
agreement to call together what became known as the Westminster Assembly of Divines.[27] The assembly's task was to formulate a common form
of governance, worship, and statement of belief for Scotland, England,
and Ireland. *The Westminster Confession of Faith*, and the *Larger* and
Shorter Catechisms were its products, along with *The Form of Presbyterial
Church-Government* and *Directory for the Publick Worship of God*. In the

---

24. Eccl 5:4–6, modified by author.

25. Matt 5:33–37, modified by author. In this passage, Jesus seems to be telling
his followers to vest their integrity in themselves rather than any outside source or
authority, even the name of God.

26. The Solemn League and Covenant formed an alliance between the Scottish
Covenanters and English Parliamentarians in opposition to Charles I.

27. It met in the Jerusalem Chamber of Westminster Abbey from 1643 to 1649.
The participants were clergy, and some laity, drawn from the various churches of England, Scotland, and Ireland. Although the Scots had only four representatives in the
assembly, provisions in the Solemn League and Covenant meant that those four had
virtual veto power over the final outcome.

end, however, the Scottish parliament adopted all of these Westminster Standards but the English parliament did not.[28] The Standards nonetheless served as the basis for all the various branches of Presbyterianism established in Scotland, the United States, and throughout most of the former British Empire.[29]

The covenantal context of the Westminster documents, both in their restatement of covenant theology and in their linkage to the civil covenants of the time, explicitly provides the rationale as to why they so strongly stress the importance of oaths and vows:

1. A lawful oath is a part of religious worship, wherein upon just occasion, the person swearing solemnly calleth God to witness what he asserteth or promiseth; and to judge him according to the truth or falsehood of what he sweareth.

2. [Addresses swearing by the Name of God only, noting that it is allowed by scripture, etc. . . .]

3. Whosoever taketh an oath ought duly to consider the weightiness of so solemn an act, and therein avouch nothing but what he is fully persuaded is the truth. Neither may any man bind himself by an oath to anything but what is good and just, and what he believeth so to be, and what he is able and resolved to perform.[30] Yet is it a sin, to refuse an Oath touching any thing that is good and just, being imposed by lawful Authority.

4. An oath is to be taken in the plain and common sense of the words, without equivocation or mental reservation. It cannot oblige to sin, but in anything not sinful, being taken, it binds to performance, although to a man's own hurt: nor is it to be violated, although made to heretics or infidels.

5. A vow is of like nature with a promissory oath, and ought to be made with the like religious care, and to be performed with the like faithfulness.

---

28. Parliamentary power had shifted to the supporters of Oliver Cromwell, who opposed the Presbyterian polity plan of the Assembly.

29. The theological pieces—the Confession and catechisms—were also highly influential among Congregational churches in Britain and America, and also among early Baptists in the American colonies.

30. This first portion of #3 is the later UPCUSA wording.

6.   ... it is to be made voluntarily, out of faith and conscience of duty ... whereby we more strictly bind ourselves to necessary duties ....

7.   No man may vow to do anything forbidden in the Word of God, or what would hinder any duty therein commanded, or which is not in his own power, and for the performance whereof he hath no promise of ability from God. In which respects, monastical vows of perpetual single life, professed poverty, and regular obedience, are ... superstitious and sinful snares, in which no Christian may entangle himself.[31]

Because of all this—both the biblical and historical pieces—the honoring of oaths and vows is an important theme in the ongoing saga of Presbyterianism. It has been an essential piece of our duty to God and man. More than anything else, it was Charles II's reneging of his "taking" of the Covenants—even though done under compulsion at his Scottish coronation in 1650—that turned many Scots violently against him in the 1660s and following decades.[32]

After the settlement of the Kirk in 1690, when the new sovereigns William and Mary restored Presbyterianism in Scotland, many of the most radical Covenanters still refused to be reconciled because the king and queen did not, themselves, embrace the Covenants. Betrayed, as they felt, by both church and state, they held themselves separate and apart until, eventually, they slowly came together to form the independent Reformed Presbyterian denomination in the early eighteenth century.

Presbyterian principles concerning oaths and vows also became an issue in relation to the Masonic Lodges that began to be established around the same time.[33] The vehement opposition to Freemasonry found in some of the old Presbyterian denominations was specifically due to the fact that the Freemasons were bound by their own set of vows: *secret* vows, no less. Because the Masonic vows were secret, it was held that no Presbyterian Christian could take them, because there should be no vows

31. From "The Westminster Confession of Faith" in PCUSA, *Book of Confessions,* C-6.120–126.

32. His was no mere breaking of a campaign promise. Charles's betrayal involved the re-imposition of bishops in the Kirk, the ejection of ministers like Fenwick's William Guthrie from their pulpits, and the judicial murders of men like James Guthrie and the Marquis of Argyle.

33. With roots in the seventeenth century, Freemasonry became widely popular, beginning in the early eighteenth century. Robert Burns was one of the most famous of Scottish Freemasons.

that could not be disclosed to the disciplinary oversight of the elders and ministers of the church.[34]

The interface of personal integrity with the issue of oaths and vows continued to be central in many of the church-state controversies of the eighteenth through twentieth centuries. The Secession Church in Scotland experienced a split in 1747, between the so-called Burghers and Anti-burghers, concerning whether members could take the Burgess Oath required of those holding office in Scotland.[35] In the United States, the Reformed Presbyterians split in 1833 over whether it was lawful to take the oath of office to uphold the US Constitution, since it was a secular document and did not acknowledge the sovereignty of God.[36]

Within the history of the Presbyterian churches in the US, the issue of vows often focused on the ecclesiastical matter of confessional "subscription," which became a sore sticking point. From the early 1700s into the nineteenth and twentieth centuries (and twenty-first, in some cases) ordinands in various Presbyterian denominations were required to "subscribe" to the *Westminster Confession of Faith* as part of their vows, affirming that, in their view, it was *the* system of doctrine contained in scripture. For some, this proved to be a violation of conscience and/or a compromise of principle. In the 1890s, the then-emerging fundamentalist wing of the P.C.U.S.A. instituted a strict form of subscriptionism, imposing their views onto the Confession itself, and onto those being ordained, regarding biblical inspiration, the virgin birth, substitutionary atonement, the resurrection, and the miracles of Jesus. Those of a more liberal or modernist bent in the church chafed under the imposed yoke, with some joining other denominations and others looking to bring change to the denomination.

The Auburn Affirmation of 1924, endorsed by a group of dissenters against strict subscription, proved to be a milestone in opening the P.C.U.S.A. to a broader range of understandings and interpretations of

34. The Freemasons were also regarded with suspicion as freethinkers, libertines, and sometimes as dabblers in the occult . . . all of which was true in various instances.

35. The two parties disagreed over whether the oath's affirmation of "true religion" involved a general affirmation of the Reformed faith, or a specific endorsement of the established Kirk. Thomas and Alexander Campbell, the founders of the Disciples in Christ, came out of the Irish branch of the Anti-burghers.

36. RPNA members did not vote or hold public office until about forty years ago. Sometime around 1970, a civil court case cleared the way for those with such scruples to sign a declaratory statement acknowledging the sovereignty of God and the lordship of Jesus Christ over the affairs of nations. Under such terms, RPNA members may choose to vote and hold office, so long as other circumstances do not involve a compromise of obedience to Christ.

the theological tradition. Slowly but surely the mainline Presbyterian denominations began to back away from subcriptionism. The adoption of the *Book of Confessions* in 1967 marked a decisive turn away from any notion of subscription and toward being "guided" by the confessions (plural) drawn from different periods of history. Although "the essential tenets of the Reformed faith" continue to be mentioned in the current ordination vows, the PCUSA strongly resists any effort to define them.[37]

In each of the foregoing cases or issues—the Covenants, Freemasonry, civil oaths, subscription—the central question is one of the binding of conscience. What duty can be required, or imposed, by either church or state, over against the God-given freedom of the individual conscience? What is the appropriate balance between denominational or community standards and personal conviction (and/or private behavior)? Although often violated, the basic principle adopted by the Presbyterian Church USA in 1788 has remained a standard ever since:

> God alone is Lord of the conscience, and hath left it free from the doctrines and commandments of men which are in anything contrary to his Word, or beside it, in matters of faith or worship.[38]

As the twentieth century proceeded, Presbyterian beliefs concerning vows became a significant factor in the discussions and debates that arose over the issue of divorce. Presbyterians understand marriage as a covenantal relationship and adultery as one of the most serious breaches of interpersonal covenant listed in the Bible. In earlier times (seventeenth century), the only two valid grounds for divorce recognized by Presbyterians were adultery and willful desertion.[39] A 1930 report to the P.C.U.S.A. marks a beginning of the shift in that understanding:

> Beyond the fact that the marriage relationship is terminated by death, is the further fact that it may be destroyed by either party to the agreement proving unfaithful to the vows taken.[40]

37. My personal inclination is to view the 1991 *Brief Statement of Faith* as being the closest thing we can have to a statement of essentials, but publically saying that always stirs up a hornets' nest. A portion of the "Foundations of Presbyterian Polity" section of the *Book of Order* (see F-2.03–2.05) also hints at some "essential" understandings.

38. PCUSA, *Book of Order,* F-3.0101, quoting the *Westminster Confession, Book of Confessions,* C-6.109.

39. *Westminster Confession,* 1647 edition, Chapter XXIV. See *Book of Confessions,* C-6.131, note q.

40. Quoted in Rogers, *Jesus, the Bible, and Homosexuality,* 42.

Unfaithfulness to marriage vows was no longer understood solely in terms of adultery and desertion, but increasingly as a "breach" or "death" of the relationship that could occur under various circumstances. In 1953 the P.C.U.S.A. approved a new version of Chapter XXIV of the *Westminster Confession*, allowing for divorce and remarriage to be sanctioned for reasons "implicit in the gospel of Christ" as well as for the longstanding explicit grounds previously stated.[41] Covenants, it seemed, could die, too.

As we move on to the present, since the 1970s the ordination vows of the PCUSA and its predecessor bodies have sometimes been used as a means of enforcing denominational policies in the ongoing struggles over the ordination of women and gays.[42] As noted in an earlier chapter, in 1975 the Kenyon ruling held that, in taking the ordination vows, ordinands (ministers, elders, and deacons) in the UPCUSA were endorsing the ordination of women. Scruples of conscience were not allowed—period. Case closed. "Amen." Not surprisingly, the ruling provoked serious dismay among conservative Presbyterians, some of whom were even willing to carry out the ordinations so long as they were free to say they personally did not agree with it.[43] A number of Presbyterian ministers, seminarians, and congregations found themselves led by conscience to seek another denominational home . . . including a number of those involved in founding the Evangelical Presbyterian Church in 1981.

At the opposite end of the spectrum, the strategy ultimately used by conservatives to exclude LGBT Presbyterians from full participation in the PCUSA also focused on ordination, and the ordination vows. In 1996 the denomination adopted a constitutional amendment that stated:

> Those who are called to office in the church are to lead a life in obedience to Scripture and in conformity to the historic confessional standards of the church. Among these standards is the requirement to live either in fidelity within the covenant of marriage between a man and a woman, or chastity in singleness. Persons refusing to repent of any self-acknowledged practice which the confessions call sin shall not be ordained and/or installed as deacons, elders or ministers of the Word and Sacrament.[44]

41. PCUSA, *Book of Confessions*, C-6.132.

42. Possibly race, too, though I do not know of specific cases.

43. This was still a big issue and debate among Presbyterian students at Gordon-Conwell, a conservative evangelical seminary, at the time I attended.

44. G-6.0106b in the pre-2011 PCUSA *Book of Order*. Cited from 2004/2005 edition.

The explicit content of the section was implicitly (but clearly) linked to the fifth of the PCUSA ordination vows, used for all offices:

> Will you be governed by our church's polity, and will you abide by its discipline?[45]

Because of the ordination vow, anyone who chose the path of ecclesiastical disobedience in regard to LGBT ordination—either by being ordained, or participating in the ordination or installation of a known LGBT person—was not merely violating the PCUSA constitution; he or she was also, according to the confessions, committing the serious personal sin of swearing falsely.[46]

The conundrum just described became deeply personal for me after I came out. Having been ordained as a minister of the Word and Sacrament before coming out (and while I was still "fighting my tendencies"), I responded to the ordination vows in good conscience in 1982. After coming out in the mid-1980s, however, I felt that I could no longer affirm the fifth ordination vow in good conscience in order to be installed in a "called" position. This became even more the case for me after the adoption of G-6.0106b. It was a true matter of conscience, a matter of integrity, a matter of owning who I am, both as a gay man and as a minister.

Quite a few of my LGBT friends and colleagues simply left the PCUSA over the long stretch of years between 1978 and 2011. Others, in groups like More Light Presbyterians, chose to openly violate the rules, daring those on the other side to come after them . . . which some did. Others of us chose to quietly hang in, biding our time as best we were able, on the non-installed margins of the denomination, while working for change.[47]

---

45. Ibid., G-14.0207d, and G-14.0405b(5).

46. Unlike the situation after the Kenyon decision, the deep division of opinion in the church led to sporadic enforcement of G-6.0106b, with many local congregations, and even presbyteries, choosing to openly defy (or at least quietly ignore) the ban. Nonetheless, if it became publically known that candidates for the ministry, such as my now husband, were gay, the path to ordination was, more often than not, effectively blocked.

47. There are different classifications of ministry in the PCUSA. There are those who are "installed" in a traditional pastoral setting. There are "validated ministries" for persons who work for approved organizations, such as hospital chaplaincy for instance. Others are engaged in independent ministries, or even some kinds of secular work, in which they are granted the status of "member-at-large" in the presbytery. The specific wording of the old G-6.0106b applied only to ordination and installation, creating (intentionally or not) a convenient loophole for some.

In the spring of 2011, a majority of the PCUSA presbyteries ratified a new version of G-6.0106b,[48] which went into effect in July of that year. It reads:

> Standards for ordained service reflect the church's desire to submit joyfully to the Lordship of Jesus Christ in all aspects of life. The governing body responsible for ordination and/or installation shall examine each candidate's calling, gifts, preparation, and suitability for the responsibilities of office. The examination shall include, but not be limited to, a determination of the candidate's ability and commitment to fulfill all requirements as expressed in the constitutional questions for ordination and installation. Governing bodies shall be guided by Scripture and the confessions in applying standards to individual candidates.

The change removes the last explicit exclusion of LGBT persons from ordination in the PCUSA. However, it does not explicitly sanction LGBT ordination. It is not prohibited, and may be undertaken at the level of the local congregation (for deacons and elders) or the presbytery (for ministers). Thus, unlike the Kenyon ruling, nothing is required of anyone in direct violation of their conscience. No one's integrity is violated, though not that all are convinced of that! Hence we are beginning to live into a new reality.

---

48. Now G-2.0104b in the 2011 PCUSA *Book of Order.*

12

Justice and Mercy

God hath shewed thee, O mortal, what is good;

and what doth the LORD require of thee,

but to do justly, and to love mercy,

and to walk humbly with thy God?

—MICAH 6:8

OUTSIDE OF THE TEN Commandments and Psalm 23, the preceding verse from the Prophet Micah may be the most familiar text from the Hebrew Bible, at least for many Americans. It is often the text of choice for American Presidents to be sworn in upon, and is cited regularly by social activists. I like it because it balances justice and compassion (mercy).

In the last chapter, I noted that one of the chief characteristics of God, according to the Bible, is trustworthiness. Another characteristic is that God is "kind" and "merciful." Archaeological evidence from the fourteenth century BCE shows that, even before the Bible itself was written, the chief god of the old Canaanites and earliest Israelites, El, was known as the "Father of the gods" and "Creator of all," who is also "the Holy One," "the kind," and "the compassionate."[1] Thus the oldest shared affirmation

---

1. See translations of the Ras Shamra texts in Coogan, *Stories from Ancient Canaan*, 33, 38, etc. The anti-Canaanite rhetoric of the Hebrew Bible generally seems to focus on those who honored the rival deity, Baal, while El appears to have served as a precursor to the Israelite understanding of God.

of the Abrahamic faiths, pre-dating Judaism, Christianity, and Islam, is of "God the compassionate and merciful."

Kindness, compassion, mercy, love . . . these are essential elements of God, according to what we have been taught to believe. However, these qualities are abstractions until they are lived out, and they are lived out in a two-fold way: in acts of benevolence and in the doing of justice. A 1991 report to the PCUSA General Assembly even went so far—somewhat awkwardly, but accurately—as to hyphenate the concept as "justice-love." They are two sides of the same coin, and either one suffers if separated from the other.

If there were ever two Scotsmen less likely to be found in agreement on something, they would probably be John Knox and Robert Burns, the stern prophet and the prodigal poet. However, I think they might actually agree on one thing: their fundamental belief in the common man as the basis of the social order.[2] My PhD dissertation, written (it now seems) long ago, was an analysis of John Knox's life and work viewed through the lens of Liberation Theology.[3] I read virtually every word Knox ever wrote.[4] I was actually rather amazed at what I found, for while "Brother Knox" was really quite a scary man, a true zealot with little evident graciousness or compassion in him, I think he truly laid the foundations for the emergence of the common people of Scotland from servility to empowerment.

John Knox did this by turning, first, to the laity—both nobles and commons—as leaders of the new Reformed Kirk. The exclusive power of the clergy over the church was set aside. The Lords of the Congregation and the Reformed ministers worked in tandem as the Reformation was set in place. The polity of the Kirk immediately embraced the office of Elder, with (over time) local lairds often sitting together with their tenants on Kirk Sessions. Secondly, in Knox's emphasis on ecclesial discipline, accountability was elevated over privilege in the exercise of both religious and civil power . . . as Mary Queen of Scots, among others, learned to her regret.[5] The third crucial piece of the Knoxian agenda was his promotion

2. In both their cases, unfortunately, I do mean "man" and not "humanity." In very different ways, both were quite sexist, with Knox even being something of a misogynist.

3. Gustavo Guitierrez in particular.

4. Except for his notes in the Geneva Bible which I was not, at the time, able to track down.

5. While vehemently opposed to her at every turn, Knox's denunciations went off the charts after Mary was accused of conspiring to have her second husband (Darnley) murdered and then marrying the suspected leader of the plot (Bothwell). Knox called

of the establishment of universal public education in Scotland, via parish schools. The goal was for even the poorest Scot to be able to read the Word, and to receive a basic education, with "bursaries" (scholarships) available for promising poor students to even attend university. Such schools were often extremely modest, primitive structures, stuck off in a corner of the kirkyard and taught by ill-paid but (hopefully) faithful schoolmasters. Nonetheless, they accomplished a great work.

The Covenanting struggles of the seventeenth century were ostensibly religious, aimed at preserving the liberty of self-determination in belief and practice that had become normative in the Kirk of Scotland. As it turned out, this was also a profound social struggle against the ideology of royal absolutism favored by the Stuart Kings and their minions. From the multitudes of 1638 on down to the "men of the *moss-hags*" of the 1680s, it was the common people who rose to resistance in numbers above and beyond the more privileged classes.[6]

In his day, Robbie Burns was enthusiastically embraced as the romantic "ploughman poet" who arose from among the lower classes. Being a trueborn Scot, he was not willing to submit to being patronized by his patrons. He was an ardent Scottish patriot, indeed, and, in his last years, his sympathies for the ideals of the American, and then the French, Revolutions began to emerge. He became a strong advocate for the rights and dignity of the common people—his own class. His best known work on the subject is the song-poem "Is There for Honest Poverty," dating from 1795:

> Is there for honest poverty
> That hings his head, an' a' that?
> The coward slave, we pass him by
> We dare be poor for a' that!
> For a' that, an' a' that,
> Our toils obscure, an' a' that,
> The rank is but the guinea's stamp,
> The man's the gowd for a' that.
>
> What though on hamely fare we dine,
> Wear hodden grey, an' a' that.

---

not only for Mary to be deposed, but for her to be tried and executed as an adulteress and murderer.

6. The list of Fenwick martyrs includes one member of the minor gentry, Captain John Paton of Meadowhead, but otherwise consists primarily of the ordinary cotters and tenants in the parish. Of the local gentry, the Laird of Rowallan was supportive, but did not take to the fields in like manner.

Gie fools their silks, and knaves their wine
A man's a man for a' that.
For a' that, an' a' that,
Their tinsel show, an' a' that,
The honest man, tho' e'er sae poor,
Is king o' men for a' that. [7]

Having asserted the natural dignity of the common working man, however modest the circumstances of his life, Burns turns to a bold (for his time and place) critique of the pretensions of the aristocracy:

Ye see yon birkie ca'd a lord,
Wha struts, an' stares, an' a' that?
Tho' hundreds worship at his word,
He's but a coof for a' that.
For a' that, an' a' that,
His ribband, star, an' a' that,
The man o' independent mind,
He looks and laughs at a' that.

A prince can mak a belted knight,
A marquis, duke, an' a' that!
But an honest man's aboon his micht—
Guid faith, he mauna fa' that!
For a' that, an' a' that,
Their dignities, an' a' that,
The pith o' sense, an' pride o' worth
Are higher rank than a' that. [8]

Burns then concludes with the sort of "prayer" that sent chills through the upper classes of his time (the era of the French Revolution) and that echoes still in the twenty-first century:

Then let us pray that come it may
As come it will, for a' that
That sense and worth o'er a' the earth
Shall bear the gree an' a' that;
For a' that, an' a' that,
It's comin' yet for a' that,
That man to man the world o'er
Shall brithers be for a' that.[9]

7. Burns, *The Poetical Works*, 346–347. "Gowd" is gold.

8. Ibid., 347. The "ribband, star" comment refers to the accoutrements of the orders of knighthood, including the Scottish Order of The Thistle.

9. Ibid. In a typically somewhat cheeky Scottish move, the song was particularly

The attitudes of Knox and Burns both emerge when I read the records of the farmers, cobblers, and (especially) the weavers of Fenwick from the eighteenth and nineteenth centuries. Fenwick was something of a hotbed of social and political radicalism in those times, and the first and foremost manifestation of that was found in the Fenwick Weavers' Society, a group now recognized as an early precursor of the trade union movement.

The Society of Weavers in Fenwick was founded in the spring of 1761, with sixteen members, and continued until the year 1873. The signers of the original charter included eight handloom weavers, one yarn merchant, and seven apprentice weavers, all with familiar local surnames like Gemmill, Wallace, Buntine, Barr, and even a couple of Burns.[10] Their purpose was clearly stated:

> That we shall be honest and faithful to one another and to our employers and make good and sufficient work and exact neither higher nor lower prices than are accustomed in the towns and parishes of the neighborhood.[11]

Over the years, the Society members—and their honored wives—gave mutual aid and support to one another in time of need: literally, to the widow and orphan, the sick and the dying. They are also believed to have been one of the first groups in Scotland to practice co-operative trading, as from 1770–1800 they pooled their resources to buy oatmeal (the basic staple of the poor Scots' diet) in bulk for the members' families. In later days they combined together to buy a warping mill and other necessary equipment. As the end of their era approached—handlooms having given way to the industrial weaving mills—they combined with the Stonemasons Society to turn over the building they jointly owned to become a new schoolhouse for the community.

The communal spirit of Fenwick found expression in other circumstances as well. Sometime about 1776 Gabriel Anderson[12] suffered an apparent stroke. Gabriel was a blacksmith and, according to Fenwick legend, the Andersons had been established as blacksmiths at Doghillock on lands of Rowallan since the fourteenth century. That all came to an end when the factor (land agent) of the Rowallan estate, who apparently bore Gabriel some sort of grudge, decided to evict the incapacitated smith and his

---

chosen to be sung on 12 May 1999—in the presence of the Queen herself—as the climax of the opening session of the newly re-established Scottish Parliament.

10. Later generations prominently included the name of Fowlds as well.

11. Charter of the Society of Weavers, quoted in Fairlie, *Matthew Fowlds*, 61.

12. This Gabriel Anderson (there were others) was my fourth great-grandfather.

family from their home and shop. According to the tale recounted in *The Annals of Fenwick* in the 1840s, the community rallied to the support of the family. Gabriel's son John, later known as the Auld Smith, was barely a teenager and not yet fully trained as a blacksmith, but the responsibility for supporting the family fell onto his shoulders. With the assistance of neighbors and friends, a new "smiddy" was built, called the Blackfall, at the very head of the village and there—eventually in a newer building—the Andersons and their descendants plied their trade for another hundred years.[13]

Throughout the first half of the nineteenth century, one of the major social and political issues in Great Britain was the Corn Laws. Grain imports were severely restricted in order to support the prices of the grain produced in the United Kingdom itself. The advantage in this restriction lay overwhelmingly with the wealthy landowners of the gentry and aristocracy, who were the One Percent of their time.[14] From at least the mid-1840s, the Fenwick folks were ardent advocates of the abolition of the Corn Laws, a move that ultimately opened trade and made basic food supplies more affordable to the lower classes. While some farmers felt pressured by their laird to endorse a petition opposing the reforms, *The Annals* give special note to the tenants on the Crawfordland estate, none of whom signed the petition. When the repeal occurred in 1846, the annalist James Taylor described the events:

> June 27th: A public meeting of the inhabitants of Fenwick was held this evening in the open air, to see what measures they would adopt on Monday the 29th, in honour of the passing of Sir Robert Peel's Corn Law Abolition Bill. Alex Watt, farmer, Gainleich, was in the chair.[15] It was unanimously agreed to hold a public rejoicing.
>
> June 29th: A great public meeting and rejoicing was held in Fenwick today to celebrate the abolition of the Corn Laws. In the afternoon the inhabitants were all astir. Two large bonfires blazed on the streets, the freshest of boughs and the fairest of flowers adorned the houses, the banners of Freedom waved in the breeze, the parish bell rang out its merriest peal, a numerous discharge of firearms rent the air like explosive thunder, and the

13. The last I knew, descendants by the name of Douglas still live at Fenwick, and are active in the Kirk.

14. To put it in the 2011 terminology of the Occupy movement.

15. Watt was my great-great-grandfather Cuthbertson's uncle, and the one who later wrote him the letter that accompanied the gold watch.

people with one accord joined in the nation's jubilee. The inhabitants walked through the village in procession, after which they held a meeting in the Secession Church, Alex Watt, Gainleich, in the chair. Alex Murdoch, John Kirkland, Alex Dunlop, Matthew Fowlds and Robert Lindsay were the principal speakers. All went off in a most orderly and becoming manner.[16]

One last Fenwick example of the zeal for justice among these staunch Presbyterians is perhaps the most surprising. In the spring of 1846, just three months before the repeal of the Corn Laws, there was another gathering, which James Taylor described as follows:

April 5th: Mr. Frederick Douglass, once an American slave, addressed a public meeting of the inhabitants of Fenwick in the Secession meeting house, on the subject of "American Slavery." The Rev. Mr. [William] Orr occupied the chair. In the course of his speech, Mr. Douglass made some severe animadversions on the Free Church of Scotland, for going to the slave states of America and uplifting money to support their church. Mr. Thomas Brown from Kilmarnock followed in the same strain. The Rev. Mr. Dickie of the Parish Church, also spoke in condemnation of the American slave system. An uncommonly large meeting agreed unanimously to a resolution condemning churches in this country for having fellowship with the slave-holding churches of America. Mr. Dickie closed with prayer.[17]

With this in the background, it comes as no surprise to learn that, after immigrating to America, various of the Fenwick families became strong abolitionists, and quite a number of the men served in the American Civil War . . . specifically to free the slaves. Writing in 1939, my grandfather's uncle, Matthew Cuthbertson of Sterling, Kansas, recalled an incident he observed as a child.[18] The family lived on a farm near Sparta, Illinois, just a bit to the southeast of St. Louis. Uncle Math wrote:

In the [1850s] it was common for negroes to run away from their masters in Missouri, and come to Sparta for protection and a lift by the underground railroad to Canada or elsewhere. On one occasion Mr. Luke Bottom, a merchant in Eden, drove in to Father's place early one morning and, after talking to Father

16. Taylor, *The Annals of Fenwick*, 72. The Matthew Fowlds noted here is the same one who lived on to be the centenarian weaver.

17. Ibid., 70.

18. Born in 1853, "Uncle Math" was the second youngest son of Alexander Cuthbertson (of the gold watch).

a few minutes, went to his wagon, tipped a hogshead barrel over, and out came a big [black man]. He was told to stretch his legs, for it would be the last outing he would have till he got to Belleville, which was about 40 miles away.[19]

As the United States formed itself in the late eighteenth century, the polarization that would ultimately lead to the Civil War was already beginning to fester. While the large P.C.U.S.A. faced internal divisions over the issue, smaller groups like the RPNA, the APs, and the two northern synods of the ARP came down pretty firmly in the antislavery camp. As early as 1800, it became a membership requirement in the RPNA that no one who owned slaves would be permitted at the Lord's Table. That was quite a strong stance to take, in particular because quite a number of the RPNAs lived in South Carolina, which was, even then, the most ardently pro-slavery state in the US. The AP followed suit in 1831. While the ARPs did not go as far as the RPNAs to make it a Communion requirement, many of the ARPs shared the same sentiments . . . again, including many in South Carolina.[20]

Despite their views, quite a few RPNAs and abolitionist ARPs continued to live in South Carolina until the early 1830s when, apparently in conjunction with the reaction to Nat Turner's Rebellion (1831) and the Nullification Crisis (1832), the political climate became too hot. Culminating around that time, large numbers of antislavery RPNA and ARPs relocated to Ohio, Indiana, and Illinois . . . whole congregations sometimes moving *en masse*. My mother's Gibson ancestors were part of that migration, moving in about 1833 from Chester County, South Carolina,

---

19. William C. Cuthbertson, *Memories of Ayrshire*, 28. Another story I was told, as I recall, by a Covenanter minister, tells of a Reformed Presbyterian family who were active in the Underground Railroad. As the tale goes, the family had given shelter one night to a small group of escaped slaves, hiding them in the barn as usual. Shortly after the refugees were settled in, the slave catchers arrived and asked for lodging. Unable to turn them away without arousing suspicion, the Covenanters took them in. The next morning the head of the family was up well before the usual hour and got the escapees on their way. A couple of hours later—at the normal time—the family was finishing breakfast when the slavers began to speak of heading on their way. "Oh, won't you stay and join us for family worship?" the father inquired. Good manners could not dictate otherwise in those days, so the slave catchers sat back down. "Ah!" said the father, as he opened the Bible, "I see our course of reading has brought us today to Psalm 119 . . . ." Psalm 119 has 175 verses, and is the longest single chapter in the Bible. The former slaves were some distance further down the road before their pursuers were free to follow.

20. The two northern synods of the ARP did adopt a moderate, but clear, antislavery resolution in 1830.

to near Marissa, Illinois. They were ARPs, and although some ARPs probably made the move as much for economic reasons as for principle, the obituary of my great-grandfather James Reid Gibson (1830–1898) attests that his father Robert, who made the move, was an ardent abolitionist.[21]

With both of its predecessor denominations having long since adopted antislavery stances, the UPNA was "of one mind" on the issue from its beginning in 1858. The Judicial Testimony of the UPNA adopted at the time included the following declaration:

> We declare, That slaveholding—that is, the holding of unoffending human beings in involuntary bondage, and considering and treating them as property, and subject to be bought and sold—is a violation of the law of God, and contrary both to the letter and spirit of Christianity.[22]

At that time, in the late 1850s, much of the focus of the antislavery movement was on Kansas. The 1854 Kansas-Nebraska Act had given those newly formed territories the right to choose for themselves whether they would be slave states or free states. "Bleeding Kansas" became the actual battleground of the cause, as the conflict between Free State settlers and their neighbors across the border in Missouri repeatedly resulted in guerilla warfare and retaliatory acts of violence between the two sides.[23] Among the Free State settlers at the town of Garnett—where, I believe, the very first UPNA congregation in Kansas was organized in 1858—were three sons of Rev. David Lindsay, whom we met earlier.

John G. Lindsay (1836–1898) was an original settler at Garnet in 1856, before the town officially existed and right at the height of the border violence in the area.[24] Half of his original land claim was eventually incorporated into the townsite, and he built the first house there. After studying law, he was admitted to the bar in 1860. He served in two different units during the Civil War, and later served as County Attorney and as a member of the Kansas Legislature. In 1857, John Lindsay was

21. The current ARP church descends from the southern synod of the old denomination, which stayed in place through the ensuing conflicts. Its most famous son is the Rev. Billy Graham, who was raised ARP before going over to the Southern Baptists in college.

22. Quoted in Jamison, *The United Presbyterian Story*, 61.

23. My grandma Gibson remembered knowing the last living Free State survivor of the 1858 Maris des Cygnes Massacre, when he was an old man and she was a young woman in the community.

24. Osawatomie, home of the infamous John Brown, lay a little over twenty miles to the northeast.

joined at Garnett by his brother, Thomas Lindsay, MD (1826–1901), who became a charter member of the Kansas Medical Society. Thomas Lindsay served as Garnett's first Postmaster and then as a member of the territorial legislature in 1860. During the Civil War he served as a surgeon, and was captured and held prisoner for a time. He later served a term in the Kansas Legislature as well.[25] The third Lindsay brother at Garnett was Samuel (1840–1863), who was a law student at the beginning of the Civil War, and was killed at the battle of Champion Hill in Mississippi.

Both in their settlement choices and through their service in the war, the Lindsays were clearly putting their family's AP antislavery principles into practice . . . literally risking life and limb in both instances. In addition to the brothers, their sister Martha also spent two years, immediately after the Civil War, teaching in the UPNA school for freed slaves at Vicksburg, Mississippi (established 1863). She and her husband also settled at Garnett after their marriage in 1867.[26]

While many writers in later years have endeavored to portray the US Civil War as a constitutional conflict and a struggle to save the Union, for many everyday folks in the North, like these Presbyterians, the real issue was one of morality and justice.[27] It was the struggle to end racially-based chattel slavery in the United States—period. Thankfully, as the generations passed, some stayed engaged with the ongoing efforts for justice and social equality. In due course, a portion of their descendants actively joined other Presbyterians, and other peoples of faith, in the Civil Rights struggles of the mid-twentieth century.

The nineteenth century was an era of massive shifts, both in Britain and the US, from predominantly rural to urban and industrialized economies. Fenwick lay only about fifteen miles from Glasgow, which underwent massive industrial development during the period. Many younger Fenwick folk made the move to the Glasgow area for work, and in Fenwick itself the Alexander family's weaving mill at Waterside began displacing the old handloom weavers.[28] It is fairly easy to see how the children and

25. In their retirement years, Rev. David Lindsay and his wife lived with Thomas's family at Garnett.

26. The UPNA undertook, for their size, extensive work among the former slaves, both during and in the aftermath of the war. Knoxville College at Knoxville, Tennessee, originated as part of this effort.

27. Perhaps the best evidence in support of this claim being Julia Ward Howe's "Battle Hymn of the Republic," with the line: "As He [Christ] died to make men holy, let us die to make men free."

28. My great-grandmother is said, as a young girl, to have done piecework

grandchildren of the old Fenwick radicals of the 1840s morphed into the Labour Party supporters of the twentieth century.

It was out of the grim streets of Glasgow that one of the most inspiring and influential organizations of contemporary Scottish Christianity emerged in the 1930s: the Iona Community. The following account comes from their website:

> The Iona Community was founded in Glasgow and Iona in 1938 by George MacLeod, minister, visionary and prophetic witness for peace, in the context of the poverty and despair of the Depression. From a dockland parish in Govan, Glasgow, he took unemployed skilled craftsmen and young trainee clergy to Iona to rebuild both the monastic quarters of the mediaeval abbey and the common life by working and living together, sharing skills and effort as well as joys and achievement. That original task became a sign of hopeful rebuilding of community in Scotland and beyond. The experience shaped—and continues to shape—the practice and principles of the Iona Community.[29]

George MacLeod was a grandson of the nineteenth century Christian Socialist Norman MacLeod. Like so many others (Karl Barth, C.S. Lewis, Teilhard de Chardin, etc.), he underwent a profound conversion experience in the face of the devastation and carnage he experienced in World War I. After beginning his ministry in the prestigious Edinburgh congregations of St. Giles and St. Cuthbert's, in 1930 MacLeod heard the call to live and minister among the poor of Scotland and accepted the call to Govan. It was a period, as John Phillip Newell notes, when MacLeod was moving from the High Presbyterianism of his family heritage toward the more mystical and political spirituality that came to characterize both him and the Iona Community. John Phillip quotes MacLeod as saying that Christian spirituality "Is to get one's teeth into things . . . . Painstaking service to humankind's most material needs is the essence of Christian spirituality."[30]

Out of George MacLeod's vision grew the corresponding vision of the Iona Community, rooted in "an experience of the liberating power of Jesus Christ, and a commitment to the personal and social transformation that spring from the vision and values of the gospel."[31] Iona is dedicated,

---

embroidery at home for the mill. Her first effort was too soiled when she took it back, so she was not paid for it.

29. Iona Community, "Our History: Founding," lines 1–6.

30. Newell, *Listening for the Heartbeat of God*, 79.

31. Iona Community, "Our Movement: Membership," lines 2-3.

in its community rule, to "action and reflection for justice, peace and the integrity of creation."[32] This commitment to justice, peacemaking, and care for creation has been lived out across the decades in the context of ministries undertaken in response to the long "troubles" in Northern Ireland, the struggle against Apartheid in South Africa, and in efforts against nuclear weapons and the arms trade. It also finds current expression in a commitment to inclusion of LGBT Christians in the Community, and in working to combat discrimination in society.

I clearly remember first seeing an article on Iona in *Presbyterian Life* magazine back around 1970. I was hooked from the moment I saw it. One of the most meaningful single days of my life occurred in 1988 when a group I was with made a daytrip over to Iona during our tour of Scotland. It was June, and we had driven across the Island of Mull on narrow, single-lane roads, surrounded by blooming broom, highland cattle, and sheep . . . always sheep! Once we had crossed to Iona, the sun glimmered off the textured sea like mother-of-pearl. I stood in true awe before the ancient Celtic crosses. In the dimness of the old abbey one of the caretakers came in, shod in wellington boots and with his border collie following at his heels, to place a bouquet of wildflowers on the Communion Table. It was just as I had envisioned. I marveled at the famous Descent of the Spirit statue in the cloister. I then wandered the lanes a bit, visiting the ruins of the old nunnery and climbing part way up the Hill of the Angels. Too soon, we had to leave. The great disappointment was that we were not on the little island long enough to attend a service.

An essential aspect of the vitality of the Iona Community has been that its justice work has been so firmly grounded in creative worship, prayer, and spiritual awareness. It has not been just an activist community, but one that has balanced the outer with the inner. Our good friend John Phillip Newell, who served as Warden of the resident community on Iona for several years, has, in recent years, assisted us in trying to bring some of that same spirit to the PCUSA's conference center at Ghost Ranch, and particularly to the Casa del Sol retreat house there.

In the US, there were many UPNAs in the Pittsburgh area as it developed into America's industrial giant over the course of the nineteenth century. Much like their kindred in Glasgow, the UPNA congregations there faced the daunting challenges of ministering in the great Steel City and its environs. Though some were comfortably well-off, I do not know of any

---

32. Iona Community, "Our Movement: Membership," line 8.

UPNA members amongst the great steel magnates.[33] The UPNA constituency tended to be of the aspiring middle and working classes. Some of the social causes dear to the UPNAs of the late nineteenth century, like temperance, were undertaken very much in reaction to the increased challenges and stresses of urbanized life and industrial working conditions.[34]

One of the interesting aspects about Girard, Kansas, the small town near which I grew up, was its ties to radical reform in the US during the late nineteenth and early twentieth centuries. In fact, some of the Girard families associated with the progressive causes were Presbyterian. One of the important figures in Girard's history was Alice Addams Haldeman, a sister of Jane Addams of Hull House in Chicago. Alice was a dynamic personality in her own right, a pioneering woman banker, a major organizer of the Federation of Women's Clubs, and—most unusually for the time—the longtime chair of the trustees at the First Presbyterian Church.[35] Partly through her influence, later carried on by her daughter and son-in-law Marcet and Emanuel Haldeman-Julius, Girard saw fairly frequent visits from the likes of Jane Addams and Helen Keller.[36] My late father remembered seeing and hearing both of them.

Girard was also home, for a time, to the leading Socialist weekly in the United States; *The Appeal to Reason* was published there from 1900 to 1922. Founded by Julius A. Wayland in 1895, *The Appeal* moved to Girard in 1900.[37] Over the years, it grew to the point where it was shipped out by the boxcar load . . . with circulation at 500,000 copies per week in 1912. Because of it, figures like Eugene V. Debs, the five-time Socialist candidate for President, became regular visitors to our little town.[38] In 1904, *The Appeal* sponsored Upton Sinclair's expose on the Chicago meat-packing industry, *The Jungle*, and it was originally serialized in the paper in 1905.

33. The P.C.U.S.A. of that time usually got the big-money people.

34. I was, actually, once an "affiliate" member of the Women's Christian Temperance Union, thanks to the initiative of Helen Weede, a dear but crusty old *memsahib* who had retired in Sterling. Thankfully Miss Weede had entered the "Nearer Presence" of God before I learned the pleasures of a good pint, or even a wee dram.

35. Because of her efforts, Girard was one of the smallest towns in the country to have a Carnegie Public Library, and the Presbyterian Church still has a Carnegie-donated pipe organ. The contrast between Andrew Carnegie's anti-organized labor views and actions, versus his philanthropy, raises all sorts of justice issues.

36. Jane Addams herself, while raised Presbyterian, mostly attended the Unitarian Church later in life.

37. The plant was directly across the street from Uncle Colonel Conder's livery stable.

38. Debs loved children, and once bought my Aunt Juanita—who became the matriarch—a sack of chocolates at Decker's Candy Kitchen on the town square.

Jack London, "Mother" Jones, and Stephen Crane also contributed articles over the years.

While I have never been able to find out about Julius himself, the Wayland family (son and daughters) were affiliated with the First Presbyterian Church. In 1912, depressed by the death of his wife and ongoing libels published against him, Julius Wayland shot himself. His son, Walter Wayland, whom I remember well from my childhood, tried to run the paper for several years, but Walter did not share his father's ardent Socialist views.[39] He did better at running a stationery store and writing a bit of poetry. In 1922 *The Appeal* ceased publication. The printing plant was sold to Marcet and Emanuel Haldeman-Julius, who then used the facility for publishing their Little Blue Book paperbacks . . . many of which were, themselves, on cutting edge social topics—including subjects like sex education and birth control—that rather scandalized the local folks.

While I find it hard to conceive of my great-grandparents (after retiring from the farm) and other Fenwick-borns like Alex and Maggie Gemmell, worshipping side by side with such as the Haldemans and Waylands, they really did so. People like Jane Addams and Alice Haldeman, Iowa's Henry Wallace,[40] Norman Thomas,[41] and so on, are a few of the deep social justice spin-offs from Presbyterian roots. Of course, there are many others . . . .

One of the great challenges in working for justice has always been to pursue justice without being judgmental. We Presbyterians, along with Christians of almost all stripes, have failed at this far more than we have succeeded. Given our stern and prophetic bent across the years, Presbyterians may have failed a bit more. It is something that we have to strive for, nonetheless, because we are followers of Jesus. Some of the most daunting words in the New Testament, as I read it, address the issue:

> Ye have heard that it hath been said, Thou shalt love thy neighbor, and hate thine enemy. But I say unto you, Love your enemies, bless them that curse you, do good to them that hate you, and pray for them which despitefully use you, and persecute you; that ye may be the children of your Father which is in heaven:

39. He also undoubtedly bore some scars from the vehement opposition his father had experienced.

40. Franklin D. Roosevelt's third-term Vice President, grandson of a UPNA minister . . . and a Lindsay in-law.

41. A former Presbyterian minister and the six-time Socialist candidate for President.

> for he maketh his sun to rise on the evil and on the good, and
> sendeth rain on the just and on the unjust.[42]
>
> Judge not, that ye be not judged. For with what judgment ye
> judge ye shall be judged; and with what measure ye mete, it shall
> be measured to you again.[43]
>
> Judgment will be without mercy to anyone who has shown no
> mercy; mercy triumphs over judgment.[44]

The practical meaning of these words became clear to me when we heard Rev. Allan Boesak, who was then the head of the World Alliance of Reformed Churches, speak in Chicago back in the 1990s. Rev. Boesak told of Archbishop Desmond Tutu speaking out in Soweto, at the risk of his life, during the height of the struggle against Apartheid. What Tutu said was, simply, that President de Klerk (the head of the oppressive white regime) was his brother in Jesus Christ. Baptized in the same Name, and fed from the same Lord's Table, they were members of the same family. That statement struck my heart, and through all the hard struggles in the PCUSA over subsequent years, with often horrible and hateful things said by folks on opposing sides, I have tried to remember and hold onto the knowledge that those on the opposite side from me are still my brothers and sisters, whom I am charged to love, bless, do good for, and pray.

Which brings me to the genius of Karl Barth, and the UPCUSA's *Confession of* 1967. Part of Barth's genius was his transformation of the old terminology of the doctrine of "atonement" into the theology of "reconciliation" between God and humanity, and human with human. Informed by Barth, and inspired by the statement of Paul—"In Christ God was reconciling the world to himself"[45]—the confession laid out a vision of God's reconciling work across the ages, and addressed the ongoing ministry of reconciliation that constitutes the mission of the Church. In pursuing that mission it was recognized that:

> In each time and place, there are particular problems and crises
> through which God calls the church to act. The church, guided
> by the Spirit, humbled by its own complicity and instructed by
> all attainable knowledge, seeks to discern the will of God and
> learn how to obey in these concrete situations. [46]

42. Matt 5:43–45, KJV.

43. Matt 7:1–2, KJV.

44. Jas 2:13.

45. 2 Cor 5:19.

46. PCUSA, *Book of Confessions*, C-9.43.

The "particular" and urgent issues of that day were identified as:

1. Racial and ethnic discrimination

2. Peacemaking

3. Poverty

4. The relationship between men and women

The issues cited are clearly those of the late 1960s, but they have continued to be relevant and urgent matters in our common life ever since.[47]

The particularly urgent issue for me over the years, of course, has been the PCUSA's struggle over gender and sexuality issues. From the matters surrounding women's rights, ordination, and reproduction in the 1970s, on into the long debates over gay, lesbian, and transgendered issues from the 1980s to the present, we have been constantly "in process" with the now-apparent inadequacies of the way in which issue number four was addressed in 1967.

Over these long years, I have found the ways in which our ancestors responded to the great issues of their day to be both inspirational and motivational as I have endeavored to "hang in there" with the church. I am especially taken with the example of those, like my Gibson kin and their antislavery neighbors, who literally left houses and lands to do so.[48] I have often been inspired by people like former PCUSA Moderator Jack Rogers (brought up in the UPNA), who have embraced us and realized—as he so clearly demonstrated in his book *Jesus, the Bible, and Homosexuality*—that the struggle is almost always the same. Whether dealing with slavery and race, marriage and divorce, or same-sex relationships and gender identity, it seems to have ever been the case that the "letter" of scripture used to prop up the prejudices of the status quo ultimately gives way before the "spirit" of a deepened comprehension of the implications of the gospel's message of God's justice and compassion. So may it ever be.

47. Currently I would add to the list: human sexuality and gender, marriage equality, care for the earth and its environment, and interfaith relations.

48. For LGBT Presbyterians, there have certainly been the times when—for integrity's sake and Christ's sake—we have had to let go of family and friends, jobs, homes, and so on. There have been times when we have been subjected to verbal, and even physical, abuse from those who claim religious justification for their actions. There are others whose fondest wish is that we would just go away. In the face of that, however, we simply do not, and will not, give up. It is a matter of conviction. Another old saying that comes to mind is that "I would rather face an army of a thousand drawn swords than a single Presbyterian convinced that he/she was doing God's will!"

The Last Presbyterian?

In a broken and fearful world
the Spirit gives us courage
to pray without ceasing,
to witness among all peoples to Christ as Lord and Savior,
to unmask idolatries in church and culture,
to hear the voices of peoples long silenced,
and to work with others for justice, freedom, and peace.

—*A Brief Statement of Faith*, PCUSA

13

The Great Ends

JUST OVER A CENTURY ago, in 1910, the UPNA was in the process of re-thinking, re-visioning, and reshaping itself for life in the twentieth century. One of the pieces that emerged from that process was a statement on "The Great Ends of the Church"[1] which, a century later, continues to be an important piece of Presbyterian ecclesiology:

The great ends of the Church are:

- The proclamation of the gospel for the salvation of humankind;

- The shelter, nurture, and spiritual fellowship of the children of God;

- The maintenance of divine worship;

- The preservation of truth;

- The promotion of social righteousness; and

- The exhibition of the Kingdom of Heaven to the world.[2]

In one way or another, I have touched on most of these "ends" in what I have presented here, but I want to spend a little more time on the first and the last: the proclamation of the gospel for the salvation of humanity, and the exhibition of God's commonwealth in the world.

My strong impression—backed up by quite a few years of study—is that, from the time of the Reformation up until at least the early nineteenth century, Presbyterian proclamation focused primarily on doctrine and propositional truth, and not on narrative. Although Presbyterians

---

1. "Ends" meaning "purposes" or "objectives."

2. PCUSA, *Book of Order*, F-1.0304.

were familiar with the stories of scripture through daily readings at home, preaching was focused on teaching, and was more in the style of the Apostle Paul than of the gospel writers. The parts of the gospels that did make it into a sermon were often the "teachy" bits like the Sermon on the Mount, and the narrative portions that were addressed were analyzed and expounded upon in the same sort of didactic mode.

Story, as story, was not especially appreciated, and leaders like John Calvin (for instance) distrusted the human imagination—viewing it as sinful and tending toward idolatry.[3] Because of such attitudes, and especially because the Knoxian sort of Presbyterians did not observe the church year or major "holy" days for some three centuries, it appears that the only major narrative of Jesus's life to regularly feature in the cycle of congregational life was the story of the Last Supper enacted at Communion, which was held only one, two, or (at most) four times a year.[4]

Over the course of the nineteenth and twentieth centuries, the stories of Jesus's life, ministry, death, and resurrection came to figure more prominently in the proclamation of Presbyterian churches, partly through the embrace of more liturgical forms of worship (recognizing holidays) and the increasing use of artistic depictions of Jesus.[5]

While I have not specifically tracked the corresponding shift to the use of more narrative and story-telling in preaching, my sense is that it began in earnest around the middle of the nineteenth century—in the wake of the Romantic movement—and became more common as popular culture was increasingly dominated by narrative forms, first with novels (Scott, Dickens, etc.) and later by the movies. Preaching followed popular culture, until we eventually reached the vividly imaginative pictorial style of story-telling exemplified in the sermons of Peter Marshall. As a result, I think, Jesus became far more humanized and familiar than had been the case for earlier generations . . . but with somewhat mixed results.

3. This is why some Calvinists remain leery of using imaginative modes of meditation and reflection, such as the one espoused by Calvin's Catholic contemporary, Ignatius Loyola, in his *Spiritual Exercises*.

4. By embracing believer baptism early on in their history, the Disciples of Christ also at least got the story of Jesus's baptism repeatedly set before them.

5. As I noted in an earlier chapter, the most common actual images that showed up in the churches seem to have been the Last Supper, Jesus the Good Shepherd, Jesus blessing the children, and Jesus praying in the Garden of Gethsemane . . . all depicting the pastoral role and spiritual example of Jesus, rather than the more classical "theological" themes of incarnation, atonement, and resurrection. Depictions of the crucifixion, in particular, were still seen as too idolatrous and superstitious . . . i.e., Roman Catholic.

Back in the 1990s, my friend Rev. Janie Spahr was featured in a video entitled "Maybe We're Talking about a Different God." While the topic of the video was homosexuality and the Presbyterian Church, it pointed to a deeper, ongoing conflict. In many ways the Presbyterian Churches, in the US and around the world, along with all the old Protestant mainline denominations, have been struggling over the last century with the question of who Jesus is, and what the "gospel" is, for our day. The roots of this conflict stretch back to the Fundamentalist/Modernist disputes at the turn of the nineteenth-twentieth centuries, and remain very much alive.

According to a variety of current authors—ranging from Marcus Borg to Phyllis Tickle, John Phillip Newell, and Cynthia Bourgeault—perhaps the central theological task for Christians in our time is to go back to the original sources and reassess our traditional understandings of Jesus. [6] Other related theological topics raised include the doctrine of original sin and the doctrine of the atonement. In terms of John Newton's still-beloved old hymn, what does it really mean to be "lost" and then "found"?

In the PCUSA there have been at least two versions of the gospel in play. One is the standard evangelical version: I-am-a-sinner-Jesus-died-for-my-sins-and-I-must-repent-be-born-again-and-be-saved. That version, rooted in traditional conservative views of biblical inspiration, original sin, the substitutionary atonement, and even (sometimes) predestination, remains deeply grounded in a significant portion of the church. The other view, coming from the liberal/progressive end of the spectrum, is harder to summarize easily. My attempt incorporates a popular bumper sticker: God-is-love-and-loves-the-whole-world-(no exceptions)-and-Jesus-came-to-show-us-that-and-call-us-to-follow. That is what the Bible testifies to, as many progressives see it. Humans do sin but, as beings created "in the image" of God, our most essential being is good, and our alienation from God and one another can be overcome as we respond to God's love. Over against the atonement-centered theology of the traditionalists, liberals and progressives have tended to look more to Jesus's life and teachings as prophet, wisdom instructor, and spiritual master:

> Jesus proclaimed the reign of God:
> preaching good news to the poor
> and release to the captives,

6. Cynthia Bourgeault, for instance, cites the threefold nature of Jesus's role and function as being that of wisdom teacher, spiritual elder, and transmitter of "blessing" . . . much in the mode of the Sufi *sheiks* of subsequent generations in the Near East. *The Wisdom Jesus*, 24.

teaching by word and deed
and blessing the children,
healing the sick
and binding up the brokenhearted,
eating with outcasts,
forgiving sinners,
and calling all to repent and believe the gospel.[7]

That said, it is not as though either side does, or could, exclude the other's views completely. Because we work from the same script (the Bible), both theological perspectives must deal with the life and teachings of Jesus, and both theologies must grapple with what Jesus's death and resurrection means, both individually and for all. While the two sides differ over many understandings, the *crux* of the matter seems to lie in whether we think that the cross gives meaning to the life and teachings of Jesus, or whether the life and teachings of Jesus are what give meaning to the cross. In either case, both sides find Jesus to be, in some way, the definitive embodiment of God-with-us, and together we trust the biblical proclamation that the resurrection both vindicates and gives meaning to his life and his death.[8]

So, then, what is salvation, and who is it for? There is no simple *Westminster Shorter Catechism* answer for these questions. To extrapolate a bit, salvation has been seen as occurring when the Holy Spirit, "convincing us of our sin and misery, enlightening our minds in the knowledge of Christ, and renewing our wills, doth persuade and enable us to embrace Jesus Christ, freely offered to us in the gospel."[9] The benefits of salvation were seen as the forgiveness of sin ("justification"), adoption into the family of God, and the process of being renewed in God's image ("sanctification").[10] From this flows assurance of God's love, peace of mind, joy, perseverance, eternal blessedness, and so on.[11] Such benefits were, of course, only for the predestined elect, chosen by God "from all eternity."

One of the ever-various Scottish controversies that spilled over into Fenwick in the nineteenth century concerned the views espoused by Rev.

7. PCUSA, *Book of Confessions*, C-10.2, lines 9-18.

8. In an April 2012 article in The Huffington Post, former Associated Press religion journalist David Briggs cited a variety of reputable polls, including Gallup, showing that, for all that divides Christians in the US, 97% affirm their belief in the resurrection of Jesus as being central to their faith. See Briggs, "Voices of the Faithful."

9. PCUSA, *Book of Confessions*, C-7.031.

10. Ibid., C-7.033–7.035.

11. Ibid., C-7.036–7.038.

James Morison of Kilmarnock. Morison was ordained as the minister of the Clerk's Lane United Secession Church in 1840, but from the outset his views on the ability of individuals to choose to believe (or not), and on a more universal nature of the atonement, led to controversy. He was quickly suspended from the United Secession ministry and, in 1843, co-founded the Evangelical Union out of the old Clerk's Lane church.[12] Fenwick's Rev. William Orr was appalled, both by Morison's views and by what he viewed as his young colleague's disingenuous behavior at the time of his call, but a number of Fenwick folks—including the family of another John Anderson, an ancestral uncle—embraced Morison's teachings.[13] The Morisonians proved to be pioneers of the type of emerging British and American Evangelicals that came to the fore in the late nineteenth century and continues on to the present.

I grew up in that broadly evangelical Protestantism of Middle America. In the 1960s and 1970s, our home was the type where, if a Billy Graham crusade was on TV, we watched it. As I entered my teens, every time Dr. Graham gave the invitation at the end of the service, I tried "giving my heart" to the Lord. Try as I might, though, I never really felt any different afterwards; no change, no "second birth," as far as I could tell. It was worrisome.

Thankfully my years at Sterling introduced me to a more joyful version of evangelicalism than I had known before. The old UPNAs there were clear that you could love and serve the Lord without having had a particular, dramatic conversion experience. However, I still felt like something was missing . . . and prayed harder. Then, in the summer between my junior and senior years in college, I was driving home to my folks on a Sunday evening from preaching in a little Presbyterian Church in a nearby town—and it happened, in a rather odd way. I was thinking to myself that, "I know I need God, but I am afraid to have God see me as I fear I am." (I knew, even then, that something was lurking in the inner shadows.) Without missing an internal beat, the thought carried itself on, "But that is silly! God sees me as I am whether I want him to or not." That, if I ever had one, was the moment of my conversion: the moment when I truly and finally opened my heart to God's presence and action, within me and my life, and discovered that God truly is "Love." Six months later I had the first

12. Both Eric Liddell (*Chariots of Fire*) and Dr. Peter Marshall were associated with Evangelical Union churches in their lifetimes.

13. I wonder if the Morison connection may help explain why some of the Fenwick families readily switched from Presbyterianism to Congregationalism or The Disciples of Christ after emigrating.

inkling that I might be gay, and I have no doubt that the former experience prepared the way for the latter.

This all casts the old catechism-speak about "assurance of God's love" and "peace of mind" in a new and different light. The word "salvation" comes from the same Latin root as "salve," the ointment we put on a cut, scrape, or burn. Salve is a healing ointment, the oil with which God anoints us (Psalm 23, etc.). Along with whatever else, salvation is about the healing of souls. The healing of souls comes as a gift of God's "Amazing Grace" that—to paraphrase the hymn—relieves our heartfelt fears and leads us safely home.

When I—some seven years later—finally came out as a gay man to my friend Beth, her response was perfect: "I don't know what to say," she said, "but I'll pray that you find peace." The Hebrew word for peace, *shalom*, does not just mean the absence of conflict. It also indicates a state of well-being . . . a state, I think, of salvation. Thus I think, now, that soul-healing is about finding *peace*, the peace of God that "passes understanding."[14]

In the end, then, I think all of the tangled doctrinal categories boil down to the simplicity of some biblical words we used to sing as a chorus in college: "Beloved, let us love one another: for love is of God; and anyone who loveth is born of God, and knoweth God."[15]

Lovers of God, lovers of Jesus (of whatever stripe), lovers of neighbor . . . all. And so:

> With believers in every time and place,
> we rejoice [and proclaim] that nothing in life or in death
> can separate us from the love of God in Christ Jesus our Lord.[16]

Balancing "the proclamation of the gospel for the salvation of humankind" in the Great Ends of the Church is "the exhibition of the Kingdom of Heaven to the world." The individualism of personal salvation is hereby balanced by the manifestation of God's universal reign.

Unlike many evangelical Protestants in the United States, Presbyterians have—thankfully!—mostly shied away from taking any particular stance in regard to Christ's return. To the extent that they did so, the historic Presbyterian inclination was mostly toward the now little-known view identified as post-millenialism. In general terms, post-millenialism holds that the reign of Christ commenced when "he ascended into heaven"

14. Phil 4:7.

15. 1 John 4:7, KJV.

16. PCUSA, *Book of Confessions*, C-10.5, lines 77–79.

and took his place "at the right hand of God." The Kingdom both has come, and continues to come, expand, and grow, as the gospel spreads to all peoples, *and* as good ("justice, freedom, and peace," etc.) increasingly prevails over evil in the affairs of the world until, in due course, Christ appears again at the end of time.[17]

A major benefit—in my opinion—of post-millenial thought was that it gave a sense of ultimate meaning to the work of both missionaries and progressive social reformers alike. Both efforts "exhibited the kingdom" to the world, and the two, more often than not, intermingled as the missionaries brought schools, hospitals, agricultural advances, water projects, and so on, along with the gospel.[18]

Over the last several years, the trendy word in church-speak has been "missional." The concept is that, in our increasingly post-Christian society, we cannot just "build it"—i.e. attractive church buildings with high quality programming, etc.—"and they will come." Instead, every Christian is now (more than ever) a missionary, and every local church is a mission station from which we are to go forth to engage and serve the community in Christ's name. Ironically, maybe because I grew up in such a simple tiny meeting-house type of church, I cannot remember ever thinking otherwise. The local church building may be where we go to study the Bible, pray together, and share the Supper, but the life and work of the church is everywhere.

A couple of years ago I saw a video by Diana Butler Bass in which she raised the question of how it would be if, instead of the Great Commission,[19] our faith communities focused on living the Great Commandment to love God and neighbor. It is a somewhat false dichotomy, but it makes the important point that, too often, we have concentrated on head-counts (and budgets) in measuring the success of our congregations and mission endeavors. Taking off from Diana's point, I think that the "exhibition of the Kingdom" is really just another piece of our endeavor to live the Great Commandment.

---

17. The apocalyptic prophecies of the book of Revelation, as well as those in the gospels and epistles, were viewed more as archetype than as foreseen history, showing the ever-ongoing struggle between the forces of evil and the goodness of God.

18. I say this fully recognizing, and not *at all* excusing, the corresponding cultural destruction and real abuses that, far too often, accompanied missionary efforts. I also know that the missionaries I have known best—mostly old UPNA folks who worked in Pakistan, Egypt, the Sudan, and Ethiopia—include some of the most humble, faithful, kindly, and caring people that I have ever known, people who did much true good.

19. Matt 28:19: "Go into all the world and make disciples of every nation."

The examples of two men come to mind, men who simply cared about people and really enjoyed being engaged with the community. The first was Uncle Albert Cuthbertson (1859–1932). Albert was another of my great-grandfather's brothers, along with the oft-cited Uncle Alex.[20] He was also the father of the Osage matriarch Grandma Green. While Uncle Alex was known in the community for his piety, Uncle Albert was noted for being involved. The following excerpt from his obituary amply demonstrates that:

> Mr. Cuthbertson was county assessor for one term and census enumerator in 1900, 1910, 1920 and 1930. He was a man who had a happy home and was so constituted as to be able to fit in anywhere he was needed. Several times he had the guardianship of orphans and others unable to take care of their own business interests. His mother made her home with Mr. and Mrs. Cuthbertson for 20 years and his sister, Mrs. Jennie Mann who went to her reward last Easter lived in their home for eight years. He took a great interest in anything progressive. He helped to organize the Farm Bureau and the county fair, and served on the hospital board for several years. At the time of his death he was . . . a trustee of the Presbyterian Church. He will be greatly missed in his home and in the church.[21]

Before retiring to town, Uncle Albert had also long served as a trustee and Sunday School superintendant out at Osage.[22]

My second exemplar is Uncle Albert's grandson, Marvin Green (1910–2006). I have mentioned his name several times already. As I was growing up, I came to admire Marvin more than any other man in the community (at least outside of my dad and Uncle Jesse), and more than any other person he nurtured my engagement with the larger church beyond the local congregation. Marvin never made a great living for himself. He worked his small farm and supplemented his family income by acting as the "weed supervisor" for Crawford County. I have never known anyone who was richer in his enjoyment of community service. As with his grandfather, Marvin's obituary shows a rather amazing record:

20. Again, like Alex, he was married to one of my great-grandmother's Gemmell nieces.

21. Obituary, *The Girard Press*, November 10, 1932.

22. I know for a fact—reported by my cousin Hattie in her old age—that he was the superintendant in 1897 when his one son, Ralph, was born. The birth was on the same night that my Cuthbertson grandparents were married, and the next day at church a proud Uncle Albert announced the opening hymn to be "There is Sunshine in My Soul Today!"

Prior to his retirement from farming, he was an active leader and participant in area organizations. He was a 4-H leader for many years. He served on the Board of Directors for Elm Acres Youth Home. He was recognized by the Girard Area Chamber of Commerce, receiving the Outstanding Community Service Award in 1984 . . . . He was a past member, Elder, [Treasurer,] Sunday school teacher, and Sunday school superintendent of the Osage Presbyterian Church. More recently, he was a member of the Pittsburg First Presbyterian Church. He served as a Trustee on the Board of the Presbyterian Manor of Mid-America from 1978 to 1985. He was instrumental in establishing and maintaining the Museum of Crawford County located in Girard. He was 21 years old when he became a member of the Crawford County Fair Board. He held the office of secretary [to the Crawford County Fair Board] for 50 years. A 4-H building on the fairgrounds was dedicated in his honor. He served on the Kansas State Board of Agriculture for 32 years. He was on the Board of Producers Cooperative Association for 33 years, holding the offices of president and associate vice president during his tenure.[23]

What the fulsome obituary failed to note, e'en so, was that Marvin was also very active in the presbytery, where he served both as Moderator and as a Commissioner to the General Assembly in Kansas City in 1979. For many years he organized the program and served as Master of Ceremonies for the Christmas Tree at church. As I recall, he, too, was on the board of the Girard Hospital at one time. Also, when we still had our little country school,[24] he was our school bus driver . . . using his own car. Marvin loved fried chicken, ice cream, and gooseberry pie. He truly enjoyed, loved, and served God and neighbor.

At this point, I really do not know whether I believe in a literal Second Coming of Jesus but, at the very least, I think that we each face a Last Judgment of sorts when we die. The striking thing is that the gospels—Matthew, Mark, and Luke, at least—show that the final measure of our lives will be the love we have shown our neighbors. Matthew provides the most dramatic portrayal:

23. Obituary, *The Girard Press*, May 10, 2006.

24. Crawford School, District 134, had one room, one teacher, eight grades, and eighteen students. Ellen and I went there for first and second grades before it was closed, and we constituted our entire class both years.

When the Son of Man comes in his glory, and all the angels with him, then he will sit on the throne of his glory. All the nations will be gathered before him, and he will separate people one from another as a shepherd separates the sheep from the goats, and he will put the sheep at his right hand and the goats at the left. Then the king will say to those at his right hand, "Come, you that are blessed by my Father, inherit the kingdom prepared for you from the foundation of the world; for I was hungry and you gave me food, I was thirsty and you gave me something to drink, I was a stranger and you welcomed me, I was naked and you gave me clothing, I was sick and you took care of me, I was in prison and you visited me." Then the righteous will answer him, "Lord, when was it that we saw you hungry and gave you food, or thirsty and gave you something to drink? And when was it that we saw you a stranger and welcomed you, or naked and gave you clothing? And when was it that we saw you sick or in prison and visited you?" And the king will answer them, "Truly I tell you, just as you did it to one of the least of these who are members of my family, you did it to me."[25]

Such is the exhibition of God's realm in the world.

25. Matt 25:31–40.

Postscript

"It Burned, but It Was Not Consumed"

FOR MOST OF OUR history, the primary symbol of Presbyterianism has not been a cross, but the burning bush of the desert, where Moses first encountered God. With that symbol has been the Latin motto *Nec Tamen Consumebatur* which means "Yet it was not consumed."[1] It was at the burning bush where God revealed the Name, YHWH, a verb meaning "I AM" or "I WILL BE." My friend Nahum, a Rabbi in Santa Fe, New Mexico, has suggested that a good translation for the Name is Living Presence. God is the Living Presence who—in the words of John Phillip Newell—is the "Ground of all Being, Mother of Life, Father of the Universe" whose Name is "sacred beyond speaking."[2] The Mystery of that Living Presence was manifest in the burning bush and, in the Christian understanding, again in the transfiguration of Jesus, where the Living Presence shone forth in him, and from him, but he was not consumed.

At our best, I think, we Presbyterians have been a people of the Mystery of the Living Presence. We have been seekers of the Mystery in the Word and in Sacrament, in Psalm and in prayer. We have sought the Mystery in Sabbath time, and in daily life. We have looked for it in Jesus, and in one another. We have both feared it and loved it. At our worst, we have forgotten it, turning away from Presence itself, and from the presence of Presence in neighbor and in creation.

I sometimes think that it is one of God's great ironies that the Presbyterians were given Ghost Ranch back in 1955.[3] The Ranch is a fairly vast

1. Exod 3:2.

2. From "The Casa del Sol Prayer of Jesus." See Newell and Poole, *Liturgies from Casa del Sol*, 3.

3. I am not sure we were, or are, the people best suited to appreciate the Word

property of 20,000 acres in northern New Mexico, set among the splendors of red and golden cliffs in the so-called Valley of the Shining Stone (*Piedre Lumbre*). Its red hills and high desert landscape inspired the artist Georgia O'Keefe, and John Phillip Newell refers to it as one of Earth's "thin places," where little divides the divine realm from creation.

In the autumn, the skies at Ghost Ranch are bluer than sapphire, and the cottonwood leaves are all shimmering gold in the bright sun. It is then that I have accidentally stumbled upon the burning bush, on a couple of occasions. Once, I was out wandering in the badlands below Chimney Rock, and when I turned around, the sun had caught the rusty leaves of a small scrub oak just right, so that they were ablaze with color illuminating the edges of each leaf. Another time, I was back near the Campo Santo burial ground and chanced upon an old dead chamisa bush near the pond that had brilliant Indian Paintbrush growing up through the branches. Both times I stopped and took off my shoes, for I felt God was present.

During our years of living in New Mexico, one of the privileges that has come my way is getting to know a variety of people who follow the Sufi path. The Sufis are the mystics of Islam, and the ones I know are people who possess a deep spirituality and wisdom. They are also, in their way, great lovers of Jesus. At the heart of their spiritual discipline is the practice of *Zikr*, which means "Remember." The practice of *Zikr* is the practice of remembering God, and all that is "of God." In differing ways, it is a practice shared by Jews, Christians, and Muslims. In remembering the Sabbath, or partaking the Supper in "remembrance"[4] of Jesus, we seek to *remember* the Living Presence in a comparable sense to what the Sufis undertake in chant and dance. The desert is a good place to *remember*.

A couple of miles out from the main campus at Ghost Ranch is Casa del Sol, a lovely old hacienda-style house built in the 1930s and now used as a small retreat house. In 2006, when we were in the process of establishing Casa del Sol, it was decided that we would set up a group called The Companions of Casa del Sol that is loosely modeled on the Iona Community Associates program: a group that gives prayer, volunteer, and financial support. At the time of our founding, the vision statement of the Companions was written out by John Phillip Newell as being, "A community of the

---

hidden in its magnificence, or to listen for what the landscape has to tell us of sacred things. Albeit, maybe that is why we were given the stewardship.

4. As previously noted, the Greek word *anamnesis* (1 Cor 11:24–25) means to experience something again, as if for the first time.

Living Presence, seeking the oneness of the human soul and the healing of creation."[5] It is an invitation to remember who we are, at a very deep level.

That vision had emerged slowly over the previous year. Throughout the summer of 2005, various ones of us had gone weekly to Ghost Ranch on Thursday nights, when evening prayer was held in the courtyard of the old house amidst ongoing repair work. On those evenings there was time, around the blazing fire pit, for guests at the Ranch to voice what they longed to see and find in this emerging place of retreat and prayer, and to express their own deepest spiritual longings. The vision statement came from what they said on those high desert nights.

Casa del Sol at Ghost Ranch, Abiquiu, New Mexico
(Photograph courtesy of Ghost Ranch)

I think the Companions' vision is one expression of what is called the "emerging church" or "emerging Christianity." Part of what John Phillip calls the "new birthing" of Jesus for our time is a critically needed rethinking of how we relate to one another, especially those of other faith traditions, and how we relate to creation itself. As we undertake this as Christians, Presbyterian or otherwise, we have to discern how we understand and know Jesus—"our treasure," as John Phillip calls him—in this new setting.

5. Newell and Poole, *Liturgies from Ghost Ranch*, 34.

Strange as it may sound, I think this is an area where some of the old Presbyterian ways can help. Among the various Protestant bodies, I think our tradition has some of the deepest affinities with the beliefs, attitudes, and even practices found in the other Abrahamic faiths of Judaism and Islam. Not that we can, or should, drop all our differences and just melt into one another, but at least we can learn to respect and mutually appreciate one another as sprouts growing off a common root-stock. I think we can also learn to pray *with* one another—which is not exactly the same as *together*—to the One we all claim to worship and serve.

I have to admit that the connection to the other part of the Companions' vision, the healing of creation, is a bit harder to tie in . . . even with all the farmers and shepherds, psalm paraphrases, and sabbatical emphases found among our ancestors. Over the last century and a half, in particular, Presbyterians have very much been modern people (in the philosophical sense). For most of our history, we used the earth accordingly. However, I also know that it was my farmer father, an elder, who taught me to observe, know, and love the land and the ever-unfolding cycle of the seasons. I think also of a particular Scots-born fellow who, although he rebelled against the stern faith of his old Campbellite father, could still "preach" a fairly prophetic sermon when he wanted to. The man in question was the great American naturalist John Muir (1838–1914):

> The world, as we are told, was made especially for man—a presumption not supported by all the facts. A numerous class of men are painfully astonished whenever they find anything, living or dead, in all God's universe, which they cannot eat or render in some way what they call useful to themselves. They have precise dogmatic insight of the intentions of the Creator, and it is hardly possible to be guilty of irreverence in speaking of *their* God any more than of heathen idols. He is regarded as a civilized, law-abiding gentleman in favor either of a republican form of government or of a limited monarchy; believes in the literature and language of England; is a warm supporter of the English constitution and Sunday schools and missionary societies; and is as purely a manufactured article as any puppet of a half-penny theater.
>
> With such views of the Creator it is, of course, not surprising that erroneous views should be entertained of the creation. To such properly trimmed people, the sheep, for example, is an easy problem—food and clothing "for us," eating grass and daisies white by divine appointment for this predestined purpose, on

perceiving the demand for wool that would be occasioned by the eating of the apple in the Garden of Eden . . . .

But if we should ask these profound expositors of God's intentions, How about those man-eating animals—lions, tigers, alligators—which smack their lips over raw man? Or about those myriads of noxious insects that destroy labor and drink his blood? Doubtless man was intended for food and drink for all these? Oh, no! Not at all! These are unresolvable difficulties connected with Eden's apple and the Devil . . . .

Now it never seems to occur to these farseeing teachers that Nature's object in making animals and plants might be first of all the happiness of each one of them, not the creation of all for the happiness of one. Why should man value himself as more than a small part of the one great unit of creation? And what creature of all that the Lord has taken the pains to make is not essential to the completeness of that unit—the cosmos? The universe would be incomplete without man; but it would also be incomplete without the smallest transmicroscopic creature that dwells beyond our conceitful eyes and knowledge.[6]

Clearly the "country gentleman" puppet-God that Muir lampoons is *not* YHWH of the desert. However, the "Lord" of that last paragraph surely may be. Clearly, the starting place for a truly Presbyterian rethinking of our relationship to creation itself simply has to be a covenant—in this case, probably the one made with Noah . . . and all living things:

YHWH said in his heart:
"I will never again curse the ground because of humankind . . .
Nor will I ever again destroy every living creature as I have done.
As long as the earth endures,
Seedtime and harvest, cold and heat,
Summer and winter, day and night,
Shall not cease."[7]

God said: "This is the sign of the covenant that I make between me and you and every living creature that is with you, for all future generations: I have set my bow in the clouds, and it shall be a sign of the covenant between me and the earth."[8]

6. Muir, *A Thousand-mile Walk to the Gulf*, 77–79.

7. Gen 8:21–22.

8. Gen 9:12–13.

෬ ෬ ෬

So, then, what is my concluding word as I bring this work to an end? It comes from scripture, pure and simple: "Mercy triumphs over judgment."[9] For all the rigor of John Knox and the Covenanters, of predestination and church discipline, I think that is the true essential message of a biblically based covenant theology. It is true of God in relation to humanity, and it is the essence of how we are called to regard and treat one another. It is enough to know, and it changes *everything*!

That said, the questions I have at the end of this book are essentially the same ones I have pondered throughout. As Presbyterians moving into an unfolding future:

- How are we going to continue to be a "people of the Book"?

- How are we going to practice our faith with our families?

- How will we be mindful of the need to set aside time for God?

- How will we rightly worship and serve God, sharing in Word and Sacrament?

- What is essential to the ongoing roles of our elders and ministers?

- What does it mean to be covenanted communities of disciples?

- What is the proclamation of the gospel, and how do we exhibit God's realm to the world?

- How should we pursue the emerging vision of the oneness of the human soul and the healing of creation?

Unlike my late father, who had just a wee touch of the Second Sight,[10] I do not know what is going to happen in the future—thanks be to God! I do know that the day of Christian "privilege" is mostly at an end in

9. Jas 2:13.

10. According to my late brother, one Sunday back in 1953 our dad started crying during church at Osage. On the way home he said he had "seen" his dad's funeral there in the church. Shortly after they got home they got the call from California that my grandfather had suffered a major stroke, from which he died a few days later. In 1984 dad told a cousin at church that he had a "feeling" something was going to happen to "Sis." A few days later Auntie suffered a major stroke, and died later that summer. Then, in 1989, while in the hospital himself, he warned my brother not to go on their planned family vacation because something bad was going to happen. Merle took the precaution of checking with dad's doctor, who thought things were alright for them to go. Later that very same day Merle broke his leg, and decided that was the fulfillment of dad's premonition. The family went on vacation, and a few days later my grand-nephew died in an accident at the campground where they were staying.

western culture. Proud establishmentarian Presbyterianism is over and done with. Like our Covenanter kin (the RPNAs) who have been living on the margins since the seventeenth century, if we believe we are called by God to do so, the rest of us Presbyterians will have to find ways to journey on and be faithful to the truth—as best we perceive it—from the edges of society. We can learn many things, some helpful and others less so, from their example.

Back in Ayrshire, the Fenwick Kirk is hanging in there, though, like most Church of Scotland parishes, it faces an uncertain future. Osage, my beloved home church, was closed by presbytery in 2002 and, although a remnant tried to hang on as an independent congregation, my impression is that services are no longer held. There are still a handful of Cuthbertsons and Gemmells hanging around the area, but only one or two cousins remain Presbyterian. Ellen, my dear childhood friend and churchmate, died in January 2011 after a long struggle with breast cancer. Sterling College continues, and has actually grown in enrollment over the last thirty years, but its ties to the Presbyterian Church have grown more tenuous over the decades as a variety of presidents from other evangelical traditions have taken the helm. It is now over fifty years since the UPNA got swallowed up (as many saw it) by what is now the PCUSA, and the last few elders and ministers formed and ordained in that tradition—including my husband's father—are now into their eighties.

I remember a day, back in college, when Harriette Stafford sighed a bit wistfully and said that the world she had grown up in—the mission field of the northwest frontier of India in the final years of the British Raj—no longer existed. I am beginning to better understand that sigh, but I also have hope. I truly believe that God is still working in the PCUSA, and I trust that we still have a future ahead of us. It will be very different from what we have known before, but the Living Presence calls from the unknown and the old fire-bush is "not yet consumed."

As the current PCUSA moves through a new season of "sorting out" in the wake of the changed policy on LGBT ordination, we are sad to hear of various relations and old friends who have left, or are considering leaving. Such is their choice. May God be with them. At the same time, I also celebrate the fact that, in January 2012, one of Uncle Albert Cuthbertson's great-grandsons became the third openly gay minister ordained since the policy change.[11] In addition to that, in March 2012, after twenty-five years

11. Rev. Paul Mowry, who is now serving the congregation at Sausalito in Marin County, California.

of life together, Doug Calderwood and I were able to be legally married, and have our marriage blessed in God's name, at Niagara Falls, New York.[12]

With all that said, I think I have finished what I set out to do. I knew that this book was something I had to write, and my sense is that it may, somehow, be the most important thing that I have ever done. What I have said here is what I truly felt *called* to say, as a witness to those who come after us, and I trust the Spirit will use it accordingly. My heartfelt hope is that this will, at least, be a book of remembrance of those who have encountered the Living Presence we call God on a particular path, "the way" of the venerable but odd sect of Christian elders known as the Presbyterians. As I said at the outset, it is my great fear that, in this era of such profound transformation and change, much that is worth knowing will be forgotten and lost. To remember who we have been is important in knowing who we are, and in discerning who we may be called to become. We are called to remember. I hope this *wee buke* helps.

> Our God, our help in ages past,
> Our hope for years to come,
> Our shelter from the stormy blast,
> And our eternal home.
>
> Before the hills in order stood,
> Or earth received its frame,
> From everlasting Thou art God,
> To endless years the same....
>
> Time, like an ever rolling stream,
> Soon bears us all away;
> We fly forgotten as a dream
> Dies at the opening day.
>
> Our God, our help in ages past,
> Our hope for years to come,
> Be Thou our guard while life shall last,
> And our eternal home.
>
> —PSALM 90, (TUNE: DUNLAP'S CREEK, CM)

12. The ceremony was conducted by a wonderful minister of the United Church of Christ, a woman who co-officiated at the mass wedding of forty couples at the Falls on the day the New York law went into effect in July 2011. Presbyterian ministers are still (in 2013) prohibited from performing same-gender marriages, but some of us are working hard to change that.

The Author, wearing a Clergy Tartan stole, 2013
(Author's personal photograph)

Ken Cuthbertson and Doug Calderwood, lawfully married
by a Minister of the United Church of Christ at Niagara Falls, NY,
25 March 2012 *(Author's personal photograph)*

Postscript 2 – May 2023

Still Presbyterian!

WE LIVE IN A very different world in 2023 than we did in 2013. So much has changed in the U.S., the world at large, and also in the PCUSA, in my husband's and my shared life, and in my own life. Sadly, our country and the world feel much meaner, more violent, more desperate, and less hopeful than they did a decade ago, leading many of us to ponder and fear what lies ahead. The PCUSA is smaller. We are older. And yet—as Presbyterians are ever-reminded to affirm, we believe and trust that "God is faithful still."[1]

Looking anew at my original postscript, I am actually a *wee bit* surprised, and truly pleased, at how much of it still rings true for me. I am much less involved with Casa del Sol at Ghost Ranch than I was in 2013, but it remains dear to me, and what I experienced there in those years continues to be a profound and meaning-*full* part of my journey. Creation care remains a particularly high priority—ever more so, in fact, not just for myself, but for all of us. And, thankfully, this includes the PCUSA.

This book focuses on a particular tradition of spiritual formation and living—and its ongoing evolution. My foundational questions, posed at the end of the original postscript (see page 144), remain, and I believe that the PCUSA as a whole has become somewhat more existentially aware of them. If we want to continue as a *living* tradition, we must remain aware. The denominational "sorting out" I wrote about in 2013 has left us much diminished in numbers but somehow rather oddly renewed in spirit. First and foremost: "We are still here!" And, as the journey goes onward, it feels to me like we are finding ways to stay true to the best of our heritage while

---

1. *A Brief Statement of Faith*, C-11.3, line 51.

adapting to the conditions of the present. We are, in the classic Reformed sense, *persevering!*[2]

A brief review of how the last decade has unfolded seems in order....

In the PCUSA, following the change in ordination standards and the adoption of the revised *Form of Government* in 2010–2011, the denomination at last moved in 2014–2015 to revise our constitutional description (a term I prefer over "definition") of Christian marriage. Our *Directory for Worship* now terms marriage "a unique commitment between two people, *traditionally* a man and a woman" and otherwise simply refers to the "couple" being married.[3] Since that change, ministers are fully permitted—but *not* required—to officiate same-sex marriages, and congregations are free to host same-sex weddings in their facilities—or not. The *Directory for Worship* is permissive in this, not prescriptive. Nonetheless, from what I can see, officiating has quickly become a fairly universal practice among PCUSA ministers.

At the 223rd General Assembly in St. Louis in 2018—a full biblical forty years after the beginning of the denominational debate and struggle over LGBTQIA+[4] issues—a resolution affirming LGBTQIA+ "gifts for ministry"[5] and a second affirming the church's "commitment to the full welcome, acceptance, and inclusion" of transgender, nonbinary, and people of all gender identities into "the full life of the church"[6] were adopted

---

2. From "The Westminster Confession of Faith": "They whom God hath accepted in his Beloved, effectually called, and sanctified by his Spirit, can neither totally nor finally fall away from the state of grace; but shall certainly persevere to the end." PCUSA, *Book of Confessions*, C-6.0904.

3. PCUSA, *Book of Order*, W-4.0601, *italics* added. A key emphasis in the discussions at the time was the emphasis on *mutual* love and commitment found in Eph 5:21: "Be subject to one another out of reverence for Christ." Christian marriage is, first and foremost, a mutual commitment between equals. Another illuminating insight was that the phrase "bone of my bones and flesh of my flesh" in Gen 2:23 points to our *like*ness to one another as human beings, not our gender differences. The gender distinction in the next line is linguistic, but the focus is clearly on the likeness. It is about kinship. Compare Gen 29:14, where Laban (a man) uses the phrase in speaking with his nephew (and future son-in-law) Jacob. Similarly, in 2 Sam 5:1, the tribes of Israel use it when they come to David to make him king: "Look, we are your bone and flesh," i.e., "We're kin!"

4. The LGBTQIA+ acronym stands for: Lesbian, Gay, Bisexual, Transgender, Queer/Questioning, Intersex, Asexual, etc.

5. PCUSA Overture 11–13 (2018), "On Celebrating the Gifts of People of Diverse Sexual Orientations and Gender Identities in the Life of the Church," *PC Biz,* https://www.pc-biz.org/#/search/3000313.

6. PCUSA Overture 11–12 (2018), "On Affirming and Celebrating the Full Dignity

by unanimous consent, without any debate. Enough had, apparently, at last been said. The statement affirming LGBTQIA+ gifts for ministry included the following:

> Celebrating the expansive embrace of the gospel of Jesus Christ and the breadth of our mission to serve a world in need, the 223rd General Assembly affirms the gifts of LGBTQIA+ people for ministry and celebrates their service in the church and in the world.
>
> The Assembly celebrates that over the years, LGBTQIA+ people have faithfully, lovingly, and courageously served in every kind of service to which Christian disciples are called—notwithstanding the church's efforts to exclude them from particular types of service.
>
> The Assembly laments the ways that the policies and actions of the PC(USA) have caused gifted, faithful LGBTQIA+ Christians to leave the Presbyterian church so that they could find a more welcoming place to serve, as they have been gifted and called by the Spirit.
>
> At the same time, the Assembly gives thanks for the LGBTQIA+ pioneers of the faith who have persisted in relationship with the Presbyterian church, at great personal cost and sacrifice, together with the whole of the LGBTQIA+ community, moving the church toward a more generous, loving, and just understanding of God's grace.
>
> The Assembly also gives thanks for those who continue to seek deeper understanding, and more authentic welcome, even amid discomfort or uncertainty about how best to show hospitality, in the spirit of continuing Reformation.[7]

For obvious reasons, I took those words rather personally, and they actually brought me to tears. Along with many others, I had literally been waiting for most of those forty years to hear my church say that. Clearly, we have come a very long way.

That way, however, proved very costly in terms of denominational membership and associated financial resources. Drawing on statistics from the Office of the General Assembly, the PCUSA went from a membership of 2,140,165 in 2010 to a membership of 1,482,767 in 2017.[8] The

---

and Humanity of People of All Gender Identities," *PC Biz*, https://www.pc-biz.org/#/search/3000312.

7. PCUSA Overture 11–13 (2018). In the PCUSA, deacons, ruling elders, and ministers are all ordained.

8. Statistics for 2021 show 1,193,770 members (Office of the General Assembly,

massive drop (-657,398) of basically one third between 2010 and 2017 came in the wake of the changes in ordination standards and marriage policies. During that time period, many large conservative evangelical congregations disaffiliated with the PCUSA, despite the repeated assurances of "local option" and freedom of conscience. Some congregations split.[9] Other members withdrew as individuals and families. This was very much to the regret and chagrin of those of us who felt we had for so long bent over backward in trying to accommodate them without giving up ourselves.

The massive loss of membership set into motion new and ongoing rounds of institutional transitions and restructuring. Then came COVID-19: From one Sunday to the next, in March 2020, we went from "church as usual" to a full pandemic lockdown that lasted—in varying degrees of severity—for about a year and a half, with a couple of later relapses. We are all still in the process of reemerging.

I was really quite amazed and pleased at how quickly and well so many Presbyterians adapted to the prevailing COVID situation. Simplified, yet often wonderfully creative, worship services quickly appeared via livestream and Zoom. Dispersed choirs quickly figured out the necessary technologies to keep on singing. The PCUSA Office of Theology and Worship advised that Communion could be held remotely, with all joining together online for the prayers and basic liturgy but with each household using its own elements at home. Of course, it wasn't as good as being together in person, but the Word was shared, we prayed together, we waved at and greeted one another on Zoom, we sang together, and we could still share the Communion bread and cup. It made a world of difference in those many months.

In our Presbytery of Santa Fe, we had a group of (mostly young*ish*) ministers who joined together to provide a weekly livestream service via YouTube for any in the presbytery who wished to tune in. There were some particularly good children's messages—especially including the ones done in one minister's chicken coop, his garden, and baking bread in his

---

"PC(USA) 2021 Statistics Continue to Show Declining Membership," *PCUSA*, April 25, 2022, https://www.pcusa.org/news/2022/4/25/pcusa-2021-statistics-continue-show-declining-memb/). Along with the earlier impact of the LGBTQIA+ struggles, the further decline also reflects overall trends in various denominations and the impact of COVID-19 on church participation. The "hemorrhage" of 2010–2017 of about 100,000 members per year has, at least, slowed to something more like 50,000 per year. Statistics for 2022 are still forthcoming.

9. Including, I'm sad to say, my in-laws' church in Wichita, Kansas.

kitchen. Folks took part from all over the presbytery (which covers half of the State of New Mexico), the country (households in Pennsylvania, Chicago, and other places signed in), and even abroad (a mission coworker in Honduras was a regular).

We even figured out how to do ordinations and installations online, with a well-masked and be-gloved minimum quorum showing up together for the laying on of hands and the rest of us raising our hands in blessing from home. Remote session and presbytery meetings proved tolerable, at least. We have now had a totally remote General Assembly (2020, essential business only) and our first hybrid one as well (2022). In all this, the church changed—probably more than any of us yet realize. We are still seeking the way ahead into what a "new normal" may look like....

The third great shift in the PCUSA over the last decade has been a renewed focus on social justice and missional connection with the larger community. The Matthew 25 Initiative[10] and Earth Care Congregations[11] movements have both gained increased visibility and momentum. As with various more "Progressive" Christian constituencies, many Presbyterians now look more to *following* Jesus in loving service than to the more Evangelically oriented emphases on right belief and personalized moralism. As Reformed—and *ever-reforming*—Christians[12] have always attempted, we seek to be true to the original impetus of the life and teachings of Jesus in the context of our day. This current focus feels authentic to me and true to the Jesus of the synoptic gospels in particular.[13]

While the PCUSA is still a very privileged, largely white, Euro-American denomination, we have been truly blessed with an increasingly diverse leadership drawn from our African American, Hispanic, Native,

---

10. Emerging out the 222nd General Assembly (Portland, Oregon, 2016), the Matthew 25 movement in the PCUSA focuses on the words of Jesus that when we minister to and with "people who are hungry, thirsty, naked, sick, imprisoned, strangers, poor or oppressed in other ways and in need of welcoming," *aka* the "least of these, my siblings," we are truly ministering to Jesus in and through them. The programmatic foci of the initiative are to address building congregational vitality, the dismantling of structural racism, and the eradication of systemic poverty. (From the PCUSA Matthew 25 brochure: https://www.presbyterianmission.org/wp-content/uploads/Matt25-big-brochure-2021.pdf.)

11. See "Earth Care Congregations," *Presbyterian Mission*, https://www.presbyterianmission.org/ministries/environment/earth-care-congregations/.

12. As the Reformation-era motto has it, "*Ecclesia reformata semper reformanda secundum Verbum Dei*" ("A church community reformed and always in the process of being reformed according to God's Word").

13. See Appendix 4 for more on this topic.

and other racial-ethnic constituencies. While it is not their "job" to do so, nor should they *have to*, these leaders have together played an essential role in raising awareness and sensitizing us all to the persistent realities of structural racism and systemic poverty and to our historical and communal role in it.

For those of us in the Southwestern U.S., much of the focus has been on Native American issues. There are things past (though still present) like the Doctrine of Discovery and its ongoing effects[14] and the truly atrocious history and impact of the Indian boarding schools of the nineteenth *and* twentieth centuries. I am thankful that our Presbytery of Santa Fe has been willing to look honestly into this history and address, as best we can, what can be addressed. During the COVID-19 pandemic, the Synod of the Southwest and its presbyteries also responded vigorously in providing assistance to disproportionately hard-hit reservations (Diné/Navajo and Apache) and pueblos.

Along with all this, I remain mindful of what I was once told by the late Rev. Hank Bremer, a ministerial colleague who was quite an "out there" activist in the 1960s. When I once asked him, "How did you get away with it?" as an activist pastor, the gist of his words was to this effect: "You can get away with a lot, so long as you make sure to show up and do the pastoral work too." Religious formation, spiritual nurture, and being present with the community's joys and sorrows are as important now as ever, even as we experiment with what is appropriate and workable moving forward. There is, I think, still a role for institutional "church," and in some ways I am rather more hopeful for it now than I was ten years ago.

As for us two, my husband and I are now into our thirty-seventh year of committed relationship and our twelfth year of legal marriage. Both of Doug's parents have now passed from this life into what Lord George MacLeod of Iona so beautifully called the "Nearer Presence" of God.[15] The Rev. Don Calderwood died at the beginning of 2015, aged nearly 84, and Evelyn Campbell Calderwood followed in the autumn of 2022, aged 91. Their ashes are interred in the cemetery at Sterling, Kansas, Don's hometown, with pinches of dirt from both Fenwick, Scotland and Murree, Pakistan[16] added into the Kansas soil.

---

14. See "Doctrine of Discovery," *Facing Racism: PCUSA*, https://facing-racism.pcusa.org/item/41901/.

15. Newell, *Listening for the Heartbeat of God*, 93.

16. Murree Christian School, where the Calderwoods taught from 1956 until a couple of years before their retirement in the U.S., permanently closed in 2021.

We have reached that age where it feels like too many beloveds are dying, and too frequently. The ranks of our elder generations are rapidly thinning out, and more and more of our own peers are now going too. Two particular people come to mind in relation to what was written in this book.[17] In late 2020, my longtime spiritual director, colleague, and great friend, Dr. Wallace Ford, passed away. Wally was a Disciples of Christ minister, and we shared many a conversation on the interface between the Presbyterian and Disciples traditions. Then, in early 2021, Doug's cousin Carol Sieverling died after many years of ill health. We both loved Carol very much. She'd been in college with us and had been a wonderful ally and support in the family across the years. Neither Wally nor Carol succumbed to COVID-19. Through both, however, we had our most direct exposures to livestreamed memorial services.[18]

Fewer and fewer among our own families, either biological or chosen, are still Presbyterian. From our generation, I have one first cousin and Doug has two who belong to PCUSA congregations. Doug has a couple of other relatives who belong to other Presbyterian bodies. We do have some much-beloved *chosen* family in Albuquerque—the sort of "friends who are closer than siblings"[19]—who are members of the Las Placitas congregation. That, however, is basically all. So, in this, we nearly are the *last* Presbyterians!

With Sterling College, while we retain our ties with many old friends, faculty members, and classmates alike, we have realized we can no longer support the institution itself. Although Louisville (PCUSA national headquarters) doesn't seem to be quite fully aware of it,[20] I was told some time back by a representative of the college that they had cut their ties to the PCUSA, and that seems to be reflected in various ways in what we see and read. Their published standards of conduct are also very clearly, strictly, and pointedly heteronormative. (All in Jesus's name, of course!) There are still truly good things about Sterling College, but not in their staunchly prohibitive stance on LGBTQIA+ matters. None of this surprises us, but it makes us deeply sad. We know we (and folks *like* us) are not *truly* welcome

17. See also those names marked with an * in the Acknowledgments.

18. For Carol's service, her siblings and cousins came together to create a beautifully done remote choral rendition of a portion of Psalm 139. See Emmanuel Bedford, "Wings of the Dawn," *YouTube*, February 21, 2021, https://www.youtube.com/watch?v=oOXs6C6juXs&list=RDMMLeRXNIyJq6c&index=3.

19. Prov 18:24b.

20. As of 2022–2023, Sterling still appears on the list of PCUSA-related institutions in the Presbyterian Planning Calendar.

there, at least not as who we really are.[21] We tread carefully when family ties occasionally bring us to town.

My personal journey of this last decade began with my becoming somewhat of a same-sex marriage activist, both locally and nationally, in the church and also in our state. It just sort of *happened*. In preparation for the 2014 General Assembly in Detroit, I renewed my old connections to and with two of our national advocacy groups, More Light Presbyterians and the Covenant Network of Presbyterians. At the 2014 Assembly, I worked with Covenant Network to promote an "Authoritative Interpretation" of *The Book of Order* to immediately clear the way for same-sex marriages to take place in the PCUSA in civil jurisdictions where they were legal. It was a wonderful moment when that passed at the Assembly, along with the proposed revision of the marriage section of the *Directory for Worship*.[22] Around the same time, back home in New Mexico, I also happily cooperated with a younger friend who was working with the ACLU to gain faith-leader support for civil same-sex marriage in the state. To our amazement, that all came together even more quickly than PCUSA approval, thanks to a bold county clerk in Las Cruces and a subsequent New Mexico State Supreme Court ruling in late 2013.

Following the 2014 General Assembly, I began to ponder how I wanted to engage in an ongoing way with the organized church and ministry. At age fifty-eight and after so many years on the margins, I knew I did not feel called into full-time professional ministry. My first decision was to take official retirement. Having been a "member at large" of various presbyteries for most of my (then) thirty-two years of ordained service, I was particularly weary of the required annual process of being re-approved in that capacity—of having, in essence, to continually re-justify my ministerial status and existence. When I realized that I could continue doing everything that I was then doing as a retiree, including my service as a parish associate at Las Placitas Presbyterian Church, it was a total no-brainer—and a decision I've never regretted for a second. I was "honorably retired" by the Presbytery of Santa Fe, effective the beginning of November in 2014.

That, however, has not stopped me from pursuing matters of importance—to my heart and mind, at least—in the national church. In the

---

21. I also fully acknowledge and "own" that my strongly held views were once very much the same as theirs are still. (See page 101, including note 18.)

22. As an amendment to *The Book of Order*, the latter had to go on to be ratified by a majority of PCUSA presbyteries.

PCUSA, one of the ways that business comes before our national General Assembly is by "overtures" (proposed legislation) sent by local presbyteries with the concurrence of at least two other presbyteries. In addition to my involvement with those that brought about the changes in ordination and marriage, over the last decade I have originated several overtures in and through our Presbytery of Santa Fe:

1. Starting in 2012, but finally moving forward in 2016–2017, I proposed an overture that would restore the traditional nomenclature designating us as "Ministers of the Word and Sacrament" to *The Book of Order*, in place of the term "Teaching Elders" that had been chosen by the authors of the revised *Form of Government* adopted in 2010–2011.[23] After failing in 2012, a revised version of the overture was resubmitted by the Presbytery of Great Rivers (Illinois) in 2016 and was approved by the Assembly.[24] It then received overwhelming approval in the votes of the presbyteries.

2. Starting in the summer of 2017, but finally just now nearing the end of the process of presbytery voting in the spring of 2023, I proposed a series of overtures making seemingly slight, but I think substantive, changes to several sections of our new *Directory for Worship* adopted in 2016–2017. The suggested changes mostly emerged from a study of the new *Directory* that I conducted at Las Placitas in the winter of 2017. From the beginning, I also consulted with our national Office of Theology and Worship and deeply appreciated their cooperation and, as the process proceeded, support. The most important additions, from the perspective of this book, were to the sections concerning household worship and prayers at table (W-5.0104a and c) and to the section concerning services of prayer for healing and wholeness (W-5.0204). As of May 5, 2023, all the amendments have been approved.[25]

23. Emotional attachments aside, my main arguments for reverting to "Ministers of the Word and Sacrament" were that it was the common usage among Reformed and Presbyterian churches from the Reformation on, while "Teaching Elder" (as used) was a designation that only became popular in some churches from the late eighteenth to early nineteenth centuries on. "Minister" is also the more commonly used designation among most non-Anglican, non-Lutheran Protestant denominations.

24. PCUSA Overture 06–08 (2016), "On Amending the Book of Order to Clarify Titles to Ordered Ministry—From the Presbytery of Great Rivers," *PC Biz*, https://www.pc-biz.org/#/search/6328.

25. Amendments 22-T through V and X through BB may be found via: https://www.pcusa.org/resource/ga225-proposed-amendments-constitution/.

3. Currently, in 2023, I have a proposed overture being considered by the Presbytery of Santa Fe that would establish minimal requirements of Reformed polity for small worshipping communities for whom formal organization as a congregation (which includes legal incorporation) is not deemed appropriate but who wish to be officially affiliated with the PCUSA.[26] We will see where it goes.

I know—because they have openly said so—that some of my colleagues in ministry find my efforts in these matters puzzling, amusing, and/or even a bit irritating. All I can say in response is that I do deeply believe in the importance of how we say things and in doing things "decently and in good order" insofar as possible. The good news is that I think I am pretty nearly out of things to tinker with, at least for now.[27]

Turning back, however, to the subject of retirement, next steps occurred as I approached my sixtieth birthday in 2016. I knew I wanted at that milestone to find ways to mindfully undertake transitioning into my "Third Chapter" of life. I did manage to find an excellent little pre-retirement retreat put on by the Lutherans (ELCA) at a retreat center just north of Phoenix. But, in general, the sort of resources I was looking for proved to be a bit thin on the ground. Unfortunately, as some of my spiritual direction colleagues like to put it, "Jesus never got old!"—which means that we don't have much guidance from the New Testament on how to approach our later years. The Hebrew Bible is somewhat better on the topic, but I knew that I did *not* want to go the Moses route, working until I'm 120 years old and then wandering up a mountain to die with God. (A

---

26. The essential core of the proposed overture is this: "Such recognized groups shall be under the mutually agreed-upon oversight of a Minister of the Word and Sacrament approved by the presbytery, shall include at least one ruling elder in their chosen leadership, and shall function under the financial, legal, and disciplinary sponsorship of an ecclesial council (either a session or a presbytery)."

27. There is one item in my worship proposals that got culled back at the outset, in 2017. I would still very much like to see it added into the *Directory for Worship*, but I am reluctant to take the lead in pushing it through the process at this point. It addresses the sensitive issue of cultural appropriation. As I would now write it, the amendment would be: "At W-1.0304, to amend the third paragraph as follows (words to be added in *italics*): Whenever and wherever we gather in Jesus's name, we join the praise and prayer of the people of God in every time and place. Therefore, it is fitting that we share stories and sing songs from cultures other than our own as we pray for and with the Church throughout the world. *At the same time, due and sensitive care should always be taken to avoid acts of religious or cultural misappropriation of the sacred rites and practices of other faith traditions and peoples.*"

surprising number of ministers do seem to try to pursue this approach, which is fine if they want, but it is not for me!)

I very quickly realized that I'm more of a "vine and fig tree" sort.[28] Let me putter around in the garden and pray. Several years on, I'm finding *Ecclesiastes* to be a great resource, at least when read from a more Buddhist perspective of mindful nonattachment, balanced with compassion: "*How then can we learn to step back, let go, and find contentment in the basics of our living?*" My dear Wally Ford nudged me further on this, as was always his wont: "*How, as well, can we find the place in our lives for wise 'eldering' and mentoring of those coming along behind us?*" I'm still puttering and pondering.

The most startling self-realization that emerged, rather quickly, in my reflective stepping-back was a new realization about gender identity—*my* gender identity. This is not the place to recount the long journey toward new understandings about gender that stretch, for me, back into the 1990s. That is for another book at another time. Suffice it to say that for a long time I had recognized a strong *femme* aspect in myself—rather as I once recognized my "homosexual tendencies"—and had even come to refer to myself as "Auntie Ken" with various younger friends. But, beyond that, I'd not really come to terms with much of the new understanding and terminology that has emerged. Then, out of the blue, as I was driving up to Ghost Ranch on an early December day in 2017, somewhere on the "Relief Route" around Santa Fe, I suddenly realized and said out loud, "I have always been *nonbinary!*" And it was so.

I am male-bodied and essentially happily so. But, for want of a better way of putting it, I am very female-*souled*. The two are not in opposition to each other but integrated together into a nonbinary whole. That, as I now see it, is my gender *identity*. As for gender *expression*, I long ago realized that I have basically always looked to strong female role models— the "capable wife" of Proverbs 31, my mother, my aunts, Doug's mother, and other strong women like the matriarchs discussed in this book (see Chapter 8, etc.). Throughout life, I have tended toward more traditionally female roles and relational modes. I seek out the friendship of women. Now, more than ever, stereotypical "guys" feel like the most *opposite*, and toxic, of any of the sexes to me.

As for pronouns, I find myself equally comfortable with any of the *he/she/they* options. (The *zi/xe* suggestions are just a bit too odd for me.)

---

28. "But they shall all sit under their own vines and under their own fig trees, and no one shall make them afraid" (Mic 4:4).

I most love being called "Auntie!" Thankfully, Doug has proven to be to-tally accepting and comfortable with it all. I'm still a bit careful in church circles, but I'm becoming somewhat bolder over time.[29] In the current atmosphere of *anti*-trans hysteria and *phobia* in so many places, especially among conservative and traditionalist Christians, I am thankful beyond words to be in a denomination that is on record in support of us.

Best intentions notwithstanding, for various reasons—our pastor's sabbatical, followed by a crisis in his family and then his accepting a new call, etc.—I got rather distracted from my retirement progress and drawn back into church busy-ness from about May 2017 until March 2020, when the COVID-19 lockdown hit us all. I stayed engaged with the Las Placitas congregation as best I could for those first few months, but at the same time I increasingly felt an invitation and call, which I perceived as Spirit-directed, to take the next, deeper step into retirement—which I did at the beginning of August 2020. I resigned from my position as parish associate that I had held for most of the time since 2005. It is another of those things that felt right and feels right, and I have had no second thoughts.

Since 2020, my ministry has settled into a few limited—and de-creasing—commitments. Since early 2017, I have been helping out sev-eral times a year at the tiny Cuba (New Mexico) Presbyterian Church, a setting that reminds me of my childhood community at the Osage Presbyterian Church in Kansas. That continues. In 2021, after twenty-plus years, I stepped aside from my part-time teaching commitment with the Ecumenical Institute for Ministry in Albuquerque. That was another good decision. I continue to see a few spiritual directees, for now. I read a lot, study, pray, and do a bit of writing.[30] I garden—albeit more stiffly than before. And so on....

Since things have opened up again, post-pandemic, I have still kept myself distanced from any active engagement with ministry at Las Placitas, but we have become regulars at the simple and tiny early service. Each week there is a hymn, usually *a capella*; discussion of one of the day's

---

29. It was just on March 12, 2023, that I first mentioned from the pulpit that I identify as nonbinary. It was in my sermon at a small church up near Los Alamos, New Mexico, and was *apropos* to the text of the day from John 4. Concerning resources, in my opinion, the best available basic text on gender spectrum-related issues from a biblical and theological perspective is Austen Hartke's *Transforming: The Bible and the Lives of Transgender Christians* (Louisville, KY: Westminster John Knox Press, 2018).

30. Among many literary accompaniers along the way, I have come to especially appreciate Parker Palmer's works, especially his candid honesty and insights on deal-ing with depression. His book *Let Your Life Speak: Listening for the Voice of Vocation* (San Francisco, CA: Jossey-Bass, 2000) has been especially helpful.

scripture texts rather than a sermon; prayers; the offering; a second hymn; and the benediction. No frills. Communion—alas—is only monthly, but lovely to share in the circle, with different ones stepping up to serve the minister after he has served us. We meet in the adobe chapel that was the church's old 1931 sanctuary. We sit in a circle around a small central table. Attendance typically ranges from eight to fourteen, plus or minus. It is very "basic" worship, still Reformed in spirit and content, and we love it!

Looking ahead, when we recently updated our wills, advance directives, and so on, we noted that when we had done this ten years ago it was for "if" we were to die, but now it is for "when" we die. Doug's full retirement is approaching in about a year and a half. Sometimes, as we observe the growing impact of climate-change-induced aridification on our beloved New Mexico, we talk about relocating to somewhere greener—Oregon, perhaps—but I doubt that we ever will. This is home. At some point, however, we plan to look for a more senior-appropriate house and garden.

At some time in the not-too-distant future, I fear, it is also likely the beloved little Cuba congregation will decide that it is time to disband. (It is now down to nine members on the roll.) We *shall* remain Presbyterian. Otherwise, *God alone* (literally!) knows what may or will come to pass.

I am currently waiting to hear if I get chosen to be on the Special Committee to Write a New Confession of Faith for the PCUSA, a project approved by the 2022 General Assembly. I have no idea if I'll make the cut, but it feels like it would be a great final foray into the life of the larger church. I know I felt called to apply, and we will see if those in charge feel called to choose me.[31]

While feeling somewhat more hopeful for the future of the PCUSA in the near term, I share with so many an ever-deepening concern for the long-term futures of the U.S., of humanity, and of the natural environment and life on Planet Earth. That said, I also keep trying to hold on to the words of the Apostle Paul, written in his own days of challenge and uncertainty long ago, that:

> In all things, God is working toward good for all who love God, who are called according to God's purpose. (Romans 8:28, slightly adapted)

And so, God help us all. Amen!

---

31. In the meantime, see Appendix 4.

The author—February 2019
(Photo by Michael Edminster, used by permission)

IN FROM THE WILDERNESS
Metre: 10.10.10.4 (Tune: Engelberg)

Not included in this book in 2013, this hymn was written upon the final passage of Presbyterian Amendment 10-A to the Book of Order, *May 10, 2011. It was Amendment 10-A which opened the way for LGBTQIA+ ordination in the PCUSA. I deliberately modeled it on various biblical psalms and poetic accounts of the exodus tradition. Verse 4 is very slightly revised here from the original. Now, as then, it is:*

> *"Dedicated to the memory of the Rev. David B. Sindt, Elder C. Willard Heckel, Elder William P. Thompson, Elder Virginia West Davidson, the Rev. Howard Warren, the Rev. Merrill Proudfoot, and others far too numerous to mention who longed for this day."*

God through this wilderness for forty years
You've led your people in the cloud and fire,
And through each hardship you've sustained us still.
Alleluia!

Oppression's burdens slowly slip away,
As we, all children of your covenant,
Have not turned back, though faced with fearful scorn.
Alleluia!

So many died, so many turned away,
So many wondered if this faith was vain,
But still we've journeyed on through darkest days.
Alleluia!

We do not seek to conquer, but to love,
And to embrace each one who hears your call,
To be united in the bond of peace.
Alleluia!

So, as we pause along the river's side
And gaze across into a hoped-for land,
May your own Spirit go before us now.
Alleluia!

Words by the Rev. Kenneth Cuthbertson, PhD
May 2011

Appendix 1

The Confessional Statement of the United Presbyterian Church of North America (1925)

TRANSCRIBED, WITH NOTES, BY REV. KENNETH CUTHBERTSON, PHD, OCTOBER 2012

The contents of Appendices 1 and 2 have not been publicly available for many years. When I wished to consult them during my preparation of the manuscript of The Last Presbyterian? *there was no version currently available from the PCUSA. After locating an old copy belonging to a family member, I transcribed the* Confessional Statement *(including the full original scriptural notes) and extensive excerpts of the* Book of Government and Worship *of the United Presbyterian Church of North America (UPNA), and shared my transcriptions with the Office of the General Assembly of the PCUSA.[1] I include them here as background documentation for both the theological and practical (polity and worship) cultures of the UPNA during the first half of the twentieth century.*

In 1925, the UPNA adopted a Confessional Statement which sought to restate the Reformed theology of the seventeenth century Westminster Standards in terms of what the UPNA had come to believe in the context of early twentieth-century America. The statement was prepared and submitted by a committee of nine men, but was primarily the work Dr. John McNaugher of Pittsburgh (later Pittsburgh-Xenia) Theological Seminary, who chaired the

---

1. As the corporate successor body of the UPNA, the PCUSA is the current rights holder to these documents, and I include them here with the permission of the Office of the General Assembly.

group. Some of the old Westminster topics were omitted or revised, while new topics were added. The statement omitted, for the most part, distinctly theological and technical language, but accompanied all its articles with extensive citations of scripture texts (moved herein to footnotes). The Confessional Statement set a precedent for the writing of new confessional documents for Presbyterian bodies in the US, such as the UPCUSA's Confession of 1967[2] and also the PCUSA's Brief Statement of Faith.[3]

PREAMBLE

The United Presbyterian Church of North America declares afresh its adherence to the Westminster Confession of Faith and Catechisms, Larger and Shorter, as setting forth the system of doctrine taught in the Scriptures, which are the only infallible and final rule of faith and practice. Along with this it affirms the right and duty of a living Church to restate its faith from time to time so as to display any additional attainments in truth it may have made under the guidance of the Holy Spirit. Accordingly, by constitutional action consummated June 2, 1925, it adopted the following Confessional Statement. This Statement contains the substance of the Westminster symbols, together with certain present-day convictions of the United Presbyterian Church. It takes the place of the Testimony of 1858, and wherever it deviates from the Westminster Standards its declarations are to prevail.

Subscription to the foregoing Subordinate Standards is subject to the principle maintained by our fathers, that the forbearance in love which is required by the law of God is to be exercised toward any brethren who may not be able fully to subscribe to the Standards of the Church, while they do not determinedly oppose them, but follow the things which make for peace and things wherewith one may edify another.

In keeping with its creedal declaration of truth, the United Presbyterian Church believes that among the evangelical communions of the world there is "one Lord, one faith, one baptism," and therefore, shunning sectarian temper, it cherishes brotherly love toward all branches of the Church Universal and seeks to keep the unity of the Spirit in the bond of peace.

---

2. The writing of *The Confession of* 1967 occurred as part of the 1958 merger of the UPNA and the old P.C.U.S.A.

3. *A Brief Statement of Faith* was adopted in 1991 after the 1983 union of the UPCUSA with the predominantly southern-based PCUS to form the current PCUSA.

ART. I. OF GOD

We believe that there is one living and true God, a self-existent, personal Spirit, eternal and unchangeable, the creator, upholder, and ruler of the universe, a God of infinite love, mercy, holiness, righteousness, justice, truth, wisdom, and might. We believe that the one God exists as the Father, the Son, and the Holy Spirit, and that these three Persons are the same in substance, equal in power and glory.[4]

ART. II. OF DIVINE REVELATION

We believe that the works of nature, the mind and heart of man, and the history of nations are sources of knowledge concerning God and His will, though insufficient for human need; that a clearer revelation came through men who spake from God, being moved by the Holy Spirit: and that in the fullness of the time God perfectly revealed Himself in Jesus the Christ, the Word made flesh.[5]

ART. III. OF HOLY SCRIPTURE

We believe that the Scriptures of the Old and New Testaments are the Word of God and are inspired throughout, in language as well as thought; that their writers, though moved by the Holy Spirit, wrought in accordance with the laws of the human mind; that they faithfully record God's gracious revelation of Himself and bear witness of Christ; and that they are an infallible rule of faith and practice and the supreme source of authority in spiritual truth.[6]

---

4. Gen. 1:1, 26, 27; Gen. 17:1; Exod. 3:14; Exod. 34:6; Deut. 6:4; Deut. 32:4; Deut. 33:27; Neh. 9:6; Psa. 9:8; Psa. 62:11; Psa. 90:2; Psa.103:19; Psa. 108:4; Psa. 145:8,9; Isa. 6:3; Isa. 40:26, 28; Isa. 45:21, 22; Isa. 57:15; Isa. 65:16; Jer. 10:10; Jer. 31:3; Mal. 3:6; Matt. 28:19; Mark 12:29; John 4:24; John 5:19, 26; John 10:30, 38; John 17:3, 5; Acts 17:28; Rom. 2:5; Rom. 5:8; Rom. 11:33; 2 Cor. 13:14; Eph. 1:11, 19; Eph. 2:4; Phil. 2:6; 1 Thess. 1:9; 1 Tim. 1:17; Jas. 1:17; 1 Pet. 1:2; 1 John 4:8; Rev. 4:11.

5. Gen. 1:27; Deut. 32:8; Psa. 19:1–6; Psa. 119:105; Luke 1:70; John 1:1, 10, 14, 18; John 5:39; John 10:30; John 14:9; Acts 3:21; Acts 14:17; Acts 17:26, 27, 30; Rom. 1:18–21; Rom. 2:14, 15; 1 Cor. 1:21; Gal. 1:12; Heb. 1:1–3; 2 Pet. 1:21.

6. Deut. 18:15; Psa. 19:7–11; Psa. 119:160; Isa. 8:20; Isa. 11:1, 2; Matt. 4:4; Luke 16:29; Luke 24:27, 44; John 5:39; John 10:35; John 16:13; Acts 1:16; Acts 3:18; Acts 8:35; Acts 10:43; Rom. 1:1–4; Rom. 3:2; 1 Cor. 2:13; Gal. 3:16; Eph. 3:3–5; 2 Tim. 3:16; Heb. 3:7; 1 Pet. 1:10, 11; 2 Pet. 1:21.

ART. IV. OF THE DIVINE PURPOSE

We believe that all things which have come to pass, or are yet to come to pass, lie within the eternal and sovereign purpose of God, either positively or permissively, and are ordained for the manifestation of His glory; yet is God not the author of sin, nor is the free agency of moral beings taken away.[7]

ART. V. OF CREATION

We believe that God, for His own wise ends, was pleased in the beginning to create by His infinite power the universe of the worlds, and that all intelligent beings, human and superhuman, are the product of His will; that through progressive stages he fashioned and ordered this world in which we dwell, giving life to every creature; and that He created man with a material body and with an immortal spirit made in His own image, and intelligence, feeling, and will, possessed of holiness and happiness, capable of fellowship with Him, free and able to choose between good and evil, and therefore morally responsible.[8]

ART. VI. OF PROVIDENCE

We believe that God is above all His works and in them all; that He upholds all things by His own supreme will and energy, providing for and preserving His creatures according to the laws of their being; and that He directs and governs all events to the praise of His glory. We believe that, while in relation to the eternal purpose of God, the First Cause, all things are fixed immutably, they are accomplished through the operation of second causes, although as an extraordinary proof of His presence, God may dispense with natural means and instrumentalities.[9]

---

7. Gen. 45:7, 8; Gen. 50:20; Job 1:12; Job 2:6; Psa. 33:11; Prov. 16:33; Isa. 46:9–11; Luke 22:22; Acts 2:23; Acts 4:27, 28; Acts 13:29; Rom. 8:28; Rom. 11:36; Eph. 1:4–6, 11, 12;– Phil. 2:12, 13; Jas. 1:13, 14.

8. Gen. 1:1–31; Gen. 2:7, 16, 17; Deut. 30:19; Josh. 24:15; Psa. 33:6; Isa. 40:26; Jer. 27:5; Acts 17:24, 25; 1 Cor. 8:6; Eph. 3:9; Col. 3:10; Heb. 11:3; Heb. 12:9; 1 John 1:3; Rev. 4:11.

9. Exod. 15:18; Josh. 24:17; Neh. 9:6; Psa. 22:28; Psa. 47:7; Psa. 77:13–15; Psa. 93:1; Psa. 103:19; Psa. 135:6; Psa. 145:9, 15; Isa. 40:26; Ezek. 21:27; Dan. 4:25; Zech. 14:9; Matt. 5:45; Matt. 6:26; Acts 2:23; Acts 17:25, 28; Acts 27:24, 31; Rom. 11:36; Jas. 1:17; 1 Pet. 5:7.

ART. VII. OF ANGELS

We believe God created a superhuman order of intelligent and immortal beings, mighty in strength, to be the servants of His will: that these are of various ranks; that, having been placed under probation, some kept their original holiness and were confirmed therein, while some fell into sin, and remain fallen; that holy angels are the ministers of God's providence in the interests of His kingdom and the human race; and that the apostate angels, led by Satan, their personal head, are seeking to establish a dominion of evil by the temptation and corruption of men.[10]

[*The presence of this article may seem somewhat incongruous, but as the Westminster Standards—as well as scripture—address the existence and fall of the angels in various places, a statement about them in this document is understandable. While the article does not explicitly address the origin or nature of evil, it does set a context for its entry into the world.*]

ART. VIII. OF THE SIN OF MAN

We believe that our first father Adam was created sinless and that there was held out to him a promise of eternal life dependent on perfect obedience for a season, while the penalty of disobedience was to be death, bodily and spiritual; that Adam, as the common ancestor of the race, was constituted the representative head of the human family; that he broke the Divine command through temptation of the devil, by which transgression he fell from his original state of holiness and communion with God and came into bondage to sin; that in consequence all men descending from him by ordinary generation have come under condemnation and are born with a sinful nature which is alienated from God and from which proceed all actual transgressions; and that out of this condition of guilt and depravity none are able to deliver themselves.[11]

---

10. Gen. 19:1; Psa. 91:11; Psa. 103:20, 21; Matt. 4:3; Matt. 13:41; Matt. 24:31; John 8:44; Acts 7:53; Acts 12:7–11; 2 Cor. 4:4; Eph. 1:21; Eph. 6:11, 12; 1 Tim. 5:21; Heb. 1:14; 1 Pet. 3:22; 2 Pet. 2:4; Jude 6; Rev. 20:1–3.

11. Gen. 2:16, 17; Gen. 3:19; Hos. 6:7; John 6:44; John 8:34; Rom. 3:19, 20; Rom. 5:12, 14, 17; Rom. 6:23; 1 Cor. 2:14; 1 Cor. 15:22; 2 Cor. 11:3.

ART. IX. OF SALVATION

We believe that God, Who is rich in mercy, out of His infinite love for the world, entered from all eternity into a covenant of grace with His Only-begotten Son, wherein the Son, standing as the representative of sinners and their mediator with God, freely consented to secure for them a full salvation by taking their humanity and through a life of obedience and a vicarious death satisfying the Divine law and providing a perfect righteousness for all who believe on Him; that because of this covenant there was held forth from the first, immediately after the Fall, a promise of redemption, in fulfillment of which, when the time of preparation was ended, Christ Jesus came into the world and wrought out a salvation sufficient for all and adapted to all; and that they who accept this salvation, being born anew, are restored to the fellowship of God, given a desire to forsake sin and live unto righteousness, and made heirs of eternal life. [12]

ART. X. OF ELECTION

We believe that the Eternal Father, before the foundation of the world, in His own good pleasure gave to His Son a people, an innumerable multitude, chosen in Christ unto salvation, holiness, and service; that all of these who come to years of discretion receive this salvation through faith and repentance; and that all who die in infancy, and all others who are given by the Father to the Son and are beyond the reach of the outward means of grace, are regenerated and saved by Christ through the Holy Spirit, Who works when and where and how He pleases.[13]

ART. XI. OF GOD THE FATHER

We believe that within the Godhead the Father is the First Person in the order of office and operation; that in some inconceivable manner, by eternal generation, He is the Father of the Only-begotten Son; that from

12. Gen. 3:15; Psa. 40:7, 8; Isa. 42:21; Isa. 53:4–6; Isa. 55:1; Jer. 31:3; John 1:12; John 3:16; John 5:24; John 10:29; John 17:1–26; Acts 5:31; Rom. 3:22; Rom. 5:1–11; Rom. 8:5, 30; Rom. 10:4; Rom. 12:1; 1 Cor. 1:30; Gal. 4:4, 5; Eph. 1:7; Eph. 2:4, 5; Eph. 4:20–24; 1 Tim. 2:5; Tit. 1:2, 3; Heb. 7:22, 25; Heb. 8:6; Heb. 9:12, 15, 28; Heb. 12:24; Heb. 13:20; 1 Pet. 2:24; I John 4:10; 1 John 5:11, 12; Rev. 22:17.

13. Mark 10:14, 15; Luke 18:16; John 6:37, 39; John 17:6, 9; Acts 10:3; Acts 13:48; Acts 17:27; Rom. 8:29, 30; Eph. 1:4; Eph. 2:10; 2 Thess. 2:13; 2 Tim. 1:9; 1 Pet. 1:1, 2; Rev. 5:9; Rev. 7:9.

Him and from the Son the Holy Spirit proceeds; that with the Son and the Holy Spirit He abides in mutual union and fellowship; and that He is the originating source in creation and redemption. We believe that He is the Father of all men as His rational and moral creatures, made after His likeness; that, beyond His universal benevolence He so loved the world of humanity as to provide a common salvation at the cost of immeasurable self-sacrifice; and that, though men as sinners have lost the privileges of sonship and denied its obligations, they still retain traces of their heavenly Father's image and share in His providential care and bounty. We believe in the fatherhood of God in a pre-eminent sense with reference to those who become His children by regeneration and adoption, and who yield a filial response to His love; that in His parental relationship with these He attains to the satisfaction of His desires for men; that He welcomes them into communion with Himself, makes them partakers of His holiness, and works out for them His gracious purpose in all that pertain to their present and eternal well-being.[14]

ART. XII. OF THE LORD JESUS CHRIST

We believe that the Lord Jesus Christ is the Eternal Son of God, having a Sonship that is natural and necessary, inhering in the very constitution of the Godhead; that, freely laying aside His Divine glory and majesty, He became man by taking to Himself a true body and soul, yet without sin, being conceived by the power of the Holy Spirit and born of the Virgin Mary; that thus He is very God and very man, two whole and distinct natures, the Divine and the human, being joined together in His one Person, never to be divided; and that He, the God-man is the sole mediator between God and men, by Whom alone we must be saved. We believe that the Lord Jesus Christ was anointed by the Holy Spirit to be our perfect and eternal prophet, priest, and king; that He has revealed the will and counsel of God; that for our redemption He fulfilled all righteousness by His holy obedience and His propitiatory sacrifice for the sin of the world; that, having died upon the cross and been buried, He rose from the dead by a physical resurrection and ascended into heaven, where as their advocate

14. Gen. 1:26, 27, Gen. 6.2, Num. 16.22; Psa. 2:7; Isa. 63:16; Mal. 2:10; Matt. 3:17; Matt. 5:45; Matt. 6:9; Matt. 17:5; Luke 3:38; Luke 15:11–32; John 1:14, 18; John 3:16; John 5:20, 26; John 10:29; John 16:28; Acts 2:33; Acts 17:26–29; Rom. 8:11, 14, 15, 28; 1 Cor. 8:6; Gal. 3:26; Gal. 4:6; Eph. 3:14, 15; Heb. 1:2, 3, 5; Heb. 12:9, 10; Jas. 3:9; 1 Pet. 1:3, 11, 17; 2 Pet. 1:4; 1 John 4:7, 9.

He makes continual intercession for His people; that He abides in believers as an indwelling presence, communicating newness of life and power, and making them sharers of what He has and is; that He sits at the right hand of God as the Head of His Church and Kingdom, with dominion over all created persons and things; and that He will come again in glory for the vanquishing of evil and the restoration of all things.[15]

ART. XIII. OF THE HOLY SPIRIT

We believe that the Holy Spirit is a real personality, the Third Person within the Divine Being, proceeding from the Father and the Son, and together with the Father and the Son is to be believed in, loved, obeyed and worshiped; that He shared in the work of creation, and is the Lord and Giver of all life; that He is everywhere present with men, inclining them unto good and restraining them from evil; that He spoke by the prophets and apostles and inspired all writers of the Holy Scriptures to record infallibly the mind and will of God; that He had peculiar relations with the Lord Jesus Christ, enabling the Son of God to assume our nature without being defiled by sin, and guiding, animating, and supporting the Saviour in His mediatorial work; that the dispensation of the gospel is especially committed to Him, in that He accompanies it with His persuasive power and urges its message upon the reason and conscience of men, so that they who refuse its merciful offer are without excuse. We believe that the Holy Spirit is the only efficient agent in the application of redemption, convicting men of sin, enlightening them in the knowledge of spiritual realities, moving them to heed the call of the gospel, uniting them to Christ, and dwelling in them as the source of faith, of power, of holiness, of comfort, and of love; that He abides in the Church as a living Presence, giving efficacy to its ordinances, imparting various gifts and graces to its members, calling and anointing its ministers for their holy service and qualifying all other officers for their special work; and that by Him the Church will be preserved, edified, extended throughout the world, and at last be glorified in the heavenly places with Christ.[16]

15. Matt. 1:20; Matt. 3:15; Matt. 28:16–20; Luke 1:30–35; Luke 3:21, 22; Luke 4:18; John 1:1, 14, 18, 33; John 3:13, 16; John 10:36; John 14:6; John 15:5; John 17:5; John 20:19–29; Acts 1:9–11; Acts 2:33; Acts 3:21; Acts 4:12; Acts 10:38; Rom. 3:24, 25; Rom. 8:3, 17, 32, 34; Rom. 9:5; 1 Cor. 15:3, 4, 25; Gal. 1:12; Gal. 4:4, 5; Eph. 1:20–23; Eph. 3:17; Phil. 2:6–11; 2 Thess. 1:7–10; 1 Tim. 1:15; 1 Tim. 2:5; Heb. 1:5, 8, 13; Heb. 2:14; Heb. 7:25, 26; Heb. 12:24; 1 Pet. 1:7, 13; 1 Pet. 3:22; 1 John 1:5; 1 John 2:1, 2; 1 John 4:2; Rev. 1:5, 6.

16. Gen. 1:2; 2 Sam. 23:2; Job 26:13; Psa. 139:7; Zech. 4:6; Matt. 1:18–25; Matt.

ART. XIV. OF THE ATONEMENT

We believe that our Lord Jesus Christ, by the appointment of the Father, and by His own gracious and voluntary act, gave Himself a ransom for all; that as a substitute for sinful man His death was a propitiatory sacrifice of infinite value, satisfying Divine justice and holiness, and giving free access to God for pardon and restoration; and that this atonement, though made for the sin of the world, becomes efficacious to those only who are led by the Holy Spirit to believe in Christ as their Saviour.[17]

ART. XV. OF THE GOSPEL CALL

We believe that the gospel is a revelation of grace to sinners as such, and that it contains a free and unconditional offer of salvation through Christ to all who hear it, whatever may be their character or condition; that the offer is in itself a proper motive to obedience; and that nothing but a sinful unwillingness prevents its acceptance.[18]

ART. XVI. OF REGENERATION

We believe in the necessity of regeneration, whereby we who by nature are spiritually dead are made new creatures, established in union with Christ, released from bondage to sin, and made alive unto God; that this is the immediate act of the Holy Spirit, who changes the governing disposition of the soul by a secret and direct operation of His power; and that ordinarily, where years of understanding have been reached, regeneration is wrought in connection with the use of Divine truth as a means.[19]

4:1; Matt. 12:28; Matt. 28:19; Luke 1:35; Luke 4:14; John 14:16, 26; John 15:26; John 16:7–14; Acts 1:2, 8; Acts 2:1–4, 38; Acts 7:51; Acts 8:17; Acts 10:38; Acts 16:7; Rom. 8:9, 11, 13, 16, 26; 1 Cor. 2:4, 10–13; 1 Cor. 12:4; 2 Cor. 13:14; Gal. 4:6; Gal. 5:16–23, 25; Eph. 2:18; Eph. 3:16; Eph. 4:30; Phil. 1:19; 1 Thess. 1:5; Heb. 9:14; 1 Pet. 1:11; 2 Pet. 1:21; 1 John 2:20.

17. Psa. 40:7, 8; Psa. 139:7; Matt. 20:28; John 1:29; John 3:16; John 10:18; Rom. 3:25; Rom. 8.3, 4; 1 Cor. 15:3; Gal. 2:20; Gal. 3:13; 1 Tim. 2:4–6; 1 Tim. 4:10; Heb. 10:5–10, 14, 19; 1 Pet. 1:19; 1 John 2:2; 1 John 4:10.

18. Isa. 55:1; Matt. 9:13; Matt. 11:28; John 3:16; John 6:37; Rom. 1:16, 17; Rom. 10:8–10; Eph. 1:13, 14; Heb. 4:7; Rev. 22:17.

19. Ezek. 11:19; John 3:3–6; 1 Cor. 1:30; 2 Cor. 5:17; Gal. 4:5–7; Eph. 2:1, 5; Eph. 5:26; Tit. 3:5, 6; Jas. 1:18; 1 Pet. 1:23.

ART. XVII. OF SAVING FAITH

We believe that saving faith is the gift of God; that in it there is not merely an assent to the truth that the Lord Jesus Christ is the Saviour of sinners, but also a cordial acceptance and appropriation of Him, and a fixed reliance upon Him, as our Saviour; that this faith, which involves the conviction of the mind, the trust of the heart, and the obedience of the will, rests solely upon the free and unlimited offer of Christ made in the gospel to sinners of mankind; and that such faith is the necessary and all-sufficient condition and channel for the communication of every spiritual gift and the progressive realization of salvation.[20]

ART. XVIII. OF REPENTANCE

We believe that saving faith issues in repentance, which is essentially a turning away from sin unto God, accompanied not only with sorrow over sin, but with hatred of sin and with an earnest desire and sincere purpose to obey God's righteous law; that, while repentance is produced in the believing sinner by the Holy Spirit, it springs from a sense of sin as involving guilt and defilement and from an apprehension of God's mercy in Christ; that it is not to be rested in as any satisfaction for sin, or any ground of the pardon thereof, and yet it is of such necessity that none are saved without it; and that it is evidenced by humble confession of sin before God and by reparation for wrongs done to men.[21]

ART. XIX. OF JUSTIFICATION

We believe that justification is a judicial act of God by which in His free grace He places sinners in a new relation to Himself and His law, so that henceforth they are forgiven and accepted as righteous in His sight; that the procuring cause or ground of this is not anything wrought in them, or done by them, but only the perfect righteousness of Christ, embracing all that He did in the way of obedience and all that He suffered in their stead

---

20. Mark 1:15; John 1:12; John 3:16; John 20:27, 28; Acts 10:43; Acts 15:9; Rom. 10:17; Rom. 13:14: Gal. 2:16; Gal. 5:6; Eph. 2:8; Col. 2:6; 2 Tim. 1:12; Heb. 3:15; Heb. 11:6; Jas. 2:14–26; 1 Pet. 1:21; 1 John 5:4, 10.

21. Isa. 6:5; Matt. 3:2, 8; Luke 3:3, 8; Luke 5:32; Luke 13:5; Luke 15:18; Luke 24:47; John 16:8; Acts 2:38; Acts 15:9; Acts 20:21; Acts 26:20; Rom. 2:4; Rom. 7:24; 2 Cor. 7:10, 11; 1 Thess. 1:9; 2 Pet. 3:9.

while on earth, a righteousness imputed to them, and received by faith alone; and that the evidence of justification is holy living.[22]

ART. XX. OF ADOPTION

We believe that adoption is an act of the free grace of God whereby those that are justified are received into the number of His saved children, have His Name put upon them, have the Spirit of His Son given them, are the objects of His fatherly care and discipline, are admitted to the liberties and privileges of the family of God, and are made heirs of all the promises and fellow-heirs with Christ in Glory.[23]

ART. XXI. OF SANCTIFICATION

We believe that sanctification is the carrying on to completion of the great change effected in regeneration, being a progressive deliverance from the dominion and defilement of sin and a corresponding growth in holy character; that it is wrought by the power of the indwelling Spirit, whereby union with Christ is maintained and holy dispositions are fostered; that in sanctification believers are fellow-workers with the Holy Spirit, being called to faith and repentance, to true obedience in motive and act, to dedication of themselves to the will of God, and to a diligent use of the outward means of grace; and that, while, because of defective faith and human frailty, perfection never can be reached in the present life, it is nevertheless the duty of believers to aim at entire conformity to the will of God, to which, with advancing experience and fuller appropriation of Christ, they may increasingly approach.[24]

22. Isa. 53:11; Acts 13:39; Rom. 3:22–26; Rom. 4:25; Rom. 4:1, 9, 16, 18, Rom. 6:22; Rom. 8:1, 30, 33; 1 Cor. 6:11; Gal. 2:16; Gal. 3:24; Eph. 1:7; Phil. 3:9; Tit. 3:7; Jas. 2:18.

23. John 1:12; Rom. 8:15–17, 23; 2 Cor. 6:18; Gal. 3:26; Gal. 4:4–6; Eph. 1:5; Tit. 3:7; Heb. 12:7, 8; 1 John 3:1; Rev. 3:12.

24. Psa. 19:12, 13; Ezek. 36:25–27; Matt. 5:48; John 17:17; Acts 15:9; Acts 29:32; Rom. 6:1–6, 12, 14; Rom. 7:18, 23, Rom. 8:13, Rom. 13:14; 1 Cor. 1:30; 1 Cor. 6:11; 2 Cor. 3:18; 2 Cor. 7:1; Gal. 2:20; Gal. 5:16, 17, 24; Eph. 1:4; Eph. 3:16–19; Eph. 4:11, 12, 15, 16, 23, 24; Eph. 5:26; Eph. 6:10; Phil. 2:12, 13; Phil. 3:12–14; Phil. 4:13; Col. 1:10, 11; 1 Thess. 5:23; 2 Thess. 2:13; 2 Tim. 2:21; Heb. 12:1, 14; 1 Pet. 1:2; 1 Pet. 2:11; 2 Pet. 3:18; 1 John 1:5–10; 1 John 3:6, 9; 1 John 5:4.

ART. XXII. OF UNION WITH CHRIST

We believe that all who receive Christ by saving faith are made one with Him in a mystical union through the Holy Spirit; that thereby they become vitally related to Him as the Sin-bearer and the Life-giver, insuring their acceptance with God, their renewal of nature, and their growth in holiness and fruitfulness; and that believers thus joined to Christ as their Head, and nourished by His life communicated to them, are bound together in one spiritual organism, which is called the body of Christ.[25]

ART. XXIII. OF THE SECURITY OF BELIEVERS

We believe that, because of the original purpose, the unchanging love, and the constant operation of God, all who are brought into vital union with Christ, and are members of His mystical body, abide permanently in a state of grace and finally are made perfect in glory; that, while such fall into sin, and come under God's fatherly displeasure, until they humble themselves and make confession, they never become utterly apostate; and that this continuance on the part of believers is accomplished by the Holy Spirit in harmony with their rational nature, the warnings, cautions, and exhortation of Scripture addressed to them being used to foster self-examination, watching, prayer, and the faithful observance of all sacred ordinances.[26]

ART. XXIV. OF ASSURANCE

We believe that from the first the believer has a persuasion, proportioned to the strength of his faith, that he is saved, this initial confidence resting on the promise and power and faithfulness of God; that, in addition, there is the assurance of sense or feeling, to which he attains through his conscious possession of the graces of the children of God and through the inner witness of the Holy Spirit; and that it is the privilege and duty of every believer to give diligence to attain this conscious assurance of salvation

25. John 14:19; John 15:1–5; John 17:21–23; Rom. 6:3–5; Rom. 8:1; 1 Cor. 1:30; 1 Cor. 12:12, 13, 27; 2 Cor. 4:10, 11; 2 Cor. 5:17; Eph. 1:23; Eph. 5:30; Col. 2:10, 19.

26. Psa. 51:1–7; Psa. 73:23; Jer. 31:3; Jer. 32:40; Matt. 24:24; Matt. 26:69–74; Luke 22:31, 32; John 8:31; John 10:28, 29; John 17:2, 3, 11, 24; Rom. 8:31–39; 1 Cor. 8:8, 9; 1 Cor. 9:27; Eph. 4:30; Phil. 1:6; 2 Thess. 3:3; 2 Tim. 2:19; Heb. 3:12; Heb. 4:1, 7; Heb. 6:4–6, 9, 10; Heb. 7:25; Heb. 10:10, 14; Heb. 13:20, 21; 1 Pet. 1:5, 8, 9; 2 Pet. 1:10; 1 John 2:17, 19, 27; 1 John 3:9; Jude 20, 21, 24.

whereby he may live in joy and peace, may be moved the more by love and thanksgiving to God, and may be led to a fuller obedience and service.[27]

ART. XXV. OF THE LAW OF GOD

We believe that the moral law of God summarized in the Ten Commandments, proclaimed by the prophets, and unfolded in the life and teachings of Jesus Christ, is of perpetual obligation; that it demands not only right acts and words, but also right dispositions and states of mind; that it is of use to all men in setting before them the inflexibly holy will of God, in discovering to them sin in its true light, and in preparing the way for the gospel of grace; and that although believers, because of their justification, are not subject to it as a condition of salvation, they are required to obey it as a rule of action and standard of character.[28]

ART. XXVI. OF THE STUDY OF GOD'S WORD

We believe that Holy Scripture, as God's written Word, is adapted to the spiritual needs of man, containing whatever doctrine is necessary to salvation and all things that pertain to life and godliness; that, therefore, it deserves and demands our reverent attention and our deepest thought; and that the reading and study of the Word, when entered upon with a mind illumined by the Holy Spirit and with prayerful reflection, will always prove an efficacious means of grace, transforming life and character.[29]

27. Psa. 23:1–6; Psa. 73:23–26; Rom. 5:2, 5; Rom. 8:16, 38, 39; Rom. 15:13; 2 Cor. 1:21, 22; Eph. 1:13, 14; Eph. 4:30; Col. 2:2; 2 Tim. 1:12; Tit. 2:11–14; Heb. 6:11, 17–19; Heb. 10:22; 1 Pet. 1:3; 2 Pet. 1:4, 10, 11; 1 John 2:3; 1 John 3:2, 3, 14, 19, 21, 24; 1 John 4:13, 16; 1 John 5:13.

28. Psa. 19:7, 8, 11; Psa. 119:4; Jer. 31:33; Matt. 5:17–19, 21–48; Matt. 6:1–34; Matt. 22:37–40; Acts 13:39; Rom. 3:20, 31; Rom. 6:14; Rom. 7:4, 6, 7, 9, 12, 14, 22, 25; Rom. 8:4; Rom. 10:4; Rom. 13:8; 1 Cor. 7:19; 1 Cor. 9:20, 21; Gal. 2:16; Gal. 3:13, 21, 24; Gal. 4:4, 5; Gal. 5:14; Eph. 6:2; 1 Tim. 1:8; Heb. 8:10; Jas. 1:25; Jas. 2:8, 9, 12; 1 John 2:3, 4, 7, 8.

29. Psa. 1:1–3; Psa. 19:7; Psa. 119:130; Matt. 21:42; Matt. 22:29; Luke 24:27, 32: John 5:39; Acts 8:30–35; Acts 17:11; Rom. 15:4; Eph. 6:17, 18; 1 Tim. 4:6; 2 Tim. 3:15–17; Heb. 4:2; Jas. 1:21, 25.

ART. XXVII. OF PRAYER

We believe that prayer is an indispensable condition of fellowship with God and a vital requirement in spiritual growth and the obtaining of promised mercies; that it must be offered in the name of Christ, in reliance on His merits, and by the help of the Holy Spirit; that it includes adoration, thanksgiving, aspiration, the outpouring of the soul in converse with God, confession of sin and shortcomings, supplication for pardon and all blessings promised in the gospel, and petition for such temporal benefits as may be agreeable to the Divine will; that remembrance of others at the throne of grace is an obligation without which the life of prayer cannot be fully realized; and that God has given the intercession of His children an essential place in bringing about the salvation of men and in promoting the advance of His Kingdom and the doing of His will on earth.[30]

ART. XXVIII. OF PRAISE

We believe that God is worthy of all praise and adoration because of His glorious perfections as unfolded in creation, providence, and redemption; that praise as a definite ordinance of worship is expressed in words joined to music; and that in this ordinance the Psalms of the Bible, by reason of the Divine inspiration, their excellence, and their evident design, are accredited for permanent use, together with meritorious evangelical hymns in which are expressed the experiences, privileges, and duties of the Christian life.[31]

[*This statement marks the official shift of the UPNA from the historic Presbyterian practice of exclusive psalmody to the use of "evangelical hymns" in addition to the Psalms. The 1925 statement was followed in 1927 by the release of* The Psalter Hymnal *by the UPNA.*]

30. Neh. 1:4–11; Psa. 17:1; Psa. 32:5; Psa. 62:8; Psa. 122:6; Ezek. 36:37; Dan. 9:4; Matt. 5:44; Matt. 6:9–15; Matt. 7:7, 8, 11; Mark 11:24; Luke 11:2–4; Luke 18:9–14; John 14:13, 14; John 16:23, 24; Acts 9:11; Rom. 8:26, 27; 1 Cor. 1:2; Eph. 1:3, 15–23; Eph. 3:14–19; Eph. 6:18, 19; Phil. 1:9; Phil. 4:6; Col. 4:3, 12; 1 Thess. 5:25; 1 Tim. 2:1–4, 8; Heb. 4:16; Jas. 1:5–8; Jas. 5:16; 1 Pet. 2:5; 1 John 1:9; 1 John 5:14, 15; Jude 20, 21, 25.

31. 2 Sam. 23:1, 2; 1 Chron. 16:7–9, 23; 2 Chron. 29:30; Psa. 47:6, 7; Psa. 95:1, 2; Psa. 105:2; Psa. 137:3; Psa. 147:1; Psa. 150:1, 2; Matt. 26:30; Luke 20:42; Luke 24:44; Acts 1:20; Rom. 15:9; Eph. 1:6, 12, 14; Eph. 5:19; Col. 3:16; 2 Tim. 3:16; Rev. 4:11; Rev. 5:9–14; Rev. 14:3; Rev. 15:3, 4.

ART. XXIX. OF SABBATH OBSERVANCE

We believe that the holy Sabbath, originally a memorial of creation, is an institution which has its foundation in the revealed will of God, which was established for the physical, moral, and spiritual well-being of man, and which was designed for all ages and nations; that its transfer from the last day of the week to the first, commemorating the resurrection of the Redeemer of mankind, was effected by Christ's own example and by Apostolic sanction; that, in the spirit of gratitude for the blessings it conveys, the Sabbath, or the Lord's Day, should be hallowed by refraining from worldly employments and recreations and, aside from the duties of necessity and mercy, by devoting the day to public and private worship, spiritual culture, and Christian activities; and that the civil Sabbath of legally protected rest, because of its great and manifold benefits to human society, should be maintained and defended against desecration.[32]

ART. XXX. OF THE SACRAMENTS

We believe that the sacraments of Baptism and the Lord's Supper were instituted by Christ and are of perpetual validity and obligation; that they are signs and seals of the new covenant and channels of a real communication of grace to those receiving them in faith; and that through their observance the Church of Christ confesses her Lord and is visibly distinguished from the world.

We believe that baptism with water into the Name of the Father and of the Son and of the Holy Spirit is the sacrament that recognizes membership within the Church, in which are set forth union to Christ, regeneration and cleansing by the Spirit, the remission of sins, and our engagement to be the Lord's; that it is rightly administered by the pouring or sprinkling of water upon the person, but the mode is not essential; that not only are adult believers to be baptized, but also the children of believers before reaching the age of accountability, on the faith of the parents, who appropriate for their children the benefits which the sacrament offers and promise to rear them in the nurture and admonition of the Lord.

We believe that the Lord's Supper is the sacrament of communion with Christ, in which bread and wine are given and received in thankful

---

32. Gen. 2:2, 3; Exod. 20:8–11; Exod. 31:13; Lev. 19:30; Neh. 13:15–22; Isa. 56:2–7; Isa. 58:13, 14; Isa. 66:23; Jer. 17:24–27; Matt. 5:17, 18; Matt. 12:2–12; Mark 2:27, 28; Luke 4:16; John 20:19, 26; Acts 2:1; Acts 20:7; 1 Cor. 16:2; Rev. 1:10.

remembrance of Him and of His sacrifice on the cross, and they who in faith receive the same partake of the body and blood of the Lord Jesus Christ, after a spiritual manner, to their building up in grace; that it should never be engaged in without previous self-examination as to a sincere desire to be cleansed from all sin, a true and living faith in the Lord Christ, and brotherly love toward all; and that all are to be invited to the Lord's Supper who have confessed their faith in Christ and are leading a Christian life.[33]

[*As with Praise, the affirmation here, that all who have confessed their faith in Christ, etc., are to be invited to the Lord's Supper, marks the official shift of the UPNA away from the old practice of closed Communion, formerly practiced by the Church and its predecessor denominations.*]

ART. XXXI. OF LAWFUL OATHS AND VOWS

We believe that an oath is an act of religious worship in which we solemnly call upon the only true and living God to witness the truth of what we affirm or our voluntary assumption of an obligation to do something in the future, with an implied imprecation of God's judgment if we lie or prove false to our engagements; that the proper circumstances under which an oath may be taken are those in which serious and perfectly lawful interests are involved, in which an appeal to God is necessary to secure confidence and end strife, and where the oath is imposed by the duly constituted authority of Church or State.

We believe that a vow is a promise formally made to God, in way of thankfulness for mercy received, or for the obtaining of what we desire; that it is of like sacred nature with an oath, because it is God to Whom the promise is made; that a vow cannot bind to do that which is unlawful or impossible, nor where its continued observance is inconsistent with our spiritual interests; and that to vow on a trifling occasion, or, having rightly vowed, to fail in performance, is to be guilty of profanity.[34]

---

33. Gen. 17:7; Isa. 52:15; Ezek. 36:25; Matt. 26:26–30; Matt. 28:19; Mark 10:13–16; Mark 14:22–25; Luke 18:15–17; Luke 22:17–20; John 3:5; John 6:48–58; Acts 2:38–41; Acts 8:12, 37, 38; Acts 16:15, 33; Acts 22:16; Rom. 4:11; Rom. 6:3, 4; 1 Cor. 7:14; 1 Cor. 10:1–4, 16, 17, 21; 1 Cor. 11:23–34; 1 Cor. 12:13; Gal. 3:27; Eph. 5:25, 26; Col. 2:12; Tit. 3:5; 1 Pet. 3:21.

34. Gen. 24:2–9; Gen. 28:20–22; Exod. 20:7; Lev. 19:12; Deut. 6:13; Deut. 10:20;

[*This article helps to explain the historic and strong opposition of the UPNA to Freemasonry and other such fraternal organizations, which bound their members by oath and secret vows. See also Article XXXV's statement on secret associations. This understanding of oaths and vows was, also, the historical basis of Presbyterian rejection of the vows of celibacy, etc., in the Roman Catholic Church.*]

ART. XXXII. OF THE CHURCH

We believe that there is one holy Catholic or Universal Church, consisting of the whole number of those of every age and nation who have been chosen of God unto salvation and redeemed by the Lord Jesus, and who, being united by the holy Spirit to Christ their living Head, are one spiritual body in Him; that it is the will of Christ that His Church on earth should exist as a visible brotherhood, composed of all those who profess faith in Him and obedience to His laws, together with their children, organized for the confession of His Name, the public worship of God, the preaching and teaching of the Word, the administration of the sacraments, the nurture and fellowship of the children of God, the propagation of the gospel, and the promotion of social righteousness; and that all particular Churches or ecclesiastical denominations throughout the world which hold the fundamental truths of evangelical religion and own allegiance to Jesus Christ as Divine Lord and Saviour are to be regarded as within the one visible Church.[35]

ART. XXXIII. OF CHURCH ORDER.

We believe that the supreme and only head of the Church is the Lord Jesus Christ, under Whose authority and according to Whose will the worship, teaching, discipline, and government of the Church are to be administered; that through those who serve lawfully in the offices of the Church Christ

---

Deut. 23:21; Judg. 11:30, 36, 39; 2 Chron. 6:22, 23; Neh. 5:12; Neh. 13:25; Psa. 15:4; Psa. 61:8; Psa. 66:13, 14; Psa. 76:11; Psa. 116:14; Prov. 20:25; Eccl. 5:5; Isa. 65:16; Jer. 4:2; Matt. 5:33–37; Mark 6:23, 26; Acts 18:18; Acts 23:12–14; 2 Cor. 1:23; Gal. 1:20; Heb. 6:16; Jas. 5:12.

35. Psa. 2:8; Psa. 22:27–31; Matt. 16:18; Matt. 18:17; Matt. 28:18–20; John 10:16; John 17:21, 24; John 21:15–17; Acts 8:1; Acts 13:1; Acts 20:28; Rom. 15:9–12; Rom. 16:1, 3–5, 16, 23; 1 Cor. 1:2; 1 Cor. 4:17; 1 Cor. 10:32; 1 Cor. 12:12, 13, 28; 1 Cor. 15:9; 1 Cor. 16:19; Gal. 1:2, 13, 22; Eph. 1:10, 22, 23; Eph. 2:19, 20; Eph. 3:10; Eph. 4:11–13; Eph. 5:23–32; Phil. 3:6; Phil. 4:15; Col. 1:18, 24; 1 Tim. 3:15; Heb. 12:23; Rev. 7:9, 10; Rev. 22:16.

exercises mediately His own power and enforces His own laws; and that the Presbyterian form of church polity is in accordance with the Scriptures.[36]

[*See Appendix 2, the UPNA's* Book of Government and Worship, *Part I, Chapter VI, for a description of the biblical basis of Presbyterian polity and an explanation of how it differs from both episcopal and congregational forms of church governance.*]

ART. XXXIV. OF THE MINISTRY

We believe that Jesus Christ as the Head of the Church has appointed therein the official ministry of reconciliation; that He calls men to this ministry through the working of the Holy Spirit in their hearts and by the orderings of providence; and that those thus called are to be set apart by ordination, whereby they are solemnly invested with the authority, powers, and duties of their sacred office.[37]

[*The rationale and functions of the offices of ordained ministry in the Presbyterian system—Ministers of the Word, Ruling Elders, and Deacons—are detailed in Appendix 2, the UPNA's* Book of Government and Worship.]

ART. XXXV. OF CHURCH FELLOWSHIP

We believe that all who have accepted Christ as their Redeemer should unite themselves with some branch of the visible Church, in order to share in the privileges and responsibilities of its members and confess Christ before men; that under Christ they should yield the Church their supreme loyalty, honoring its ordinances and seeking its welfare in season and out of season; and that with this they should forsake all association, whether secret or open, that they find prejudicial to their Church allegiance and a hindrance to the fulfillment of Christian duties.[38]

---

36. Matt. 16:19; Matt. 18:17, 18; Matt. 28:18–20; John 20:23; Acts 14:23; Acts 15:2–29; Acts 16:4; Acts 20:17, 28; 1 Cor. 12:28; 2 Cor. 2:6–8; Eph. 4:11, 12; Eph. 5:24; Phil. 1:1; Col. 1:18; 1 Thess. 5:12; 1 Tim. 3:1–13; 1 Tim. 4:14; 1 Tim. 5:17; Tit. 1:4–9; Heb. 13:7, 17, 24; 1 Pet. 5:1.

37. Matt. 9:38; Acts 13:2, 3; 1 Cor. 3:5; 1 Cor. 4:1; 1 Cor. 12:28; 2 Cor. 5:18; Eph. 4:11, 12; Eph. 6:21; Phil. 1:1; Col. 1:7; Col. 4:7, 17; 1 Thess. 3:2; 1 Tim. 4:14; 1 Tim. 5:22; 2 Tim. 1:6; 2 Tim. 4:5; Heb. 13:7, 17; 1 Pet. 5:1–4.

38. Matt. 10:32; Acts 2:41, 42, 47; Acts 11:26; 1 Cor. 10:32; 1 Cor. 12:13; 1 Cor. 16:2;

ART. XXXVI. OF THE FAMILY

We believe that the family is the unit [*sic!*] of society and is fundamental to human welfare; that marriage is ordained of God, and is therefore an institution which involves a religious as well as a civil contract; that the law of marriage, requiring monogamy, governing the prohibited degrees of consanguinity or affinity, and establishing the permanence of the tie, is laid down in the Word of God, upon which the enactments of the State may not transgress rightfully; that the true Christian home is built on the Divine ideal of marriage, is sanctified by the Holy Spirit, and is observant of family religion; and that it is the duty of parents to dedicate their children to God and give them a moral and spiritual training for the making of character. We believe that since the standard of marriage is a lifelong union of one man and one woman, its dissolution is not to be lightly regarded; that, where warrantable, this can be effected only by competent civil authority; and that the remarriage of divorced persons is permissible, while both parties are living, only when the divorce has been obtained on the ground of adultery, and then for the innocent party alone.[39]

[*Divorce became a major issue in American churches in the wake of WWI and the social changes of the 1920s. The strong wording of this article reflects that context.*]

ART. XXXVII. OF CIVIL GOVERNMENT

We believe that civil government is an ordinance of God, instituted for His glory and the welfare of society, and that the sovereign authority of the Lord Jesus Christ extends over this province of human life, so that States and their rulers are responsible to Him and are bound to render Him obedience and to seek the furtherance of His Kingdom upon earth, not, however, in any way constraining religious belief, imposing religious disabilities, or invading the rights of conscience; that it is binding on all to yield willing submission to constituted authorities except where this very clearly conflicts with the still higher duty of obedience to God; and that the due fulfillment of our

2 Cor. 6:14–18; Eph. 4:11–13; Eph. 5:11; 1 Tim. 3:15; Heb. 10:25; 1 John 2:15, 16, 19; Rev. 18:4.

39. Gen. 1:27, 28; Gen. 2:24; Gen. 5:1, 2; Lev. 18:6–30; Deut. 6:6, 7; 1 Sam. 1:11, 28; Jer. 1:5; Amos 2:7; Matt. 5:31, 32; Matt. 19:3–9; Mark 6:18; Mark 10:2–12; Rom. 7:2, 3; 1 Cor. 5:1; 1 Cor. 7:10–16, 39; Gal. 1:15; Eph. 5:22–33; Eph. 6:1–4; Col. 3:18–21; 2 Tim. 3:15; Heb. 13:4.

duties as citizens includes a loyal consent to taxation for the necessities of the State and the lesser civic communities, the giving of aid to all worthy public causes, and faithful participation in the government of the country.[40]

ART. XXXVIII. OF THE SOCIAL ORDER

We believe that the Divine plan for mankind includes a social order in harmony with the ideals and spirit of Jesus Christ; that the triumph of the Kingdom of God in its present aspect would mean not only its establishment in the hearts of men individually, but a world in which righteousness and brotherhood should prevail; and that a primary duty of the Church is to give positive witness that the Christian principles of justice and love should have full expression in all relationships whatsoever—personal, industrial, business, civic, national, and international.[41]

ART. XXXIX. OF THE INTERMEDIATE STATE

We believe that the souls of the righteous dead are immediately made perfect in holiness, and during the interval until the resurrection, though separated from the body, continue conscious, active, and at peace in the presence and fellowship of Christ, Who, after His ascension, sat down on the right hand of God; that in the abode of woe the souls of the impenitent wicked also continue conscious and active, enduring punishment for their sins; and that this intermediate state is one of incompleteness, the supreme blessedness of the saints and the utter wretchedness of the lost beginning only with their resurrection and the judgment.[42]

ART. XL. OF THE SECOND ADVENT

We believe that the Lord Jesus Christ, Who at His ascension was received up into heaven, will come again to earth in person, visibly, with power and

40. Psa. 2:10–12; Psa. 22:28; Psa. 47:7–9; Psa. 82:1, 2; Prov. 8:15, 16; Matt. 22:21; Acts 4:19; Rom. 13:1–7; Eph. 1:20–22; 1 Tim. 2:1, 2; Tit. 3:1; 1 Pet. 2:13, 14, 17; Rev. 17:14; Rev. 19:16.

41. Exod. 20:1–17; Micah 6:8; Mark 12:30, 31; Acts 17:26; Rom. 13:1–10; Eph. 6:5–9; Phil. 1:27; Col. 3:22–4:1; Jas. 5:1–6.

42. Luke 9:28–36; Luke 16:19–31; Luke 23:43; John 8:56; John 14:3; Rom. 8:23; 1 Cor. 15:26; 2 Cor. 5:8–10; Phil. 1:6, 23; 1 Thess. 1:10; Heb. 11:39, 40; Heb. 12:23; 1 Pet. 1:7; 1 Pet. 3:19; 1 John 3:2; Jude 6; Rev. 7:9; Rev. 19:1–5.

great glory; that His coming marks the consummation of the Kingdom of God; that the time thereof is reserved in the Divine counsels; and that this blessed hope is to be cherished as an incentive to watchful living and faithful witness-bearing on the part of Christ's followers.[43]

[*Most UPNA ministers, college and seminary professors, etc., held to a post-millennial view of the Second Coming, and believed that the millennial Kingdom of Christ would be spiritual in nature. The Church deliberately never officially adopted that position as an article of faith, however, since it was felt that it would impose a particular system of interpretation, and would have enforcement implications via Church discipline, that were deemed impractical. Nonetheless, both Article XXXVIII and Article XLIV of the Confessional Statement pretty clearly imply a post-millennial perspective.*]

ART. XLI. OF THE RESURRECTION

We believe that through the power of Almighty God there will be a bodily resurrection of all the dead, both of the just and of the unjust; that to the just it will be a resurrection unto life and to the unjust a resurrection unto condemnation; and that the mortal bodies of those who are fallen asleep in Jesus, as well as of the faithful who are alive at His coming, will be fashioned anew and conformed to the body of His glory.[44]

ART. XLII. OF THE JUDGMENT

We believe that, at the resurrection, He Who alone can read the heart will judge the world in righteousness by Jesus Christ; that the wicked, being condemned for their inexcusable sin and depravity, will go away into eternal punishment; and that the righteous, although made manifest before the judgment-seat of Christ, will be acquitted and eternally accepted, and of God's grace rewarded according to their deeds.[45]

43. Matt. 24:29–51; Matt. 25:1–13, 31–46; Mark 13:33–37; Luke 9:26; Acts 1:7, 11; Acts 3:21; 1 Thess. 1:10; 1 Thess. 4:16, 17; 1 Thess. 5:1–11; Heb. 9:28; 1 Pet. 5:4; 2 Pet. 3:8–13; Rev. 1:7.

44. Job 19:26; Dan. 12:2; John 5:25, 28, 29; John 11:23–25; Acts 24:15; Rom. 8:11, 23; 1 Cor. 15:12–58; 2 Cor. 4:14; Phil. 3:11, 21; 1 Thess. 4:15, 16; 2 Tim. 2:18; Heb. 11:35.

45. Gen. 18:25; Matt. 10:15; Matt. 12:36; Matt. 25:31–46; Luke 12:47, 48; Luke 16:26; John 5:22, 24, 27–29; Acts 10:42; Acts 17:31; Acts 24:25; Rom. 2:5–16; Rom.

ART. XLIII. OF THE LIFE EVERLASTING.

We believe in, and with glad and solemn hearts look for, the consummation and bliss of the life everlasting, wherein the people of God, freed from sin and sorrow, shall receive their inheritance of glory in the Kingdom of the Father, and with capacities and powers exalted and enlarged, shall be made fully blessed in the fellowship of Christ, in the perfected communion of saints, and in the service of God, Whom they shall enjoy forever and ever.[46]

ART. XLIV. OF CHRISTIAN SERVICE AND THE FINAL TRIUMPH.

We believe that, as disciples and servants of Christ, we are bound to further the extension of His Kingdom by our prayers, gifts, and personal efforts, to defend the truth, to do good to all men, to maintain the public worship of God, to hallow the Sabbath, to preserve the inviolability of marriage and the sanctity of the family, to uphold the just authority of the State, and to live in all honesty, purity, and charity. We obediently receive the word of Christ bidding His people go into all the world and make disciples of all nations, declaring unto them that God is in Christ reconciling the world unto Himself, and that He will have all men to be saved and come to the knowledge of the truth. We confidently believe in the ultimate and complete triumph of our Saviour King, that by His grace and power all His enemies shall ultimately be overthrown, and the Kingdom of this world shall become the Kingdom of our Lord and of His Christ.[47]

8:33; Rom. 14:10; 1 Cor. 4:4, 5; 1 Cor. 6:2, 3; 1 Cor. 11:32; 2 Cor. 5:10; 2 Thess. 1:8, 9; 1 Tim. 5:24; 2 Tim. 4:1; Heb. 6:2; Heb. 9:27; Heb. 10:27; Heb. 12:23; Jas. 1:12; 2 Pet. 2:4; 2 Pet. 3:7; 1 John 4:17; Jude 6, 14, 15; Rev. 20:11–15.

46. Psa. 16:9–11; Psa. 17:15; Psa. 23:6; Psa. 73:24–26; Matt. 25:21, 23, 34, 46; Luke 23:43; John 3:15, 16; John 14:3; John 17:22–24; Rom. 6:22; Rom. 8:18–25; 1 Cor. 13:12; 2 Cor. 4:17; 2 Cor. 5:8; Phil. 1:23; Col. 3:4; 2 Tim. 4:8; Heb. 9:15; Heb. 12:22–24; Jas. 1:12; Jas. 2:5; 1 Pet. 1:3–5; 1 Pet. 5:1, 10; 2 Pet. 1:11; 1 John 3:2; Rev. 3:4; Rev. 7:13–17; Rev. 14:13; Rev. 21:3, 4; Rev. 22:1–5.

47. Exod. 20:8; Psa. 2:1–12; Psa. 22:27, 28; Psa. 72:8–17; Matt. 6:10; Matt. 13:31, 32; Matt. 16:18; Matt. 19:3–9; Matt. 24:14; Matt. 28:19, 20; Rom. 7:2, 3; Rom. 13:1–7; 1 Cor. 15:24–28; 2 Cor. 5:19; 2 Cor. 9:7–15; Gal. 6:10; Eph. 4:1, 2; 2 Thess. 1:7–10; 1 Tim. 2:4; Tit. 2:11–14; Heb. 10:25; Heb. 13:4; 1 Pet. 2:13, 14; Jude 3; Rev. 5:12–14; Rev. 11:15; Rev. 19:11–16; Rev. 22:17.

Appendix 2

Excerpts from The Book of Government and Worship of the United Presbyterian Church of North America

TRANSCRIBED BY REV. KENNETH CUTHBERTSON, PHD, OCTOBER 2012.

The general rationale for including these excerpts of The Book of Government and Worship *of the UPNA is stated in Appendix 1.* The Book of Government and Worship *was a revision of earlier constitutional documents adopted in 1910. Amendments to the document, occasioned by the adoption of* The Confessional Statement, *were made in 1925. Further amendments were made in 1936, 1938, 1939, 1943, 1946, 1947, 1948, and 1950. The following excerpts exemplify the theological rationale for the organization and worshipping life of the UPNA, along with key distinctives and directives that shaped the life of the community. Although divided into four distinct parts and various chapters, the paragraphs of the entire document were numbered sequentially throughout, and that enumeration is used in what follows.*[1]

---

1. As the corporate successor body of the UPNA, the PCUSA is the current rights holder to these documents, and I include them here with the permission of the Office of the General Assembly.

PART I. CHURCH ORGANIZATION

Chapter I. Of the Church

1. The Church Invisible.—The invisible Church, which is catholic, or universal, consists of the whole number of those who have been chosen of God unto salvation and redeemed by the Lord Jesus.

2. The Church Visible.—The visible Church is a formal organization which consists of all those throughout the world who profess publicly their faith in the Lord Jesus Christ and obedience to His laws, together with their children . . . .

Chapter III. Of the Ends of the Church

10. The Ends of the Church Defined.—The great ends of the Church are the proclamation of the gospel for the salvation of men, the shelter, nurture, and holy fellowship of the children of God, the maintenance of Divine worship, the preservation of the truth and appointments of pure religion, the promotion of social righteousness, and the exhibition of the Kingdom of Heaven to the world.

[*This section of* The Book of Government and Worship *was later adopted by the UPCUSA and PCUSA, and a slightly revised version is prominently featured in the "Foundations of Presbyterian Polity" section of the PCUSA Book of Order.*[2]]

Chapter IV. Of Church Power

13. The Ministerial Nature of Church Power.—The power of the church is only ministerial and declarative. The Holy Scriptures determine all legislation and procedure which are warrantable.

14. The Jurisdiction of the Church.—The jurisdiction of the Church extends to those only who are within its membership, and is limited to their spiritual interests and duties as the disciples of Christ.

---

2. PCUSA, *Book of Order,* F-1.0304.

Chapter V. Of Church Members

15. Requisites to Church Membership.—All who profess faith in Christ and obedience to his laws and ordinances are members of the visible Church, and are entitled to all its rights and privileges.

16. The Children of Professed Believers.—Through the covenant of God with His people the infant children of professed believers are with the Church. By reason of this they are entitled to baptism and pastoral care . . . .

Chapter VI. Of the Form of Church Government

19. Presbyterian Church Government.—Government by elders, or presbyters, is a New Testament ordinance. This form of organization is according to the plan of government developed under the Old Testament and brought to completion in the synagogue system. The first congregations of the New Testament Church were, by apostolic authority, organized after the model of the synagogue, and by the same authority the principle of government by elders was applied to the organization of the Church at large.

Chapter VII. Of Vocation to Office and of Ordination

21. What Constitutes a Call.—A call from God to a certain office is a conviction wrought in the heart of a person by the Holy Spirit, through the Word and providence of God, that he is required by the Divine will to serve the Lord in that position, together with the election thereto of God's people, and the concurring judgment of a lawful court of the Church.

25. Nature of Ordination.—Ordination is the official recognition [*by a court of the Church*] of a Divine call to an office or work in the Church, dedication thereto, and solemn investiture in the name of Christ with its authority, powers, and duties. The formal act of ordination consists in prayer and the laying on of hands, to which there should be added the giving of the right hand of fellowship.

Chapter VIII. Of the Officers of the Church

26. Ordinary and Permanent Officers.—The ordinary and permanent Church officers enumerated in the New Testament are ministers of the Word, or teaching elders, ruling elders, and deacons.

Chapter IX. Of Ministers of the Word.

27. The Nature of the Office.—The ministers of the Word are the highest ordinary officers of the New Testament Church. They are called by different names in Scripture to express the different relations and duties of their office. As they are commissioned to declare the Divine will and in Christ's stead to beseech men to be reconciled to God they are termed ambassadors. As they make public proclamation of the gospel, they are termed preachers. As they expound the Word and exhort and convince gainsayers, they are termed teachers. As they dispense the manifold grace of God and the ordinances instituted by Christ they are termed stewards of the mysteries of God. As they serve Christ and His people, they are termed ministers. As they have oversight of souls and of the activities of the Church, they are termed bishops. As they feed the flock of Christ with spiritual food, they are termed pastors. As it is their duty to be grave and prudent, and to govern well in the Church of Christ, they are termed presbyters or elders.

28. Duties of the Office.—(1) Peculiar Duties. The peculiar duties of the minister of the Word are to make authoritative proclamation of the gospel of Christ, expound the Word of God, administer the sacraments, instruct and lead the people in holy things, bless the people in the name of God, and minister the manifold grace of God to the wants of all men . . . .

29. Qualifications for the Office.—They who occupy this office should possess such a competency of human learning and be so enlightened by the Spirit of God that they may be capable teachers of Divine truth, so fashioned in character and life by the Spirit that they may stand before the people as fit representatives of the Lord Jesus Christ, and so endowed with wisdom that they may efficiently conduct the affairs of the Kingdom which are committed to their charge.

Chapter X. Of Ruling Elders

31. Authorization of the Office.—It appears from the New Testament that that the organization of a local church required a body of ruling elders, chosen by the people, to be associated with the pastor, or teaching elder, in the government and oversight of the congregation.

33. Duties of the Office.—It belongs to ruling elders to have an oversight of the spiritual interests of the congregation, to be a help to the pastor by instructing the ignorant, encouraging the weak, reproving and reclaiming the erring, and visiting and comforting the sick, and in the courts [*with the ministers*] to exercise the power of ordination and government.

Chapter XI. Of Deacons

37. Nature of the Office.—The office of deacon is one of service, without the power of ordination or government.

38. Duties of the Office.—Deacons are helpers to the pastor and the elders of a congregation in the work of the Lord as visitors to the sick, ministers to the poor, succorers to those in trial, and messengers of the gospel in the homes of the people.

Chapter XII. Of the Courts of the Church

43. Nature and Relations.—These courts are all alike presbyterial as being composed exclusively of presbyters . . . . The session exercises jurisdiction over a single church; the presbytery over what belongs in common to the ministers, sessions, and congregations within a prescribed district; the synod over what belongs in common to a group of presbyteries, and their ministers, sessions, and congregations; and the General Assembly over such matters as concern the whole Church.

[*From this point, Part I continues with organizational matters concerning each of the church courts, their members, officers, procedures, records, etc. Part II of the* Book of Government and Worship *covers matters of General Administration, including the organization of congregations, church membership, the training and call of ministers, ordination of ministers, election and ordination of elders and deacons, etc. Part III covers Discipline, with a brief excerpt included here.*]

PART III. DISCIPLINE

Chapter I. General Principles

209. Definition.—Discipline is the exercise of that authority and the application of that system of laws which the Lord Jesus Christ has given to His Church for the edification of its members and for its work in the world. In general it embraces the instruction, training, and control of the members and their children for their growth in grace, and the orderly exercise of authority by the officers and courts for the maintenance of the truth and the promotion of the spiritual life of the Church.

213. Necessity and Objects.—Discipline in this limited sense is necessary because of the imperfection of the members and officers of the Church, and their liability to depart from the truth and fall into sin, and the possibility that the constituted courts may err in judgment and violate established rules of procedure. Its object is to vindicate the honor and authority of Jesus Christ and advance the glory of God by removing offenses, reclaiming the erring, and advancing the purity and peace of the Church.

214. Grounds of Discipline.—Anything in the avowed belief or the life of a minister or member of the Church, or in the proceedings and judgments of a court, which is contrary to the Word of God and to the doctrines and regulations of the Church is a ground of discipline.

[*Along with the right preaching of the Word and the right administration of the sacraments, "godly discipline rightly administered" was one of the historic "marks" of the Church defined by the Scottish reformers in the sixteenth century. The intention was that discipline be pastoral in nature, although historically it was vulnerable to abuses that too often were ungraciously authoritarian and punitive in nature. Part III continues with guidelines and processes for both administrative discipline (questions concerning church order) and judicial discipline (dealing with persons charged with offenses against "truth and righteousness or the peace and good order of the Church"). Sentences imposed against persons found guilty of an offense included admonition, rebuke, suspension (from membership privileges, including participation in the sacraments), deposition (from office), and excommunication. Offenders could be restored to full privileges and participation in the body when there was satisfactory evidence of repentance and reformation. Decisions by a lower church court could be appealed to higher courts.*]

PART IV. WORSHIP

Chapter I. Introductory

326. Definition of Worship.—Christian worship is a sincere and reverent outgoing of the spirit to God in silent communion or outward expression.

327. Object of Worship.—Worship is due to God alone as He is revealed to us in the Scriptures as the Father, Son, and Holy Spirit, and is to be offered in the way of His appointment.

329. Necessity and Duty of Worship.—Inasmuch as the worship of God is essential to the Christian life and to growth in grace, it should be carefully and habitually observed, and the spirit of worship should be cultivated by the study of the Word of God, meditation, and prayer.

Chapter II. Of the Seasons of Worship

333. Set Times of Worship.—While a devotional frame of mind should always be maintained, yet set times for Divine worship are specifically recognized in the Word of God.

334. The Sabbath.—Under the gospel dispensation God has appointed the first day of the week as the Christian Sabbath, the Lord's Day, to be kept holy and specially devoted to His worship.

[*See Article XXIX of* The Confessional Statement *(Appendix 1) for the theological rationale of Sabbath observance.*]

335. Other Times of Worship.—In addition to the Sabbath, special days of worship may be appointed by the Church or State when circumstances make such an appointment proper or necessary. Congregations and companies of disciples should have stated times other than the Sabbath for prayer and the study of the Scriptures.

336. Morning and Evening Worship.—It is especially appropriate that the morning and evening be observed as seasons for private and family worship.

[*It is notable that, as late as 1948, when this edition of the book was published, there was no mention of the observance of Christmas, Maundy Thursday, Good Friday, Easter, or Pentecost in the UPNA directory for worship. However, earlier prohibitions against observing them had been dropped. Observance of a national day of Thanksgiving was allowed (see below, paragraph 382).*]

Chapter III. Of Places of Worship

337. Meeting Places Necessary.—True and acceptable worship may be rendered to God in whatever place offered, but as God has made special promises of His blessing to His people when they unite in His worship, it is necessary that suitable places should be provided where they may gather together in His presence.

338. Such Places Sacred.—Buildings set apart to the worship of God should be regarded as His sanctuaries, and nothing should be admitted into

them which will tend to destroy that thought in the minds of the people, or beget associations hurtful to spiritual worship.

339. Suitable.—The sanctuaries of God should be made as beautiful and suitable as the simplicity of New Testament worship and the circumstances of the people will permit.

Chapter IV. Of the Ordinances of Public Worship

341. Ordinances of Public Worship.—The stated ordinances of public worship as set forth in the Holy Scriptures are: prayer and praise; the reading, preaching, and hearing of the Word of God; the administration of the sacraments of baptism and the Lord's supper; Christian giving; and the benediction. To these a formal declaration of Christian faith may be added. Special ordinances are fasting and thanksgiving.

Chapter V. Of the Order of Worship

342. Order of Worship.—To maintain the dignity of worship, and that it may be of profit, an order of exercises is usually necessary; but to secure liberty also in worship this order should be subject to such variations as the circumstances of the occasion and the promptings of the Spirit may suggest to the officiating minister . . . .

Chapter VI. Of the Reading of the Scriptures

343. The Manner of Reading.—The reading of the Scriptures in an integral part of public worship, and should have a place in every service. The importance of this ordinance demands studious and prayerful preparation on the part of the minister. With due reverence and thoughtfulness he should so read the Word that the message of the Spirit may be clearly expressed.

Chapter VII. Of the Singing of Praise

345. Matter of Praise.—Praise as a definite ordinance of worship is expressed in words joined to music. In this ordinance the Psalms of the Bible, by reason of the Divine inspiration, their excellence, and their evident design, are accredited for permanent use. The poetical versions of the Psalms used in praise shall be such as may be authorized from time to time by the Church.

[*The UPNA Confessional Statement uses essentially the same language found here, but adds the phrase, "together with meritorious evangelical hymns in which are expressed the experiences, privileges, and duties of the Christian life." The 1925 statement was the first instance of hymnody, as distinguished from exclusive psalmody, authorized by the UPNA. The 1927* Psalter Hymnal *contained 155 hymns in addition to settings for all the Psalms.*]

346. Manner of Praise.—In praising God we should sing thoughtfully, reverently, fervently, with grace in the heart, as becometh the worship of the High and Holy One. That this service may be rendered in a proper manner, the congregation should carefully cultivate a knowledge of music.

347. All Should Sing.—The whole congregation should join in this part of worship. Some suitable person or persons should be employed to lead in the singing, but none should be appointed to this service who are not of known Christian character.

348. Regulation of Praise.—It belongs to the session to regulate the singing of praise in the congregation and to see that this important part of public worship is rendered for edification and in the best possible manner.

[*In the current PCUSA* Directory for Worship, *oversight of the musical selections lies with the minister.*]

Chapter VIII. Of the Offering of Prayer

349. Manner of Prayer.—Prayer, being a near approach to God and an essential channel of blessing, should have a prominent place in every

service and should be offered with the utmost reverence of thought, language, and manner, and with the humility that becomes a worshiper in the presence of the Most Holy God.

350. Number of Prayers.—The number of prayers in a service should be governed by the order of worship approved by the Church and the enlightened judgment of the minister. Each prayer should be adapted to its place in the service, and repetitions and injudicious length should be avoided.

[*The three principal prayers that are detailed and described are an invocation, the long prayer before the sermon, and a concluding prayer after the sermon. This follows the model of the seventeenth-century Westminster Directory for Worship.*]

Chapter IX. Of the Benediction

356. The Benediction.—The minister should conclude the services of worship with a solemn benediction.

357. Form.—The following form of benediction may be used: "The grace of the Lord Jesus Christ, and the love of God, and the communion of the Holy Spirit be with you all. Amen."

Chapter X. Of Preaching the Word

359. Importance of Preaching.—As the preaching of the Word is of chief importance as a means of salvation, it should receive special attention, and every minister should prepare for this service with much study, meditation, and prayer.

360. The Sermon.—Every sermon should be the unfolding of the truth taught in some portion of Scripture and a close application to the heart and conscience of the hearer.

361. Purpose and Preparation.—The minister should seek the aid of the Holy Spirit that he may be enabled to declare all the counsel of God, to present the Word in its variety and application to the different relations of life, and clearly and fully present the Lord Jesus as the Saviour of men.

Chapter XI. Of the Administration of Baptism

362. Administrator.—Baptism is a sacrament of the New Testament Church, and, therefore, may be administered only by an ordained minister of the gospel.

[*While it is clearly assumed throughout that worship is to be led by Ministers of the Word, the administration of the sacraments of Baptism and the Lord's Supper are the only two things explicitly restricted to them alone and, with the latter, always in conjunction with the elders.*]

363. Subjects.—Baptism, being a seal of the New Covenant, is to be administered to those who make a credible profession of their faith in Christ and to their children.

364. Mode.—Baptism is administered by the application of water to the person by sprinkling or pouring. The Church recognizes the validity of baptism by immersion.

365. Obligations.—Baptism involves solemn obligations on the part of the parents and those to whom the ordinance is administered . . . .

[*The section continues with the questions asked of parents at the baptism of children, or of adults at their own baptism. Additional directions for conducting the service of baptism include the prescribed use of the words, "I baptize thee in the name of the Father, and of the Son, and of the Holy Spirit. Amen." Baptism was ordinarily administered in the church as part of public worship. Exceptions were allowed if authorized by the session and done in connection with religious exercises.*]

Chapter XII. Of the Administration of the Lord's Supper

368. Administrator and Communicants.—The Lord's supper, being a sacrament of the New Testament Church, is to be administered under the direction of the session by an ordained minister, and only to those who have confessed their faith in Christ and are leading a Christian life.

[In the earlier practice of the UPNA, and the antecedent AP and ARP Churches, the ministers and elders were expected to examine the faith and life of prospective communicants, then issue them a communion token admitting them to the table on that day. The UPNA originally practiced "closed" Communion until, in the 1925 Confessional Statement, the official position of the church changed to allow baptized believers from other churches to participate.]

369. Time and Place.—The Lord's supper should be observed frequently, but how often the session of each congregation must determine . . . .

[The common practice of many congregations in this era was to have communion four times a year, at the beginning of January, April, July, and October.]

The ordinance should, ordinarily, be administered in the stated place of worship. Being a service for the communion of the saints, it may not be administered privately by the minister; but in a case of sickness or long-continued inability to attend upon the public service, it may be administered in a private house under the direction of the session.

370. Preparation.—The minister should be careful to instruct his people from time to time in the nature and purposes of the sacrament and the duty and privilege of every follower of Christ to observe it regularly. As those who receive the sacrament are required to examine themselves as to their fitness for the solemn act, the ordinance should be preceded by preparatory services carefully arranged to aid them in their preparation for coming to the Lord's table, to commune with one another, to commemorate the Lord's death, and enter into the New Covenant in His blood.

372. The Administration.—After the introductory services, the communicants shall reverently take their places for the communion during the singing of an appropriate Psalm. The minister shall then read the words of institution, and, after the example of the Lord, give thanks to God and ask His blessing.

He shall then take the bread, break it, and give it to the communicants, saying: "The Lord Jesus in the night in which He was betrayed . . . ."

He shall also take the cup and give it to the communicants, saying: "In like manner also the cup . . . ."

While the elements are being passed by the elders the communicants may be left to their own reflections.

Chapter XIII. Of Prayer Meetings.

[*Guidelines are given for regular congregational prayer meetings held on a regular basis, with the suggestion that like services be held on Sabbaths "when there is no stated preaching of the gospel."*]

377. Sessional Prayer Meetings.—Sessions should frequently meet for conference and prayer, when they should consider the spiritual condition of their congregations, and implore Divine guidance in all that pertains to their office.

Chapter XIV. Of Family Worship

378. Time.—Family worship is essential to the development of household religion, and its daily observance should be faithfully maintained in every Christian home. Parents, and children, and servants should be present at this service.

379. Leader.—The head of the family should ordinarily conduct the service. If the husband is absent or disqualified, the believing wife or other competent person should perform the duty.

380. Order.—Family worship should consist of praise, reading the Scriptures, prayer and such exercises as may be conducive to spiritual life in the home.

Chapter XV. Of Private Worship

381. Its Necessity.—In private worship the believing soul is alone with God. This is essential to growth in grace and the realization of holiness in character and life. Because of the tendency of the human heart to depart from God, and the constant temptations of the world, private worship should be a daily practice.

Chapter XVI. Of Thanksgiving

382. Occasion.—When God gives special tokens of His favor to a nation or the Church, men should unite in public thanksgiving. An annual thanksgiving day by the nation in recognition of Divine mercies bestowed is highly appropriate, and should be observed.

[*Further directions indicate that such days were to include public worship. It was recommended that an offering be received for benevolent purposes, and that a part of the day include works of Christian charity.*]

[*Unlike earlier directories, this version of* The Book of Government and Worship *did not include guidelines for public fasting. Historically, such days were to be observed in response to communal calamities and disasters, at times of communal repentance, and as a means of seeking the guidance and blessing of God, etc. Fast days were kept like a Sabbath, with the community resting from labor and gathering for public worship. Besides food, the people were expected to abstain from "worldly amusements" and to refrain from any sort of ostentatious dress or ornaments.*]

Chapter XVII. Of the Sabbath School.

Chapter XVIII. Of Pastoral Visitation.

[*This was a duty of both ministers and elders, both here and in the section on ministering to the sick.*]

Chapter XIX. Of Systematic Beneficence

392. A Christian Obligation.—The scriptures make it an imperative duty to give a portion of our worldly substance to the Lord. Every member of the church should reduce the duty of beneficence to a system.

393. Spirit and Measure.—The Word of God requires all to give cheerfully, regularly, liberally, and according as God has prospered them.

394. Duty of Instruction.—Ministers and elders should frequently instruct their people in regard to the important duty and privilege of supporting the ordinances of the Church and general Christian charities. They should particularly explain the design of the different missionary agencies and educational institutions of the Church, and the character and necessity of the work which they have in charge.

395. Neglect of the Duty.—If any person of known pecuniary ability fails in this duty, the session should point out his obligation as revealed in the Word of God, the importance of the duty, and the reward attending its faithful discharge. If he still withholds from the treasury of the Lord, it is the duty of the session to deal with him as an offender.

[*No similar disciplinary direction is given under any other heading concerning the ordinances of worship.*]

Chapter XX. Of the Solemnization of Marriage

396. Marriage.—Marriage is a solemn contract between one man and one woman, instituted by God, and sanctioned and acknowledged by the civil law. Marriage is not peculiar to the Church of Christ; yet it is the duty of Christians to marry only in the Lord, and it is becoming to have the marriage solemnized with a religious service and by an ordained minister of the gospel.

397. Parties in Marriage.—The parties in marriage must not be within the degrees of consanguinity or affinity prohibited in the Word of God, nor persons divorced on unscriptural grounds. They must be of years of discretion and capable of making their own choice. If they are under age, the consent of their parents or guardians should be obtained by the minister before solemnizing the marriage.

398. Ceremony.—The minister, having satisfied himself that the parties have complied with the forms required by the laws of the State, shall cause the parties to stand together in the presence of a proper number of witnesses, and shall briefly address them in regard to the institution of marriage and the obligations they are about to assume. They having joined their right hands, he shall address this marriage vow to the man: "Do you, A.B., take this woman whom you now hold by the hand to be your wedded wife; and do you solemnly

promise, in the presence of God and these witnesses, to be a loving and faithful husband unto her till God shall separate you by death?" When this question is answered in the affirmative, he shall address this similar vow to the woman . . . . When this question is answered in the affirmative, the minister shall say: "I pronounce you husband and wife; what, therefore, God hath joined together, let no man put asunder." He shall then conclude the ceremony with a prayer for the Divine blessing to rest upon the newly-constituted family.

[*The giving and receiving of a wedding ring is not mentioned. Before WWII it was common for Protestant marriages to take place in the home, not the church building.*]

399. When Solemnized.—Ordinarily marriage should not be solemnized on the Sabbath.

Chapter XXI. Of Ministering to the Sick.

Chapter XXII. Of the Burial of the Dead

404. Time.—No funeral should take place on the Sabbath except in cases of absolute necessity.

405. Simplicity.—Everything which savors of vain display or fulsome eulogy should be avoided.

406. Service.—Before removing the body to the grave the minister should conduct brief and suitable religious exercises. After interment appropriate words of Scripture may be spoken, followed by prayer and the benediction.

[*Funerals were often held at the home of the deceased, or at a Funeral Home, rather than at the church building.*]

Appendix 3

A Brief Overview of What the Bible Says Concerning Homosexuality

BY KENNETH L. CUTHBERTSON, PHD, 2004

Appendix 3 is included to show the author's understanding of the biblical texts widely seen as dealing with homosexual practice. It seemed appropriate to offer this because of the Presbyterian emphasis on scripture as the guide of faith and life.

1. Jewish and Christian scriptures do speak against sexual acts between persons of the same gender in several circumstances, but heterosexual sex is equally prohibited under all the same circumstances.

The circumstances in which homosexual acts are forbidden or condemned include rape and acts of prostitution associated with idolatry. Heterosexual rape and acts of prostitution associated with idolatry are equally forbidden or condemned.

Compare Genesis 19:1–11 and Judges 19: 22–30 concerning gang rape. See Leviticus 18:21–23, describing acts associated with pagan cults in Egypt and Canaan, and also Deuteronomy 23:17, which deals with both heterosexual and homosexual cult prostitution. Paul's statement in 1 Corinthians 6:9–10 draws on the Greek (Septuagint) translation of Leviticus 18:22 for terminology, suggesting a similar concern with sexual acts connected with prostitution and the practice of idolatry. Paul's statement in Romans 1:26–27 is also clearly focused on idolatry, and seems to be based on an argument found in the Apocrypha, in Wisdom of Solomon 14:12–31.

2. Jewish and Christian scriptures do speak positively about affectional relationships between persons of the same gender.

Loving, covenantal relationships between persons of the same gender are used as some of the highest examples of human relationship in the stories of Naomi and Ruth, David and Jonathan, and the gospel account of the Centurion and his servant.

See Ruth 1:16-17, 1 Samuel 18:1–5, 1 Samuel 20, and 2 Samuel 1, especially verse 20. See also Matthew 8: 5–13, which does not use the usual Greek word for "slave" or "servant," but instead uses the word *pais*, a word that is often used in non-biblical texts to designate the younger and dependent partner in a homosexual relationship in the Greco-Roman world. The atypical behavior of the Centurion in the story—where he is described as "begging" Jesus—certainly implies a deeply affectional relationship between the two.

3. Jewish and Christian scriptures do not speak at all about sexual relations in the context of affectional relationships between persons of the same gender.

Sexual relations in covenanted partnerships are simply not spoken about, positively or negatively. They fall into a gray zone that is not clearly addressed by either the prohibitions addressed in #1 or the affirmations mentioned in #2. (Caveat: there are implicit elements in some #2 texts.)

4. In questions concerning the strict requirements of the Levitical Purity Code versus the dynamics of the Law of Love, the Christian scriptures indicate that Jesus, Peter and Paul consistently set aside the old law in favor of inclusive love and covenantal fidelity.

Jesus's consistent actions were to break down barriers of exclusion for marginalized persons who were previously viewed as unclean or unacceptable. He reached out to women, to persons accused of sexual immorality, to lepers and others who were ritually impure, to social outcasts who had compromised themselves with the occupying powers, to Samaritans, and even to a Roman officer and his personal servant. Love for God and neighbor is the only law of Christ (Matt 22:36–40). Peter's rooftop vision at Joppa, which led to the welcoming of the first Gentile converts, included a command to symbolically embrace non-kosher "abomination" (see Acts 10). Paul similarly strove for full inclusion of the "unclean" gentiles in the early church, without forcing them to embrace the Jewish purity laws of circumcision and diet, vehemently arguing that, in Christ, all such distinctions have been abolished (see Gal 3:27–29).

It is therefore respectfully suggested that there is no biblical basis for continuing to bar sexually active homosexual persons, living in committed relationships characterized by covenantal fidelity, from full inclusion in the Body of Christ, or to discriminate against them in society.

Appendix 4

A New Confession: Following Jesus— A Community of Disciples

I CREATED THIS DRAFT *statement in response to the mandate of the PCUSA 225th General Assembly (2022) to establish a Special Committee to Write a New Confession of Faith. I have applied to be on that committee but have not yet heard if I will be among those chosen to serve. In the meantime, I decided to try my hand at writing my own version of such a statement. While it is thus the work of one author—as are several of our PCUSA Confessions—it has emerged from months, and even years, of ongoing prayerful listening, reading, and reflection. It incorporates many voices and sources, past and present, and is hopefully guided by the Spirit.*

The document is very much shaped by the philosophy of The Book of Confessions.[1] *It is particularly intended to complement, not supersede, A Brief Statement of Faith (1991) which so beautifully and succinctly summarizes the creedal and doctrinal emphases of the Catholic-Ecumenical and Reformed faith traditions. But, whereas the Brief Statement of Faith focuses on affirming our beliefs, this document emphasizes the teachings of Jesus in regard to our shared life and practice of faith as disciples in community. The Brief Statement of Faith's statement on Jesus's life and work is of particular importance as a jumping-off point for this statement (see C-11.2.9–18).*

This draft statement is intended to be very much in continuity with the emphases of the Confession of 1967—along with the Barmen Declaration and the Confession of Belhar—concerning the Christian community (the ecclesia) in the world, addressing civil rights, peacemaking, and economic

1. See the Preface to *The Book of Confessions*, pages iii–iv. See also Chapter One of "The Foundations of Presbyterian Polity" in *The Book of Order* (especially F-1.01 and 1.03–1.0404).

justice. It addresses new discernments concerning human sexuality and gender that have emerged amidst profound controversies and deep struggles over the six decades since the Confession of 1967 was written. It speaks to the question of Christianity in relation to other faith traditions, and it addresses the critical and urgent issue of climate change and earthcare.

The content and format of the statement are closely based on those of the gospels and apostolic letters. The design reflects the insight of various current scholars that Jesus's focus was on instructing and forming his disciples in a new way of living rather than on creating a new creedal system and/or institution. In distinction from most other confessional documents, it includes a candid "confession" of our own communal and institutional sins as well as an affirmation of the "better way" to which Christ calls us all. This Confession is focused on the call of Jesus to "repent" and to "follow" him, individually and communally. It is intended to be a basic, honest, and simple restatement of Jesus's core message, speaking still in and to the twenty-first century. The focus is on the "good news" of the "realm of God/heaven" that Jesus proclaimed.

In addition to the primarily New Testament texts, this draft is par-ticularly influenced by the very early document the Didache,[2] *especially its opening baptismal confession of "the Two Ways" of life and death. In that vein, this is a Confession focused on* praxis. *Another, later influence—which is not included in the* PCUSA's Book of Confessions—*is the* First Helvetic Confession *of 1536 which, unlike its later successor, deeply reflects the imme-diate and basic core emphases of the Reformed Community in Switzerland relatively early on. While more traditionally doctrinal and ecclesially focused than the* Didache, *it is also very practically oriented.*[3]

From our own era, the following content is very much shaped and influenced by the work of recent teachers such as Marcus Borg, Richard Lovelace, J. Mark Dyer, Howard Rice, Andrew Dreitcer, John Philip Newell, Eric Elnes, Diana Butler Bass, Phyllis Tickle, Jack Rogers, Fred Rogers, Cyn-thia Bourgeault, Nadia Bolz-Weber, Victoria Loorz, Sarah Augustine, Rachel

2. See J. B. Lightfoot, *The Apostolic Fathers* (Grand Rapids, MI: Baker Book House, 1978).

3. I know of no English translation of the First Helvetic Confession currently available in print or online. After much searching a couple of years ago, I did finally locate an old book with the sixteenth-century English translation made ca. 1540 by the Scottish Reformer George Wishart, which I transcribed and rendered into relatively modern English.

Srubas, and many others in the Queer, Feminist, Native American, Latinx, African American, Interfaith, and Ex-Evangelical spiritual communities.[4]

NOTE: *The paragraph numeration used below is based on how it would appear if included in* The Book of Confessions.

A NEW PCUSA CONFESSION

Following Jesus—A Community of Disciples

12.01 We trust in a Compassionate and Merciful God,[5] the God of Love,[6] the Ground of All Being,[7] the Source and end of life, light, and all goodness.[8]

12.02 We believe that in every age, including our own, God speaks in and through Christ Jesus, Mary's Child,[9] the Anointed,[10] the Savior[11] of humankind, in whom the fullness of God dwelled bodily[12] in and through the eternal Word and the Spirit of Wisdom.[13]

4. Many of the names here are sufficiently well known as to require no further introduction. Of those who may not be as well known, I would particularly note Andrew Dreitcer, author of *Living Compassion: Loving Like Jesus* (Nashville, TN: Upper Room, 2017); Victoria Loorz, author of *Church of the Wild: How Nature Invites Us into the Sacred* (Minneapolis, MN: Broadleaf, 2021); Sarah Augustine, author of *The Land Is Not Empty: Following Jesus in Dismantling the Doctrine of Discovery* (Harrisonburg, VA: Herald Press, 2021); and Rachel Srubas, author of *The Desert of Compassion: Devotions for the Lenten Journey* (Louisville, KY: Westminster John Knox, 2023).

5. A shared core affirmation of the Abrahamic faiths: Judaism, Christianity, and Islam. For example, see Exod 33:19, 34:6–7b.

6. 1 John 4:8b, 16. Also John 3:16.

7. See Paul Tillich, *Systematic Theology, Vol. 1* (Chicago, IL: University of Chicago Press, 1973). See Gen 1:1–3; Exod 3:13–14; Prov 8:22–31; John 1:1–3b; Col 1:15–17; Heb 1:1–3b.

8. John 1:3c–5, 5:39; Gen 1:1–31; Rev 1:8, 22:13.

9. The full, embodied humanity of Jesus is traditionally expressed in relation to his being born of Mary. In our day, there are many differing opinions among Christians concerning the tradition of the "virgin" birth of Christ, ranging from the very literal to more symbolic understandings. In essence, however, believers in all branches of Christianity are united in affirming the *mystery* of Christ Jesus somehow being both fully human and fully divine, embodied in one and the same person.

10. The *Messiah/Christ*.

11. "Savior" (Greek *soter* from the verb *sozo*) variously encompasses concepts of deliverance and protection, healing, preservation, wellness, soundness, and wholeness.

12. Col 2:9.

13. The *Logos* and the Spirit of *Sophia*. See the Gospel of John. See corresponding

12.03 In following Christ, we believe that the writings contained in the canonical Jewish and Christian scriptures are always to be read and interpreted in light of the life and teachings of Jesus, the Word incarnate among us,[14] as illumined by the Spirit[15] and guided by the all-inclusive rule of love.[16] For the "letter" of literalism and legalism kills, but the Spirit gives life.[17]

12.04 All are beloved by God.[18] Enlivened and united by Holy Spirit,[19] we are invited and called together to be a welcoming family and community of Christ's disciples and friends, trusting together in Christ.[20] We are washed in the triune name and raised to new life.[21] We are fed together at table with one bread of life and cup of salvation, always remembering and giving thanks in the communion of Christ's body and blood.[22]

12.05 Jesus calls each and all of us to repentance and conversion,[23] to renounce and turn from the ways of evil and its power in the world.[24]

---

texts on Holy Wisdom in Prov 8 and Wisdom of Solomon. See also Isa 61:1–2a and Luke 4:16–21; Rom 8:14–17; 1 Cor 2:6–7, 10–13; Eph 1:17–18; Heb 1:1–2.

14. John 1:14; Col 1:19–20, 2:9.

15. John 14:26, 16:12–15; 1 Cor 2:1–13.

16. John 5:39, 15:9–15; 1 Cor 13; Phil 2:5; 1 John 4:7–12. See also PCUSA, *Presbyterian Understanding and Use of Holy Scripture (1983)*, https://www.pcusa.org/site_media/media/uploads/_resolutions/scripture-use.pdf.

17. 2 Cor 3:6. See the Confession of 1967, C-9.27–30, 9.41–42, and 9.49. See also Jack Rogers, *Jesus, the Bible, and Homosexuality* (Louisville, KY: Westminster John Knox, 2006), for case studies on the evolution of Presbyterian thinking about race, women, divorce, and LGBTQIA+ issues.

18. Mark 1:11; Matt 3:17; Luke 3:22; John 3:16, 15:9, 12–13.

19. John 17:20–21; Acts 10:34–35, 44–48a; Rom 8:14–17; 1 Cor 12:12–13.

20. Mark 1:17, 3:33–35; Matt 11:28–29, 28:19–20; John 13:34–35, 14:1–6a, 15:14–15; Acts 2:39, 10:34b–35. Greek *ecclesia* refers to the community of those "called out" together and gathered in Christ.

21. Matt 28:18–20; Rom 6:3–4. In New Testament usage, Greek *baptizo* refers to washing or cleansing by ceremonial ablution. See also **12.19** below.

22. Matt 26:26–29; Mark 14:22–26; Luke 22:14–23; 1 Cor 11:23–26. Also Lev 17:11; Matt 8:11; John 6:32–35; Acts 17:24–28; 1 Cor 10:16–17; Didache 9:4. Note the New Testament understandings of "remembering" (*anamnesis*), "giving thanks" (*eucharistia*), and "communion" (*koinonia*).

23. Matt 4:17; Mark 1:15. The Greek word for "repentance," *metanoia*, refers to a "change of mind" that transforms both understanding and behavior.

24. Traditional phrase used in the baptismal liturgy.

12.06 In these deeply troubled days, we confess our individual and corporate sins, failings, and wrongdoings:[25]

12.07 We are complicit and guilty of the exploitation and abuse of the Earth, our common home: its natural environment, resources, and our fellow creatures with whom we are meant to share it.[26] Our human actions have now led us to the brink of global catastrophe, threatening the very survival of life itself.

12.08 We are complicit and guilty of injustice in ongoing systemic racism, classism, and sexism.

As, historically, a community of predominantly privileged and wealthy Euro-Americans, we acknowledge our sad heritage of greed, prejudice, and violence expressed in domination of others by imposed social and economic norms and structures and in white supremacy, colonialism, imperialism, and idolatrous nationalism. We continually struggle with Jesus's call to put away our weapons and to share what we have with the poor.[27] For too long we have exploited peoples and nations around the globe for our own gain.

12.09 We have grossly sinned by acts of enslavement and genocide committed against African Americans, Native Americans, and other peoples of color, past and present.

12.10 We have grossly sinned against women and children and against God's beloved offspring across all spectrums of sexual orientation and gender identity in acts of hetero-patriarchal discrimination, abuse, oppression, prejudice, hate, and deadly violence.

12.11 We have also sinned in our discriminatory attitudes and actions of ableism and ageism.

12.12 In these and other ways we have deeply wronged, marginalized, and excluded those we are expressly called by God to welcome and love.[28]

12.13 In all this, we have blasphemed God's Name, Being, and Will.[29] Too often, we have embraced false and toxic religiosity rather than a living

---

25. Matt 3:1–12; Mark 1:1–8; Luke 3:1–18.

26. Gen 1:29–30, 2:15–20a; Isa 11:6–9; Rom 8:18–21.

27. Isa 2:4; Mic 4:3; Matt 26:52. Matt 6:24, 19:21; Mark 10:21; Luke 12:33–34, 18:22.

28. Lev 19:9–17, 32–34; Isa 56:1–8; Mark 10:13–16 and parallels; Matt 25:41–45.

29. Exod 20:7; Mark 3:23–30; Matt 25:41–45; John 10:31–38.

faith, hope, and love in Christ.[30] We have sought to be "nice" and respectable rather than loving and good. We have sought personal and institutional power and privilege rather than humbling ourselves in faithful obedience and service to Christ.[31] In this, we betray and condemn Christ Jesus anew, justifying ourselves even as we continue to judge others and assuming worldly domination over others rather than embracing mutual and loving service to *all* in God's realm.[32]

12.14 And yet, in God's compassion and mercy, Jesus calls us to come and follow in a better way.[33]

12.15 Jesus calls us to turn from self-interest to "take up the cross" and accompany him daily, in life and in death.[34]

12.16 Jesus calls us to be no longer conformed to the old ways of the world, but to be transformed by the renewal of our hearts, minds, and spirits.[35]

12.17 Jesus calls us to embrace and trust the good news that God's realm of justice, peace, and wellbeing is ever at hand, here and now, in our midst.[36]

12.18 With those who have followed Christ Jesus across the ages, we proclaim the mystery of our faith: "Christ has died. Christ is risen. Christ abides and comes again."[37]

12.19 As we proclaim the mystery of Jesus's reconciling life, death, resurrection, and abiding presence in and through the Spirit, we also affirm that:

30. Matt 23:1–35; Mark 8:15; 1 Cor 13. Jesus's critique of the scribes and Pharisees of his tradition is applicable to abuses committed by religious authorities in any and all religious traditions, including our own.

31. Phil 2:5–8; Matt 5:3–12 and Luke 6:20–26; Matt 16:24–26; Matt 20:20–28 and Mark 10:35–45.

32. Matt 7:1–5; John 18:36; Phil 2:5–8.

33. Mark 1:17; Matt 11:28–30; John 14:6–7; 1 Cor 12:31b–13:13.

34. Mark 8:34–38; John 21:18–19. Also Heidelberg Catechism question 1 (C-4.001) and A Brief Statement of Faith (C-11) in PCUSA, *The Book of Confessions*.

35. See Rom 12:2, as these words of Paul very much convey the invitation of Christ.

36. Mark 1:15; Matt 4:16; Luke 17:20–21.

37. Based on the widely used eucharistic affirmation, additionally incorporating Matt 28:20b, etc. The New Testament is clear in affirming the historical death and resurrection of Jesus and the anticipated Second Coming. After over twenty intervening centuries, there are many opinions concerning them all, ranging from the very literal to more symbolic, spiritual, and mystical understandings. However understood, these affirmations remain central to Christian faith and life.

In Christ "there is neither Jew nor Greek"—which is to say that presumed privilege and barriers of culture, race, and ethnicity are abolished.[38]

In Christ "there is neither slave nor free"—which is to say that economic and class divisions are, and are to be, overcome.[39]

In Christ "there is neither male nor female"—which is to say that socio-culturally determined distinctions and barriers concerning gender roles, sexual orientation, and gender identity are removed.[40]

For each and all are made equally in the divine image and called as God's beloved children in whom God delights. "All are one in Christ."[41]

12.20 In a world of many faith traditions and spiritual paths, Jesus teaches that we are to welcome and work together with any who willingly do good in his name and in whose lives the fruits of the Spirit are evident. "Whoever is not against us is with us."[42]

12.21 Believing this, with the Spirit's help we endeavor to follow the greatest of commandments, "to love God with all our heart, soul, mind, and strength and to love neighbor and stranger as ourselves."[43] This love extends even to those we regard as enemies.[44]

---

38. Gal 3:28a.

39. Gal 3:28b.

40. Gal 3:28c; Isa 56:3–5; Acts 10: 34–35; Rom 3:21–24; 2 Cor 3:5b–6. The bulk of the scriptures themselves are deeply grounded in the heteronormative and cisgendered assumptions of the cultures in which they were written. Over the last half century, emergent understandings of the spectrums of sexual orientation and gender identity have led us to seek anew the illumination and guidance of the Spirit. In Isaiah 56 and Acts 10, the prophet and the apostle, guided by the Spirit, directly set aside prohibitions of the Law for the sake of the inclusion of those previously regarded as unclean and banned. Compare Matt 8.5–18 and Luke 7:2–10 with Acts 10. Also note Jesus's overall inclusion of women and others in non-culturally sanctioned roles throughout the gospels.

41. Gen 1:26a, 27; Matt 3:17, 17:5, 5:9; John 1:12–13; 1 John 4:7–8; Gal 3:28d.

42. Mark 9:40; Gal 5:22–23. In Matt 12:30, Jesus also says, "Whoever is not with me is against me," speaking there of the exclusivistic understanding of the religiously privileged, who ascribed to evil the working of God's Spirit among the poor and marginalized.

43. Deut 6:4–5; Lev 19:17–18, 34; Matt 22:36–39; Mark 12:28–31; Luke 10:25–18.

44. Matt 5:43–45; Luke 6:27–31.

12.22 Our love for God, others, and self is manifested in our actions of faithful compassion in obedience to Christ.[45]

12.23 With the Spirit's help, we therefore endeavor to "do unto others as we would have others do unto us" in our daily lives, individually and communally.[46]

12.24 For, as Jesus teaches, "On these commandments hang all the Law and the Prophets."[47] And in so doing unto the "least of these" among us— the poor, the hungry and thirsty, the naked and unhoused, the sick, the sorrowing, the asylum seeker, and the prisoner—we believe we do it unto Christ.[48]

12.25 Obeying Christ, we also undertake to forgive one another as we hope to be forgiven,[49] even as Jesus prayed for and forgave those who were killing him.[50] In this, we are reconciled to God and each other.[51]

12.26 And, for God's sake and the good of all, we urgently undertake to restore health and wellbeing to the planet as a whole, "tending and caring for" the good earth and all that lives upon it as, we are told, was intended for humankind from the beginning.[52]

12.27 We can do none of this on our own, either individually or communally,[53] but only with God's help, God working in us through the Holy Spirit to will and to work for God's good pleasure;[54] saving, sustaining, justifying, and sanctifying by divine grace and favor;[55] assisting us in

---

45. Luke 6:32–36; John 15:10–14; Jas 2:14–17, 26. Scriptural "love" is not so much about feeling as behavior, acting in a compassionate and caring way. See also John 14:15.

46. Matt 7:12; Luke 6:31; Gal 5:22–25.

47. Matt 7:12, 22:40. Also Mic 6:8.

48. Matt 25:40. Also Matt 5:3–12 and Luke 6:20–21.

49. Matt 6:12, 14–15, 18:21–22.

50. Luke 23:33–34. Beyond all theologizing, this is a fundamental basis of atonement-reconciliation theory.

51. Matt 5:23–24; 2 Cor 5:14–20; Col 1:19–20.

52. Gen 1:29–30, 2:15–20a; Isa 11:6–9.

53. John 15:5; Rom 8:1–4; 1 Cor 12:14–27.

54. John 14:15–17, 20:21–23; Phil 2:12–13.

55. Luke 2:14; Rom 3:21–26.

prayer and the disciplines of spiritual formation, nurture, and service.[56] "We love because God first loved us."[57]

12.28 In all this, we believe that God is alive and working with and through us in the world. As we do these things, trusting in God, we live into the hope that we and all creation may yet live,[58] dwelling together in unity with all life and being;[59] that God's universal reign of redemptive justice, peace, and wellbeing may yet be realized among us;[60] and that, as all things have come into being through God-in-Christ, so all may come to fulfillment in Christ.[61]

12.29 And so, we trust and follow Christ Jesus, our Savior, who calls us to:

Faith in a time of doubt and distrust,
Hope in a time of cynicism and despair,
Love in a time of alienation and hatred,
Joy in a time of grief and deep sadness, and
Peace in the midst of anxiety, conflict, and great need.[62]

12.30 And, day by day, we continually pray: Help us, O Christ, "to see you more clearly, love you more dearly, and follow you ever more nearly." May it be so. Amen.[63]

56. Acts 2:44, 46–47; Rom 8:26–27; 1 Cor 12:4–11; Heb 10:23–25.

57. 1 John 4:19.

58. Rom 8:18–21.

59. John 17:20–21; Gal 3:28d.

60. Isa 65:17–25; Matt 6:10; Luke 3:17–21; Rev 21:1–5.

61. John 1:1–5, 3:16–17; Col 1:15–20; Heb 1:1–4.

62. 1 Cor 13:13; Gal 5:22–23.

63. Based on the prayer of Richard of Chichester (1197–1253).

Bibliography

Anderson, Fred R. *Singing Psalms of Joy and Praise*. Philadelphia: The Westminster Press, 1986.

Barclay, William. *The Lord's Supper*. Philadelphia: The Westminster Press, 1967.

Bedford, Emmanuel. "Wings of the Dawn." *YouTube*, February 21, 2021. https://www.youtube.com/watch?v=oOXs6C6juXs&list=RDMMLeRXNIyJq6c&index=3.

Bell, John L. "The Summons." Iona, Scotland: Wild Goose Resource Group, 1987.

Borg, Marcus. *The Heart of Christianity: Rediscovering a Life of Faith*. New York: HarperSanFrancisco, 2003.

Bourgeault, Cynthia. *The Wisdom Jesus: Transforming Heart and Mind—A New Perspective on Christ and His Message*. Boston: Shambala, 2008.

Briggs, David. "Voices of the Faithful: Belief in Resurrection at Core of Christian Identity." *The Huffington Post* (April 5, 2012). Online: http://www.huffingtonpost.com/david-briggs/resurrection-of-jesus-core-belief-in-christian-identity_b_1405840.html.

Brock, Rita Nakishima, and Rebecca Ann Parker. *Saving Paradise: How Christianity Traded Love of This World for Crucifixion and Empire*. Boston: Beacon, 2008.

Burns, Robert. *The Poetical Works of Robert Burns: With Memoir, Notes, And a Complete Glossary*. New York: The American News Company, undated (pre-1909).

Campbell, Alexander. *The Christian System: In Reference to the Union of Christians, And A Restoration of Primitive Christianity, As Plead in the Current Reformation*. Third Edition. Pittsburg: Forrester and Campbell, 1840. No pages. Online: http://books.google.com/books?id=zHsXAAAAYAAJ&printsec=frontcover&source=gbs_ge_summary_r&cad=0#v=onepage&q&f=false.

Chaucer, Geoffrey. *The Canterbury Tales*. Online: http://www.canterburytales.org/.

Cuthbertson, Kenneth L. "'I Have Been Fighting Satan': John Knox and the Quest for Godly Liberation in Sixteenth Century Britain." PhD diss., University of Iowa, 1992.

Cuthbertson, William C. *Memories of Ayrshire, Illinois, and Kansas*. Privately published, 1972.

Dickinson, William Croft. *John Knox's History of the Reformation in Scotland*. 2 vols. New York: The Philosophical Library, 1950.

Douglas, James D. *Light in the North: The Story of the Scottish Covenanters*. Grand Rapids: William B. Eerdmans Publishing Co., 1964.

Douglass, Jane Dempsey. *Women, Freedom, and Calvin*. Philadelphia: The Westminster Press, 1985.

Eire, Carlos M. N. *War Against the Idols: The Reformation of Worship From Erasmus to Calvin*. New York: Cambridge University Press, 1986.

Bibliography

Ellis, Peter Berresford. *Celtic Women: Women in Celtic Society and Literature*. Grand Rapids: William B. Eerdmans Publishing Co., 1996.

Fairlie, J. Kirkwood. *Matthew Fowlds, Centenarian Weaver, 1806–1907: and Other Fenwick Worthies, etc.* Memphis, TN: General Books, 2010. First published 1910 by Kilmarnock: Standard Printing Works.

Fields, S. Helen. *Register of Marriages and Baptisms performed by Rev. John Cuthbertson, 1751–1791*. Baltimore: Genealogical Publishing Company, 1996. Originally printed 1934.

Free Presbyterian Church (Scotland). *The Confession of Faith*. Inverness: Free Presbyterian Publications, 1981.

Guthrie, William. *The Christian's Great Interest*. Inverness: Free Presbyterian Publications, 1969. First published 1658.

Hartke, Austen. *Transforming: The Bible and the Lives of Transgender Christians*. Louisville, KY: Westminster John Knox Press, 2018.

Heschel, Abraham Joshua. *The Sabbath: Its Meaning for Modern Man*. New York: The Noonday Press / Farrar, Straus & Giroux, 1951. Reprinted 1976.

Hewison, James King. *The Covenanters: A History Of The Church In Scotland From The Reformation To The Revolution . . .* 2 vols. Glasgow: John Smith & Sons, 1908.

Howie, John. *The Scots Worthies*. Carlisle, PA: The Banner of Truth Trust, 1995. First published 1781.

Iona Community. "Our History: Founding." No pages. Online: http://iona.org.uk/about-us/historty/.

———. "Our Movement: Membership." No pages. Online: http://iona.org.uk/movement/membership/.

Jamison, Wallace N. *The United Presbyterian Story: A Centennial Study 1858–1958*. Pittsburgh: The Geneva Press, 1958.

Lambert, Malcolm. *Medieval Heresy: Popular Movements from the Gregorian Reform to the Reformation*. Barnes & Noble edition, 1998. First published 1992 by Blackwell.

Larner, Christina. *Enemies of God: The Witch-hunt in Scotland*. London: Chatto & Windus, 1981.

Lightfoot, J. B. *The Apostolic Fathers*. Grand Rapids, MI: Baker Book House, 1978.

Lorimer, Peter. *John Knox and the Church of England: His Work in Her Pulpit and His Influence Upon Her Liturgy, Articles, and Parties*. London: Henry S. King & Co., 1875.

Macksoud, Anne, and John Ankele. *Maybe We're Talking About a Different God: Homosexuality and the Church*. National Film Network, 1994. DVD.

MacLeod, John. *Scottish Theology in relation to church history since the Reformation*. Carlisle, PA: The Banner of Truth Trust, 1974. First published 1946 by Free Church of Scotland.

Marshall, Catherine. *A Man Called Peter: The Story of Peter Marshall*. Grand Rapids: Chosen Books, 2002. First published New York: McGraw-Hill, 1951.

———. *Mr. Jones, Meet the Master: Sermons and Prayers of Peter Marshall*. Old Tappan, NJ: Fleming H. Revell, 1949.

McCrie, Thomas. *Life of John Knox*. First complete American Edition, Philadelphia: Presbyterian Board of Publication, undated. First published 1831 in Edinburgh.

McGrath, Alistair. *Historical Theology: An Introduction to the History of Christian Thought*. Malden, MA: Blackwell Publishing, 1998.

McNeill, John T. *Calvin: The Institutes of the Christian Religion.* 2 vols. Translated by Ford Lewis Battles. Philadelphia: The Westminster Press, 1960.

Merrill, Nan C. *Psalms for Praying.* New York: Continuum, 2001.

Miller, Thomas. *The Selected Writings of John Witherspoon.* Carbondale and Edwardsville: Southern Illinois University Press, 1990.

Muir, John. *A Thousand Mile Walk to the Gulf.* San Francisco: Sierra Club Books, 1991. First published 1916.

Muller, Wayne. *Sabbath: Finding Rest, Renewal, and Delight in Our Busy Lives.* New York: Bantam Books, 2000.

National Archives. "Declaration of Independence." No pages. Online: http://www.archives.gov/exhibits/charters/declaration_transcript.html.

Newell, John Philip. *Celtic Treasure: Daily Scriptures and Prayer.* Grand Rapids: William B. Eerdmans Publishing Co., 2005.

———. *Christ of the Celts: The Healing of Creation.* San Francisco: Jossey-Bass, 2008.

———. *Listening for the Heartbeat of God: A Celtic Sprirtuality.* New York / Matwah, NJ: Paulist Press, 1997.

———. *A New Harmony: The Spirit, the Earth, and the Human Soul.* San Francisco: Jossey-Bass, 2011.

Newell, John Philip, and David Poole. *Liturgies from Casa del Sol.* Abiquiu, NM: Ghost Ranch, 2008.

Office of the General Assembly. "PC(USA) 2021 Statistics Continue to Show Declining Membership." *PCUSA*, April 25, 2022. https://www.pcusa.org/news/2022/4/25/pcusa-2021-statistics-continue-show-declining-memb/.

Palmer, Parker. *Let Your Life Speak: Listening for the Voice of Vocation.* San Francisco, CA: Jossey-Bass, 2000.

Parker, G.H.W. *The Morning Star: Wycliffe and the Dawn of the Reformation.* Grand Rapids: William B. Eerdmans Publishing Co., 1965.

P.C.U.S.A. *The Book of Common Worship.* Philadelphia: The Presbyterian Board of Publication and Sabbath-School Work, 1906.

———. *The Book of Common Worship.* Philadelphia: The Board of Christian Education of the Presbyterian Church in the United States of America, 1946.

———. *The Hymnal.* Philadelphia: The Presbyterian Board of Christian Education, 1933.

PCUSA. *The Constitution of the Presbyterian Church (U.S.A.): Part I, Book of Confessions.* Louisville: The Office of the General Assembly, 2002.

———. *The Constitution of the Presbyterian Church (U.S.A.): Part II, Book of Order 2004/2005.* Louisville: The Office of the General Assembly, 2004.

———. *The Constitution of the Presbyterian Church (U.S.A.): Part II, Book of Order 2011–2013.* Louisville: The Office of the General Assembly, 2011.

———. "Doctrine of Discovery." *Facing Racism.* https://facing-racism.pcusa.org/item/41901/.

———. "Earth Care Congregations." *Presbyterian Mission.* https://www.presbyterianmission.org/ministries/environment/earth-care-congregations/.

———. "Matthew 25 in the PC(USA): A Bold Vision and Invitation." *Presbyterian Mission.* https://www.presbyterianmission.org/wp-content/uploads/Matt25-big-brochure-2021.pdf.

Bibliography

————. Overture "[06–08] On Amending the Book of Order to Clarify Titles to Ordered Ministry—From the Presbytery of Great Rivers." *PC Biz*. https://www.pc-biz.org/#/search/6328.

————. Overture "[11–12] On Affirming and Celebrating the Full Dignity and Humanity of People of All Gender Identities." *PC Biz*. https://www.pc-biz.org/#/search/3000312.

————. Overture "[11–13] On Celebrating the Gifts of People of Diverse Sexual Orientations and Gender Identities in the Life of the Church." *PC Biz*. https://www.pc-biz.org/#/search/3000313.

————. *The Presbyterian Hymnal: Hymns, Psalms, and Spiritual Songs*. Louisville: Westminster / John Knox Press, 1990.

————. *Presbyterian Understanding and Use of Holy Scripture (1983)*. https://www.pcusa.org/site_media/media/uploads/_resolutions/scripture-use.pdf.

Pitts, William S. "Little Brown Church in the Vale." No pages. Online: http://nethymnal.org/htm/l/i/littlebc.htm.

Reid, John. *The Best Little Boy in the World*. New York: Ballantine Books, 1976.

Rogers, Jack. *Jesus, the Bible, and Homosexuality*. Louisville: Westminster John Knox Press, 2006.

RPNA. *The Book of Psalms for Singing*. Pittsburgh: The Board of Education and Publication of The Reformed Presbyterian Church of North America, 1973.

Rutherford, Samuel. *Lex Rex, or The Law and the Prince*. Harrisonburg, VA: Sprinkle Publications, 1980. First published 1644.

Sellers, Ernest O. "Thy Word Have I Hid in My Heart." No Pages. Online: http://nethymnal.org/htm/t/h/y/thywhihh.htm.

Smellie, Alexander. *Men of the Covenant: The Story of the Scottish Church in the Years of the Persecution*. Carlisle, PA: The Banner of Truth Trust, 1975. First published 1903.

Taylor, Tom Dunnachie. *The Annals of Fenwick: by James Taylor (1814–1857)*. Kilmarnock: Ayrshire Archaeological and Natural History Society, 1970.

Tickle, Phyllis. *The Great Emergence: How Christianity is Changing and Why*. Grand Rapids: Baker Books, 2008.

Tillich, Paul. *Systematic Theology, Volume 1*. Chicago, IL: University of Chicago Press, 1973.

UPCUSA, et al. *The Hymnbook*. Richmond/Philadelphia/New York: Presbyterian Church in the United States, The United Presbyterian Church in the U.S.A., Reformed Church in America, 1955.

————. *The Worshipbook: Services*. Philadelphia: The Westminster Press, 1970.

UPNA. *The Confessional Statement and The Book of Government and Worship*. Pittsburgh: Board of Christian Education of the United Presbyterian Church of North America, 1948.

————. *The Psalter of the United Presbyterian Church of North America*. Pittsburgh: United Presbyterian Board of Publication, 1887.

————. *The Psalter: With Responsive Readings*. Pittsburgh: The United Presbyterian Board of Publication, 1912.

————. *The Psalter Hymnal: The Psalms and Selected Hymns*. Pittsburgh: The United Presbyterian Board of Publication and Bible School Work, 1927.

CPSIA information can be obtained
at www.ICGtesting.com
Printed in the USA
JSHW011946260623
43726JS00001B/3